PENGUIN BOOKS

KANSAS CHARLEY

Joan Jacobs Brumberg is the author of *Fasting Girls: The History of Anorexia Nervosa*, which won the Berkshire Prize in history, and the John Hope Franklin Prize for American Studies, among other awards, and of *The Body Project: An Intimate History of American Girls*, which won the Choice Award from the American Library Association. She has been a resident of the MacDowell Colony and is a fellow of the Society of American Historians. A professor at Cornell University where she teaches history, human development, and women's studies, she lives in Ithaca, New York.

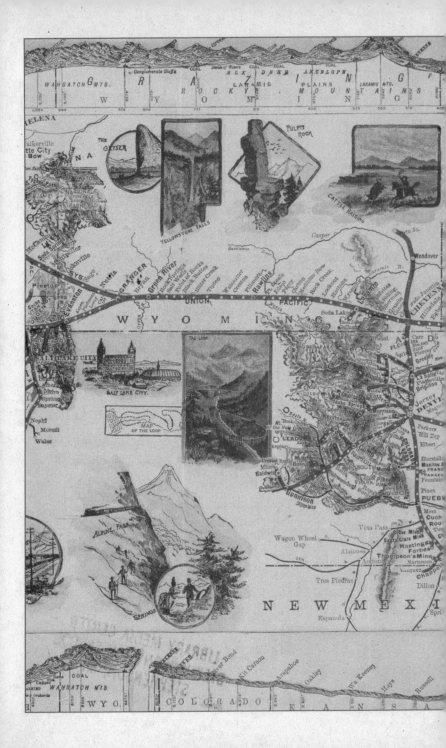

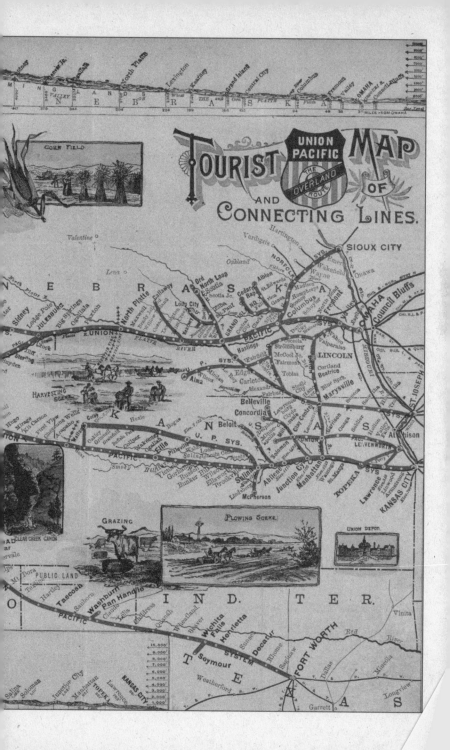

TOURIST MAP OF CONNECTING LINES.

UNION PACIFIC
THE OVERLAND ROUTE
AND OF

CORN FIELD

HARVESTING SCENE.

GRAZING

PLOWING SCENE.

UNION DEPOT.

PUBLIC LAND

KANSAS CITY
10,000
9,000
8,000
7,000
6,000
5,000
4,000
3,000
2,000
1,000

Joan Jacobs Brumberg

KANSAS CHARLEY

THE BOY MURDERER

PENGUIN BOOKS

PENGUIN BOOKS

Published by the Penguin Group

Penguin Group (USA) Inc., 375 Hudson Street, New York, New York 10014, U.S.A.

Penguin Group (Canada), 10 Alcorn Avenue, Toronto, Ontario, Canada M4V 3B2 (a division of Pearson Penguin Canada Inc.)

Penguin Books Ltd, 80 Strand, London WC2 0RL, England

Penguin Ireland, 25 St Stephen's Green, Dublin 2, Ireland (a division of Penguin Books Ltd)

Penguin Group (Australia), 250 Camberwell Road, Camberwell, Victoria 3124, Australia (a division of Pearson Australia Group Pty Ltd)

Penguin Books India Pvt Ltd, 11 Community Centre, Panchsheel Park, New Delhi – 110 017, India

Penguin Group (NZ), cnr Airborne and Rosedale Roads, Albany, Auckland, New Zealand (a division of Pearson New Zealand Ltd)

Penguin Books (South Africa) (Pty) Ltd, 24 Sturdee Avenue, Rosebank, Johannesberg 2196, South Africa

Penguin Books Ltd, Registered Offices:
80 Strand, London WC2R 0RL, England

First published in the United States of America by Viking Penguin,
a member of Penguin Group (USA) Inc. 2003
Published in Penguin Books 2004

10 9 8 7 6 5 4 3 2 1

THE LIBRARY OF CONGRESS HAS CATALOGED THE HARDCOVER EDITION AS FOLLOWS:
Brumberg, Joan Jacobs.
    Kansas Charley: the story of a nineteenth-century
  boy murderer / by Joan Jacobs Brumberg
      p. cm.
    ISBN 0-670-03228-X (hc.)
    ISBN 0 14 20.0488 X (pbk.)
    1. Miller, Charley, 1874–1892. 2. Murderers—United States—Biography. I. Title.
    HV6248.M4975B78 2003
    364.15.23.092—dc21
    [B] 2003043282

Printed in the United States of America
Set in Eldorado Text
Designed by Francesca Belanger
Photo insert designed by BTD/nyc

For Bernard Weisberger

"There is an entire series of difficulties directly traceable to the foolish and adventurous persistence of carrying firearms. . . . What might be merely a boyish scrap is turned into tragedy because some boy has a revolver."

—Jane Addams, *The Spirit of Youth and the City Streets*, 1909

"Murder is murder, and I myself believe that the murder the State does in punishment of killing is the worst murder of all."

—Willam Dean Howells, *Harper's Weekly*, 1895

"The Light of Lights
Looks always on the motive, not the deed,
The Shadow of Shadows on the Deed alone"

—W. B. Yeats, *The Countess Cathleen*, 1909

ACKNOWLEDGMENTS

IN WRITING THIS BOOK I owe an enormous debt to two historians who are part of my everyday life—my husband, David Brumberg, and my longtime friend Faye Dudden. Both listened to my relentless chatter about Charley long before I had a coherent story to tell. And both also wrestled with chapters in the rough, bringing me to the mat with their individual knowledge and insight about nineteenth-century America. David graciously traveled with me to places that were not exactly holiday destinations and then joined me in the archives looking for traces of Charley Miller. Faye endured long lunches at which I ruminated periodically about the mind-set of a fifteen-year-old boy.

When I needed help making sense of what happened to Charley in court, Anu Chaturvedi Connor and Anjali Chaturvedi, both Cornell alumnae and attorneys, pitched in. Because Anu was once my undergraduate student, her collaboration as a young professional felt especially sweet to me. When I needed advice about a rhetorical strategy for the book, I was also fortunate to be able to turn to my own undergraduate teacher and mentor, Bernard Weisberger, an octogenarian who is also a prolific writer and historian. His savvy advice about the structure of my narrative pointed me in the right direction, just as he had in my college days with undergraduate papers. In the early stages of research, Larry Brown, Wyoming's resident expert on Charley Miller, was consistently generous in answering questions and directing me to sources; Lois Brown, Frederick Hodges, Joseph Kett, Roger Lane, Philip Mackey, Eric Monkkonen, Michael James Pfeifer, and Bill Pretzer each answered my questions promptly (and electronically) when the moment was right. Paul and Ellen Grebinger read a problematic chapter for me in the midst of an Adirondack vacation. And when the manuscript was nearly done, I profited from astute readings by Steven Drizin, Nina Miller, Phil Roberts, Carla Bittel, Victor Streib, Nancy Tomes, and Randolph Werner.

There are many people at Cornell University who helped make this book possible, and also better. Within the Cornell University Library System, I am indebted particularly to Michael Cook, Julie Cophenhagen, Lenore Coral, Patricia Court, Brandy Kreisler, Robert Kibbee, Ida Martinez, Fred Muratori, Suzanne Schwartz, Susan Szasz Palmer, and Donald Schnedeker for their consistent, skillful assistance. In thinking about the psychological development of a boy like Charley Miller, I profited from lively conversations with Wendy Williams, Howard Feinstein, Steve Ceci, and James Garbarino, intellectually generous colleagues who were especially interested in a project that brought psychology and history together. Jan Jennings and Kathleen Gibson introduced me to the world of Internet searching. Carolyn Merrithew and Mary White provided able research assistance, however briefly, and a number of Cornell undergraduates—Somjen Frazer, Jillian Greenberg, Leigh McMullan, Jennifer Scheff, Carolyn Stein, and Amy Stutius—helped me in myriad ways over the four years it took to produce this book. Production of the manuscript was assisted by my longtime secretary Jolan Balog, but also by Benjamin Rockey-Harris, an undergraduate, whose enthusiasm for "Macs" and his cheerful willingness to make an occasional house call got me through some technological crises. I am also grateful to everyone in University Photography at Cornell who helped me reproduce visuals for this book.

Charley Miller's story spanned the continent, requiring me to travel and also to get some research assistance. While I was in Cheyenne, Sharon Lass Field actually came into the State Archives to help me dig for answers to my questions about local women, but I am also indebted to Julie Curry, a Cornell graduate student, who conveniently became a visiting member of the history faculty at the University of Wyoming. Julie served as my eyes and ears when I had last-minute questions about Wyoming material, and she did so with an unsparing attention to detail and accuracy. I am grateful to others in Wyoming: to Holly Geist and Cindy Brown at the Wyoming State Archives; to Carol Bowers and Leslie Shores at the American Heritage Center; to Tony Lewis at the Wyoming Bar Association; to Gary C. Anderson and Linda Newell at the Johnson County Jim Gathcell Memorial Museum; and to Betty Schroll, historian of St. Mary's Parish.

In New York City, Victor Rehmer at the Children's Aid Society graciously opened the archives for my pursuit of Charley and his siblings; Julie Miller shared her knowledge of custodial institutions for children in that city; and Megan Elias did some searching for me in the municipal archives. In Philadelphia, Jessie Bluebond-Langner skillfully gathered information about Holmesburg Prison; in Boston, Elyssa Engelmann did some local research about a juvenile homicide case in that area. Nancy Martin at the University of Rochester was an invaluable guide to sources in that city, as was Terry Lehr, who shared ideas about local materials. Donald Moore helped me find information about Charley's adopted family in Virginia.

As a I moved into the Midwest in pursuit of Charley, I got the opportunity to meet some of the people who had been helping me at a distance, often electronically. In Ohio, Denise Montbarren at the College of Wooster provided useful responses to my requests. In Missouri, my queries were answered by Jackie Lewis at the St. Joseph Museum and Mary Beth Rowe at the River Bluffs Regional Library. Paul Lubotina, William Glankler, and Suzanne Lehr all provided brief research assistance. In Kansas, a number of archivists gave generously of their time: Pat Patton at Kansas State University; Linda Glasgow at the Riley County Historical Society; and Jane Kelsey and Susan K. Forbes at the Kansas State Historical Society. I am especially grateful to Linda Glasgow for providing access to Phyllis Swanson, who invited me to her home in Leonardville to talk about the history of the town and what she had heard about Charley Miller from her own grandparents, who lived there at the same time as Fred

Miller. Mary Clement Douglass helped me trace a number of Kansas women who were involved in the story. My knowledge of Charley's experience in Minnesota was enhanced by assistance from Howard Sanborn at the Filmore County History Center; Kathy Schuler at the Winona County Historical Society; Nancy MacMahon at the Chatfield Historical Society; Maurice Bennett at the Olmsted County Historical Society; and Charles Rodgers, Debbie Miller, and Jennifer Hanson at the Minnesota Historical Society in St. Paul. Dallas Lindgren provided useful research support in the early stages of the Minnesota investigation. In Iowa, Catherine Denial briefly gave me some useful research assistance. In Nebraska, Ann Billesbach at the Nebraska State Historial Society; Catherine Renschler at the Adams County Historical Society; and Ada Ammerman and the Research Team at the Cheyenne County Historical Association in Sidney were all extremely helpful.

There are some final debts that are harder to describe. To Laurence Steinberg and the members of the John D. and Catherine T. MacArthur Foundation's Research Network on Adolescent Development and Juvenile Justice, a hearty thank you for giving me the opportunity early in my research to talk to a sophisticated audience about my historical interest in "kids who kill." That experience actually clarified my commitment to the issue and to the idea of telling only one story instead of many. To the MacDowell Colony, I am profoundly grateful for the privilege of another wonderful residency, which provided me with time and space to pay close attention to the literary quality of my work. To DeAnna Heindel and especially to my agent, Georges Borchardt, a thank you for your belief in this project even when I was uncertain about it; and to Kathryn Court and Sarah Manges, my editors at Viking, an enthusiastic declaration of gratitude for being such smart, supportive critics. I also owe a debt to Ali Bothwell for her intelligent and reliable support during the book production process. Finally, I owe a great deal to my family, not only to David, but also to Adam and Sarah, Madeline and Isabel. My writing life is, in large measure, sustained by their love, interest, and good humor.

CONTENTS

Prologue

O N THE NIGHT before he died, Charley Miller knew that
he could count on Sheriff Kelley to bring him as many
fresh doughnuts as he wanted. Everyone in the Laramie
County Jail was being especially nice and accommodating, because they knew he would be dead before noon the next day. As
the boy envisioned the sweet warmth of his favorite doughnuts, he
tried not to think about the thick hemp rope and scaffold waiting
outside his jail cell.

The year was 1892, and the place Cheyenne, capital city of the
new state of Wyoming. Charley Miller was small and fair-haired—
with steely blue eyes—an orphan from New York City, who had
been calling himself "Kansas Charley" for a number of years.
Equipped with this cocky nickname and a stylish black felt hat, he
began at fourteen to tramp the country on his own, looking for
both work and adventure. Instead, at fifteen, he killed two boys in
a Union Pacific boxcar and was sentenced to death for that crime
in a Wyoming court after a short but well-publicized trial. By the
night of April 21, 1892, the eve of his execution, Miller was seventeen. He had been confined to the Laramie County Jail for nearly
eighteen months, and he was so accustomed to the place that it felt
like the home he had longed for but never really had.

Despite his horrible crime, and the ways in which he was demonized by the press, Charley was popular with both his jailers
and fellow inmates. In addition to Sheriff Kelley's doughnut runs
to a local restaurant on his behalf, there were good times with Mr.

Sharpless, the deputy, whose job it was to watch him and keep him occupied on the final evening of his life. Oscar Sharpless was a Civil War veteran who had survived some hard times himself. When he arrived at the boy's cell that evening for the "death watch," Charley was sitting on his cot playing one of his two harmonicas. He was fond of composing poems and ballads and putting them to music, so Sharpless sat down to listen before they began a card game of Seven Up.

Sharpless noted that the walls of the cell were covered with clippings from newspapers: engravings of men on horses; advertisements with pictures of the most fashionable new shoes, topcoats, and mustache waxes; illustrated covers from the popular dime novels that Charley liked to read. There were also some elaborately decorated, handmade signs with sayings, such as "Home Sweet Home" and "What Is Home Without a Mother?"

When the songs were over, the boy showed the deputy his latest creation, a poem written for Sheriff Kelley, and then copied into an autograph book—the kind young people Charley's age carried around for collecting signatures and sentimental verses when they left school or moved to a new town. Instead of "roses are red, violets are blue," Sharpless read the words of a boy about to die:

> They talk about daring exploits
> Which they say I have done,
> And keep right on talking
> 'Cause I am to be hung.
>
> Now tell me which is worse,
> With your own will and breath.
> Don't speak too fast, but—
> Life sentence or death?

Charley had been telling people lately that he preferred hanging to confinement in the penitentiary, but in his final poem he begged Sheriff Kelley to make sure that the execution was speedy—that it would not hurt:

> All I ask of Sheriff Kelley
> That is to do his work good;
> And not have me suffering
> In this western neighborhood.

With the reading over, Sharpless suggested that Charley cut the deck and start playing cards as a way of passing time. As they played, the boy alternated between doughnuts, which he gulped down quickly, and cigarettes, smoked intensely until their heat burned his hand. At one point, he stopped to clean off his sticky fingers and wondered aloud if the governor of Wyoming might still grant him clemency in the final hour. Sharpless, eating a doughnut himself, said little in response, but at the end of the third hand, when the score was Sharpless six, Miller three, he proposed a wager that would be a good distraction for his tense and frightened charge. "Your chances for life are shown by the standing of this game," he told Charley Miller. "If you win [tonight] your sentence will be commuted. If you lose you will be hanged." With that incentive, the two played until midnight, and the boy was buoyed up when he won eight games in succession.

Despite the diversion, Charley was never really very hopeful. Before the evening was out, he admitted to Mr. Sharpless: "I think the die is cast, that I shall be hanged tomorrow, but I want here and now to say that Kansas Charley will walk to the doom which cruel fate has made necessary with as much firmness and composure as he would go to a wedding."

When the deputy finally left, Charley did one more thing before going to sleep. Using some of the old brown paper sacks that he usually saved for composing and drawing, he assembled the belongings that made up his small "estate" and sorted them into bundles marked with the names of a number of people important to him. With this accomplished, he undressed, put on his nightclothes, and went to bed.

The following morning, Charley Miller was executed by the state of Wyoming. A gallery of invited guests watched his slight body—he only stood about five feet four inches tall and weighed less than 120 pounds—drop with great velocity, and then jerk upward, until he was strangled and his neck broken. It was the first execution in the history of the new state of Wyoming. And it was also the first time that anyone had been legally executed in Wyoming since the 1870s.

A newspaper in Cheyenne recognized how unique the case was: "The criminal history of America discloses no parallel case to that of Charley Miller. It will ever remain a question as to whether the ends of justice have been satisfied by hanging him. It can safely be said that young Miller never enjoyed the comforts or was surrounded by the civilizing influences of a Christian home, but at the same time it is equally true that the fault was his alone." Oscar Sharpless, who walked to the scaffold behind Charley, was disturbed by what happened to the youngster who had beaten him at cards the night before. "I know it is justice," the veteran said to some others who watched the execution. "I have been in thirty-six battles and have seen my comrades fall by my side, but this hurts me worst of all."

＊＊＊

Who was Charley Miller? How and why did a boy his age come to be hanged in Cheyenne? These and many other questions followed me from the moment I first saw a ten-line notice of his execution in the *New York World* of April 23, 1892. I was poking around in nineteenth-century newspapers in the University Library at Cornell looking for evidence of youthful homicide in the American past. It was only a few days after the tragic school shooting at Jonesboro, Arkansas, in 1998, and I was motivated by the question posed by the students in my class on the "History of American Childhood": "Were there ever boy murderers before?"

Except for the murder of Bobby Franks by teenagers Nathan Leopold and Richard Loeb in the 1920s, I seemed to have historical amnesia about boy murderers, like most Americans. Yet, within weeks of the provocative student question, I would find dozens of cases involving homicidal adolescent boys whom I had never heard of before. It quickly became apparent, however, that, unlike today, schools were rarely the setting for adolescent homicide in the nineteenth century, because most boys that age were in the workplace, not in school. Although four adolescent males in Canton, Massachusetts, stoned their teacher, Etta Barstow, to death in 1870, there was no subsequent string of "copy-cat" incidents. When I found cases of youthful male homicide, almost all were boys acting alone, and their weapons included pitchforks, shovels, knives, guns, even string.

Because I am a historian, accustomed to spending time at the microfilm machines in research libraries, I began to look for Charley Miller's name in other newspapers in the 1890s in order to see if they made any mention of his case. In fact, they did: Charley Miller's execution was widely reported, and all the reports used similar language to talk about him. He was billed as "the boy murderer" not because he had killed two other boys but because of his own youth, a factor that made his behavior all the more troubling and fascinating. His picture was published on the front page of the *San Francisco Chronicle*, *Rocky Mountain News* (Denver), *Chicago Daily Tribune*, and *New York World*. Then, as now, the horror of homicide by the young drew public attention, and provoked heated debate about what was wrong with both the perpetrator and American society.

Charley Miller's story grabbed me immediately, because it neatly undercut any assumption that "kids who kill" are a distinctly modern phenomenon. In the wake of well-publicized boy violence in America—but also in Bootle (England), Calgary (Canada), Erfurt (Germany), Kobe (Japan), and Volgograd (Russia)—most experts in the press, on television, and in the academy are quick to imply that murder by young boys is something new, generated by late-twentieth-century cultural life, and without historical precedent. Some American commentators have suggested that we must protect ourselves from a strain of "superpredators" while others claim that homicidal youth are a symbol of our current cultural confusion and loss of discipline.

In public discussions about "kids who kill" there has been the presumption that juvenile homicide is generated principally by violent images in contemporary media combined with the easy availability of guns. Although I do not reject that theory completely, Charley Miller's story confirms that long before *Rambo* and *The Matrix* there were homicidal boys—and also well-meaning adults who pointed an accusatory finger at cheap, sensational fiction, the influential popular culture of that day, as the cause. I began to look at Charley more closely, telling my students about what I found. There were actually many cases to talk about, but Charley quickly became the best case, because my historical detective work was producing a rich file of documentary material that made it possible for me to imagine him as a real boy, and more than just a name.

Charley Miller was a murderer—there is no doubt of that—but, like most boys who kill today, he was not a psychopath, a fact that made his story even more relevant and important. He never tortured small children, killed cats, or found sexual satisfaction in the act of murder. Charley's crime was commonplace: it was an adolescent impulse killing and a robbery, similar to many we see today. And it was rooted in the particular social and economic circumstances of being young, poor, and male in late-nineteenth-century America.

Until the fatal incident in the Union Pacific boxcar, Charley Miller was absolutely ordinary and, by and large, ignored. There were thousands of poor boys just like him in the 1890s, and he only garnered special attention because of his age at the time of his crime and execution. His notoriety, fueled by an enterprising commercial press anxious to sell newspapers, made it possible for me to reconstruct his life even if the facts and details were sometimes carelessly reported. I trailed Charley Miller—step by step, month by month—from birth until his execution in Cheyenne seventeen years later. In early adolescence, Charley was a rolling stone, moving from place to place, making his way around and across the country, on his own, in search of a youthful dream. There was real detective work involved in trailing him, and in that process, I got to walk the streets he walked, and survey the cornfields he once helped to plow.

Although I admit to some degree of intuitive reconstruction at certain moments in this story, my historical imagination was always constrained by the facts and sources I uncovered in pursuit of Charley. I have been absolutely true to his words, recorded in interviews, on the witness stand, and in his poems and ballads. The fact that Charley's voice survived helped me understand what kind of young man he was, what made him tick. Though I wish he had said more, his terse, gruff assertions feel like a familiar form of adolescent verbal swagger, allowing me to see how boyish he really was. In this respect, his case provides a unique perspective on the long-standing connection between adolescent boys and violence in American life. Despite the passage of more than a century, Charley's experience rings true in terms of the way young males behave when they are stressed by harsh, unfortunate circumstances and face only a bleak future. Not all juvenile murderers are poor today, but they are often social outcasts with feelings of hurt and resentment that Charley would have understood.

Until now, very few Americans have ever heard of Charley Miller. If my readers take this as a romantic tribute to a forgotten boy murderer, they are mistaken. My intention is not to glamorize Charley or his crime: the murder he committed was undeniably ugly and merited serious punishment. In reconstructing his life (and the lives of his victims), I tried to understand him—both as an adolescent boy and as a historical figure—and it's the blending of the two that gives the story its meaning. The more I learned about Charley Miller, the more I realized that his grim tale was the flip side of the famous Horatio Alger story, a challenge, in fact, to the myth that opportunity and success come easily in America.

For the boy who called himself "Kansas Charley," the American experience was about emotional and economic scarcity, not opportunity. In the end, vested economic interests and local politics, not charity or forgiveness, determined his fate. In many ways, both large and small, his experience anticipated the thorny mix of social, economic, and legal issues that surround juvenile homicide and juvenile justice today. That's the point of my retelling. If there are moments in Charley's story when you feel a sense of déjà vu, you are not alone.

PART ONE

CHAPTER ONE

The Cradle of Youth

AT THE END of the nineteenth century, two streams of childhood experience collided visibly on the streets of New York City. There were pampered, middle-class children pushed about in fancy carriages by proud parents eager to show them off, but also plenty of poor children, alone or with only minimal supervision, collecting coal, rifling through piles of garbage, and looking for small handouts. The pampered child had a full stomach, smelled sweet, and clutched a toy—a sharp contrast to those with dirty, open palms, anxious about the next meal, and hoping to bring a few coins home to the family.

The sons and daughters of the American middle class had already begun to experience the pleasures we associate with modern childhood: reliable and constant care by adults; time for play; prolonged schooling extending into the adolescent years. Their mothers, assisted at home by domestic servants, had enough leisure to attend "Child Study Clubs," where they read and discussed the latest scientific ideas about child-raising that were percolating into the middle class. The child-study movement, along with the new specialty of pediatrics, popularized the idea that childhood was a distinct stage of life and that adolescents, in particular, progressed through a sequence of distinct developmental stages that their parents needed to recognize and understand. (G. Stanley Hall, a Clark University psychologist, first advanced the idea that storm and stress were absolutely normal in adolescence.) When youthful exuberance or disrespect had to be tamed or corrected, this generation of parents was more likely than any before them to spare the rod and spoil the child. Expectations had changed: middle-class youngsters—even adolescents—were no longer expected to do much work. They had become "emotionally priceless but economically useless," an exchange that felt comfortable, even desirable, to many middle-class Americans who put their children at the center of their universe.

This kind of thinking was alien in a less affluent, more traditional America, where children were still regarded as mini-adults expected to function like cogs in the wheel of the family's economic machinery. Among the urban poor, but also among farm families, children as young as six or seven had to assist in the support of their parents and their siblings rather than studying and socializing at the local schoolhouse. A remarkable number of them were also separated from their parents, even left homeless, because of periodic unemployment, chronic illness, and high mortality rates. Dependent on begging and rudimentary forms of charity, these urban street urchins were regarded as an economic problem— even a social threat—but not as priceless. If they were taken in by other families, their desirability more often then not hinged on what kind of slot they could fill in someone else's family economy. Children like these still had utility, and the chores they were assigned were far more demanding than the make-work invented by middle-class parents to justify paying their youngsters a weekly allowance.

The idea that childhood in a civilized society ought to be prolonged and protected—a time for personal growth and development—was a luxury of the privileged. Although poor parents certainly loved their children, they had neither time nor resources to invest in pampering them. Poor children expected less of adults, and they learned to survive without many of the emotional and material supports provided to their peers in more secure environments. Even when they were very small, life was precarious, demanding, and harsh, a reality that left its unpleasant imprint on Charley Miller.

Charley was born on November 20, 1874, in a small, dark apartment at 248 West 37th Street in Manhattan, a tenement crowded with a mix of German and Irish immigrant families, all anxious to make a better life in America. His parents, Frederick and Marie Elise Muller, named him "Karl" and spoke German to him, their third child. An older girl, Caroline, had been born in 1872, on the trip to America, and Frederick, the father's namesake, followed in 1873. When the Mullers first arrived, they probably headed for Kleindeutschland, a bustling German community on Manhattan's Lower East Side, where the conversation, newspapers, even the tastes and smells all felt familiar. Only Vienna and Berlin had larger German populations than New York City at this time, so there were plenty of other German-speaking families to help the young couple adjust to life in the great metropolis.

Despite the advantages provided by this ethnic "city within a city," the Mullers' American experience soured within five years, in part because of Frederick's inability to find work as a *Pallischer* or nickel-plater. In the 1870s and 1880s, nickel was still applied as a coating to dishes, candlesticks, and cutlery, all made in a variety of New York factories and shops, but Muller never had much luck finding regular employment in any of them. In order to keep food on the table, he began to work in a neighborhood saloon, an economic expedient which was his undoing. Like many immigrants stressed by the transition to a new environment, he turned to alcohol— probably cheap beer—to soothe the pain of an insecure existence, which became even worse with the birth of William, a fourth child in 1877. Then, three years later, on January 20, 1880—with four children under the age of ten—his wife, thirty-year-old Marie, died suddenly of a "miscarriage and septicemia," an infection of the blood. (The official description may well have hidden a botched abortion performed to prevent the birth of a fifth child.) Karl Muller, the boy who became Charley Miller and then Kansas Charley, was five at the time of his mother's death.

Fathers with children to raise on their own were fairly common-place in this era because of the high maternal mortality rate. Al-though it was an unhappy last resort, many men in Muller's situation surrendered their children to orphan asylums, in the hopes of being able to live with them again once they had accumulated enough resources to provide for their care. After the passage of the New York State Children's Law of 1875, which gave per-capita sub-sidies to children's institutions, the orphan asylum became a more popular choice than the poorhouse and the dole. At the asylum in Albany, one of the nation's largest, most of the children had one par-ent alive. (To reflect common practice, there were institutions called "half orphan" asylums.)

Frederick Muller chose not to give up his children even tem-porarily. Instead, he looked for help among the other families in the tenement at 346 West 37th Street, where he moved after his wife's untimely death. In the new location, there were at least a half-dozen adult women staying at home, many with children, but their ability to keep track of someone else's kids was limited because they had daily wages to earn—as laundresses taking in soiled gar-ments and bedclothes, or as silk winders, warpers, and weavers, all forms of work that brought extra money into their struggling households. The Muller children were expected to help their fa-ther, who continued to earn a pitiful living at the nearby saloon. Fred and Charley—now six and five—were old enough to look for valuable material dropped or discarded on the street. And Caro-line, at only eight, was a competent, obedient child, able to provide a semblance of care for her brothers, especially three-year-old Willie. Caroline was not the only young girl in the neighborhood who stayed at home to prepare meals, do the wash, and carry water and slops. Although the New York state legislature passed a mandatory-school law in 1875, it went unenforced for decades, es-pecially in New York City's immigrant quarters.

With Carrie acting as a little mother, Muller continued to drown his sorrows in drink and lose his temper with the children. Instead of providing them with the solace and comfort they needed after the loss of their mother, he became despondent and spoke of killing himself. Perhaps Muller tried to find himself another German-speaking wife, but he certainly was no catch: he was responsible for four small children, had no material resources, and lacked any marketable skills. On March 25, 1881, the forty-four-year-old father of four committed suicide by drinking Paris Green, a cheap, readily available insecticide that was close to 45 percent arsenic. Because the poison did not work efficiently, Muller lingered, ending up in a New York City hospital, an unexpected development that generated the family's American newspaper debut: "Frederick Muller, a nickel plater, residing at No. 346 West Thirty-Seventh Street died yesterday at Roosevelt Hospital from the effects of Paris Green, which he had swallowed the previous evening with suicidal intent. His wife died some months ago, and at time since [ever since] Muller had been subject to fits of despondency and had frequently threatened his life."

Suicide was not well understood in the 1880s. For some Americans it connoted crime and immorality; for others it was increasingly regarded as a symptom of insanity and mental disease. Among the German immigrants of New York, it was not uncommon. They had the highest incidence of any ethnic group in this era. For the Muller children, however, it must have been more devastating than the loss of their mother only fourteen months before. In all likelihood, the children were told that their mother had died in childbirth, that she was taken by God to a better place. But there was no easy way to sweeten the fact that their father killed himself, probably in their apartment, leaving them alone. Within the tenement and neighborhood where they lived, news of the event was upsetting, generating concern about what would become of the youngsters. Somehow, the neighbors who watched Frederick's decline managed to overlook his sinfulness and bury him, along with Marie, in the Lutheran cemetery instead of the anonymous potter's field, the final resting place of the truly indigent and isolated.

Authorities at Roosevelt Hospital probably were responsible for bringing the Muller children to the attention of the New York

Orphan Asylum (NYOA). Admission there was not guaranteed, however; it was granted only at the discretion of the Executive Committee of the Orphan Asylum Society of the City of New York, a group of six estimable matrons who received applications every Wednesday, from ten to noon, at the East 29th Street home of one of its well-heeled members. Apparently, when the case was presented, the children of Frederick and Marie Muller were deemed worthy of care and protection despite their father's disreputable end. Only six days after his death, on April 1, 1881, they were admitted to the asylum on West 73rd Street, between Eleventh Avenue and Riverside Drive. There, in new surroundings, only a few miles from the dark rooms where they experienced a potent mixture of loss and abandonment, they became Carrie, Fred, Charley, and Willie Miller, and they probably never spoke much German again. Charley was now six years old.

Founded in 1806, the New York Orphan Asylum was a mature presence in New York City when the Muller children were taken in. By this time, the asylum cared for nearly two hundred children, ranging from infants to early adolescents. Children of German descent were the largest group. The annual report for 1882 stated proudly that "the fair hair and blue eyes of Germany" were met "at every turn" within the asylum. Visually, at least, the Miller children fit in.

In keeping with the Victorian ideal that the care of children and the home should be a women's special responsibility, the board of directors and the trustees of the asylum were almost entirely women, both married and single, who combined a sense of civic responsibility with solid bank accounts. Since there still were many restrictions on women's equality in matters of law and commerce, a few men served as an Advisory Committee. Not all these women were rich, but the organization clearly had its fair share of wealthy benefactresses, women with family names like Auchincloss and Sloane Coffin, who represented the city's elite and gave significant annual contributions as well as tangible gifts, many reflecting the latest middle-class ideas about the special needs of children. There were donations intended to please the orphan's appetites—such as apples and oranges, candies and fruitcakes—but also objects intended for play, sociability, and learning: pails and tea sets, drawing slates, blocks, dolls, wagons, and books. Unlike middle-class children, the orphans did not own their own toys; they were expected to share.

There was little need for the Miller children to worry now about being hungry: they got their food at set hours, in reasonable amounts. They also had clean, individual beds, set out in long rows, as well as a basic wardrobe and a place to store it: four shirts (or chemises in Carrie's case): two suits of clothes and four pairs of stockings, all marked with their names. Even though they were required to wear aprons when they were playing, their clothes were washed regularly. In fact, they had to change their underwear twice a week and bathe every Saturday. In the asylum, well-scrubbed faces and clean clothing were considered important outward signs of good character and morality.

Although these middle-class hygienic routines were unfamiliar at first, everything was so orderly and predictable that it probably afforded the Miller children a sense of security after the wrenching events of the previous two years. Each morning, when the boys were awakened at 6 A.M., they were greeted and directed by the boy's caretaker. Immediately they aired their beds, opened windows, washed, dressed, and prayed. (Carrie did exactly the same under the direction of the girl's caretaker.) Then the children were led to chapel for a service conducted by George E. Dunlap, the asylum superintendent, usually accompanied by his wife, Harriet, the asylum matron. Breakfast and school followed. Classes were held from 8:30 to 10 A.M., and from 10:30 to noon. After lunch, there were classes again from 1:30 until 3 P.M., and, when they finally ended, a brief opportunity to use the playroom (where toys were stored) or the outside yard before another round of evening chapel, supper, and private prayers. Occasionally, the routine was broken with an exciting trip to Central Park, the American Institute Fair, or even P. T. Barnum's circus.

Wary about visitors who might upset the routine, the asylum opened its doors only once or twice a year for public "exercises," which took the form of recitations, poems, choruses, duets, and calisthenics. After one such performance, the *New York Herald* lauded the "chubby and happy set of juveniles" on display. Asylum directors and supporters adored this kind of positive publicity and tended to blow their own horn in their annual reports: "The voice of joy and health has been clearly sounded in our Institution throughout the whole of the past year," they announced in 1883. Public impressions were important, because there were many in the city (and the nation) who did not believe in the effectiveness of orphan asylums. Consequently, on those few occasions when their charges were out in public, the adults who ran the asylum made order, decorum, and a sweet, neat appearance paramount concerns.

The Miller children must have recognized quickly that propriety, compliance, and piety were valued in this new environment. Whatever they had learned from their parents about Jesus was now reinforced on a daily basis through required prayers as well as exposure to moralistic evangelical religious texts, such as the *Wide Awake*, a popular magazine that was a part of the Chautauqua Young Folk's Reading Union. (Even asylum youngsters were urged to give the few pennies they might have—usually gifts from relatives or visiting trustees—to save the heathen in foreign lands.) Education in the asylum generally stuck to the basics, since there were some Americans, then as now, who thought that the children of the poor should not be indulged in frivolous or stimulating subjects such as music, art, or literature. When music was first introduced into the asylum in 1881, the year the Millers matriculated, trustees felt that they had to justify the innovation, known as the "tonic sol-fa" notation system, on the grounds that music was healthful for children and not simply enjoyable.

In general, asylum teachers taught only the rudiments—reading, writing, spelling, arithmetic, grammar, and geography—because so many orphans left the asylum at a young age, and this was likely to be the only formal education they would ever receive. Most children did leave soon after their twelfth birthday, the moment when they were placed out on indenture into families with good credentials. (These were established by trustworthy sources, almost always Protestant clergymen.) In an indenture, the orphan and the employer had a three-month trial period; if things worked to the satisfaction of both, the employer then paid twenty-five dollars to the alma mater, where it was kept in trust until the youngster was eighteen and ready to get a start in life.

The Miller children absorbed what the asylum had to offer, including a sense of the structure of authority in the idealized middle-class home. In order to model what youngsters were likely to find on the outside, Mr. and Mrs. Dunlap's responsibilities were set up to mirror those of a normal father and mother. Mr. Dunlap supervised all male employees and boy orphans, buildings and grounds, official record-keeping, and financial accounts; Mrs. Dunlap was in charge of housekeeping—food, clothes, and bedding—as well as direction of all things concerned with female orphans and female employees. The annual reports were explicit about the Dunlaps' role as surrogate parents: "From time to time entertainment and relaxation are provided, and the Superintendent and his wife do all in their power to act the part of true parents to these orphans." The organizational directives also made it clear that the Superintendent, like a good father, was the head of this huge artificial family, and that his authority prevailed.

There was one exception, however, which would have consequences for Charley Miller. On questions requiring medical judgments, such as the severity of an illness, the need for a quarantine, or methods for treating certain behavioral problems, Dunlap was likely to defer to the asylum physician, John L. Campbell. Dr. Campbell, an 1845 graduate of Union College, received his medical degree from the College of Physicians and Surgeons in New York City in 1850, and by 1881 had been with the asylum for over fifteen years. In 1890, he was elected to the prestigious New York Academy of Medicine. Campbell always maintained a private practice at 259 West 42nd Street, a reasonable walk from the asylum where he spent most of his professional life.

The Dunlaps worked hand in hand with Dr. Campbell to modernize the asylum and keep it free from contagious diseases, the kind that could devastate an institution with so many young children in close proximity to one another. At the instigation of Campbell, the board authorized expenditures for improvements in plumbing and drainage, including refitting of the water closets. Campbell encouraged the staff to be absolutely fastidious about personal hygiene—their own as well as the orphans'—and vigilant about the cleanliness of all communal areas involving food and bodily fluids. Given the well-known carelessness of children, and the fact that so many poor youngsters had no prior experience with indoor plumbing, the boy's and girl's caretakers were required personally to flush all the water closets at least four times a day. Together, the Dunlaps and Dr. Campbell lived and modeled the idea that "cleanliness is next to Godliness."

Just like powerful parents, Mr. and Mrs. Dunlap loomed large in the minds of the children because they dispensed special treats as well as punishments. The asylum had its own reward system: for those who were quiet and mindful there was an occasional apple, a piece of rock candy; for responsible older girls, an opportunity to assist with infants in the nursery; for those who performed especially well in their schoolwork, a "Roll of Honor" where names were inscribed. Those who remained on the honor roll for an entire year won copper and silver medals entitling them to read alone in the evenings. In the case of misbehavior, boys were taken to Mr. Dunlap, girls to his wife, and both used vocal chastisement and moral suasion initially.

Yet everyone knew that Mr. Dunlap maintained his own higher court, where some children were whipped. Although asylum regulations maintained that "no teacher, or employee, shall under any circumstance, strike or maltreat a child," the superintendent was

allowed to inflict corporal punishment if "necessary for the mainte-
nance of good discipline." When a whipping did occur, the of-
fending child's teacher or caretaker was supposed to be at the
superintendent's side in order to make sure that the punishment
was not excessive. Naturally enough, stories of beatings by Dunlap
and company were repeated among the children, making most of
them wary of bringing any particular notice to themselves, no matter how badly they needed emotional attention. Although the asylum provided ample food and a modest education, it was not a
sanctuary where emotional wounds were healed, or tears brushed
away by the soft embrace of a loving adult.

<hr>

Carrie was the first of the Miller children to be noticed in any special way. She was actually "placed out" of the asylum at the age of
ten, two years before the conventional age for this momentous
transition. Female orphans were easier to place than boys, especially when they had well-honed domestic skills the way Carrie
did. In the 1880s, the demand for adolescent girls to help with domestic work was so heavy that the managers of the asylum in New
York City felt the need to tell the public that it was not an employment agency for female servants, even though its graduates were
"good little seamstresses" by the time they left. In addition to
cleaning, ironing, and sweeping, ten-year-old Carrie could darn
and mend, piece together a simple garment, and tend a kitchen
garden. She may also have been one of the coveted helpers in the
asylum nursery, a role that was excellent preparation for placement
with a young family desiring a pleasant girl.

   A perfect family appeared on the scene in the fall of 1882, when
Esther Mead Weaver, a young mother with a six-month-old son,
came to New York City to visit her parents and introduce them to
their new grandchild. Esther and her husband, George, lived in
Ilion, an upstate New York city of almost five thousand people on
the Erie Canal. George Weaver graduated from Syracuse University in 1878 and tried his hand at teaching for two years in Troy,

New York, but this failed to satisfy his entrepreneurial spirit. He quickly moved from the classroom to the print shop to become editor of the *Ilion Citizen*. In addition to writing and editing the weekly, Weaver did commercial jobbing, experimented with new typographies, and applied for patents for his many inventions. Under his energetic leadership, the paper expanded its advertising by 25 percent and it soon claimed to be the "best looking paper" in Herkimer County.

The Weavers were expansive in other ways: they expected to have more children, and they eventually did. (Between 1882 and 1889, they had four.) With this prospect in mind, Esther Weaver envisioned the possibility of domestic help, an idea that led her to the New York Orphan Asylum, where, she was told by her friends, good helpers were likely to be found. Carrie Miller must have been well recommended and attractive because the match was arranged quickly. Carrie left Manhattan, the asylum, and her three younger brothers in December 1882, just in time for the Weaver baby's first Christmas at home in Ilion. A year later, she was listed in the Ilion census, living with the Weavers and helping with the baby but also attending school. To the Weavers' credit, Carrie Miller attended school until she was sixteen, an opportunity that was unusual among poor and working-class adolescent girls.

Fred, the next oldest of the Miller children, left the asylum in 1886 in a very different way when he was almost thirteen. Fred was sent westward by train with a group of orphans under the care and supervision of an agent representing the Children's Aid Society of New York (CAS). The "orphan trains" were the brainchild of Charles Loring Brace, the son of a prominent Connecticut family, who founded the CAS in 1853 and wrote *The Dangerous Classes of New York* in 1880. Brace was opposed to orphanages because he believed that home care was superior to institutional care. He feared that the regimentation of the asylum did little to build the kind of self-reliance that practical living required. The best solution, he maintained, was to remove poor children from vicious urban environments and send them westward to live in farm homes where, he assumed, the families were welcoming, generous, and anxious for their labor. It was an idealistic, pastoral solution that allegedly cost a tenth of what it did to maintain a child in an asylum. Between 1853 and 1893, over ninety thousand American youngsters were placed in this way, 91 percent of them in New York State, New Jersey, Illinois, Iowa, Missouri, Ohio, Indiana, Kansas, and Michigan.

Whatever Brace's differences with orphan asylums, the CAS collaborated with NYOA to send youngsters west for placement. According to the annual reports of the asylum, the male youngsters in their care sorely wanted this opportunity: "The boys, God bless them! [They] begin to look so eagerly toward the West, emulating the successful career of those already gone, that we often find them rebelling against indenture nearer home." Placement out west was attractive because it raised the prospect of land ownership, a point that the asylum board repeatedly hammered into its annual reports to benefactors: "The letters received from our boys in the West are always interesting. One boy placed on a farm in 1880 at the age of twelve now owns 168 acres of land, and another owns three town lots worth $500."

On June 9, 1886, Fred Miller left the asylum for the last time, leaving Charley and Willie behind, as he headed out on an orphan train bound for St. Louis and then on to Kansas. The children ate food provided by the CAS and slept in their seats until they reached their destination three days later. The CAS agent who accompanied them made sure that they were all washed and had their hair combed so that they would look their best. Now they faced the critical moment—known as "the distribution"—when local farmers and their families came to see if there were any among them whose age, size, appearance, and general demeanor were appealing enough to take the boys home. Sometimes, there were announcements of an upcoming distribution in the newspapers or a poster in a local church. CAS placements were free, so news of an event like this could generate a sizable crowd to watch the selection process. Recognizing that this might be their chance for adoption, the children were understandably excited, but also nervous about how they would fare in what was, ultimately, a competition. In order to calm them, the CAS agent talked enthusiastically about their future prospects and handed out Bibles, a conventional prop, so that each child could carry one onto the stage of the opera house, church, or auditorium where the distributions typically took place.

Although nothing is known about Fred's reaction to the distribution, there was a great deal of preparation for it in Leonardville, the Kansas town where he found himself on June 12. Founded only five years earlier, Leonardville was a small Riley County village, overshadowed by neighboring Manhattan, a town of three thousand, twenty-six miles to the southeast. Leonardville was thought to be coming into its own, however, because of its fortuitous location on the Kansas Central, a division of the Union Pacific Railroad, the great national highway that spanned the continent when it was completed in 1869. One of the men on the committee responsible for bringing in the New York orphans was John Crans, a physician, who had his house moved by a mule team from nearby Riley in order to take advantage of the developing action in Leonardville. By the time Fred Miller arrived, Leonardville had two banks, four general stores, both telegraph and express offices, and a money-order post office with two rural-delivery routes. Most of the people were hardworking farmers earning their livelihood from the state's celebrated fertile soil—sometimes called the "golden grain belt"—but there were also enterprising merchants, such as the Erpelding and Sikes families, whose stores on the main street sold a wide variety of staples and desirable manufactured goods.

Leonardville's only newspaper, the weekly *Monitor*, offered repeated reminders about the arrival of the orphan train bearing Fred Miller: "Don't forget that the New York boys will be here a week from Saturday." And: "The New York boys will meet the public at the schoolhouse. They are hunting homes with the farmers." In this town, as in many others throughout the Midwest, there was enormous optimism about the human shipment coming from the great metropolis. The *Monitor* assured everyone that the New York City orphans were "all bright, well trained, and very fairly educated." As a result, there was considerable disappointment when there were not enough to go around. "The number brought in last Friday was entirely inadequate to supply the demand and a large number were disappointed," explained the local newspaper editor, Preston Loofbourrow, whose prose reverberated with his zeal for the project: "The boys were all taken to good homes, and will no doubt grow up to be worthy members of society." Loofbourrow was quick to claim a promising orphan for himself. That boy was Fred Miller, whom he intended to have work at his side, as a helper, in the printing trade.

Within weeks, Fred was comfortably settled in the Loofbourrows' home smack in the center of town, enjoying the kindness and the stimulation of his new employer, a hardworking man with many talents. The son of an abolitionist, Loofbourrow graduated from Liber College in Jay County, Indiana, and served briefly with Company E of the 139th Indiana Infantry in the Civil War. Afterward, he taught school for a number of years in a variety of situations that familiarized him with boys and their ways. In addition to editing the weekly *Monitor*, he was a farmer, an amateur attorney, an insurance agent, and a Republican of conviction. He was also the local postmaster and a representative of the 58th District in the Kansas legislature, both at the same time. The Loofbourrow family— including his wife, Sarah, and their daughter, Orpha, who was almost fourteen—were active members of the Methodist Episcopal church. (Another daughter, Mary, had died at age two.) Preston and Sarah had never had a son of their own, so the prospect of having a good, healthy adolescent boy around the house held out emotional as well as economic promise. When a CAS agent came to observe the situation a few months later, he told his colleagues back in New York: "Fred has a good home is happy and contented and intends to learn printing."

Newspaper offices and print shops were an important center of community information and activity in nineteenth-century America, as well as a place where adolescent boys had a significant role running errands, sweeping floors, and carting papers from storage to the pressroom. They could also learn specific trade activities that were the start of a printing career, such as how to wash ink off used type and then distribute the type back into the typesetter's case. A galley boy carried type that was already set in a shallow wooden tray to a proof press, where a print was made, read, and then corrected by the foreman, before the type was set in a metal frame on the press. Boys also fed blank sheets into the machine press and then removed them to be dried—a process called "flying the press." And, before electrification, a strong teenager pulled or cranked the newspaper press by hand. Boys also worked the treadle press with their feet, producing attention-getting handbills, fancy trade cards, and impressive business stationery, the kind of small jobs that kept many newspaper operations solvent. Author William Dean Howells, who spent his youth in his father's Ohio print shop, admitted there was a "halo of romance about the old-fashioned country [printing] office" that was hard for him to shake even as he matured. "The printing office was the center of civic and social interest," he explained, and although the place was gritty—the walls were blotched with ink and the floor was littered with refuse—it was frequented by visitors all the time, most notably schoolgirls and young ladies, who appeared in noisy, chattering groups on publication day.

Fred enjoyed this new life, regardless of whether or not he understood the opportunity in it. He took to the work easily, confirming that his schooling in the New York Orphan Asylum had prepared him sufficiently to become a printer. When he was not in the shop, he made friends among his peers in the village, and he quickly felt comfortable in his new home. Sarah Loofbourrow, who had no comparisons to make with any other sons, cooked good hearty meals and enjoyed Fred's liveliness. Some years later, Preston Loofbourrow reflected on what the orphan train meant to him and his wife: "Fred was selected by ourself [sic] from the number and has been a member of our family since that time. He has been a remarkably industrious, faithful and upright boy ever since, as the entire community will attest." On another occasion, he told the Children's Aid Society how pleased he was with Fred, now sixteen: "He has no bad habits and detests the use of intoxicants and tobacco." Because Fred was so industrious and reliable, Loofbourrow began to train him to keep the books and handle his money. He was a boy with "push and snap," he said, worthy of being treated like a son.

Fred's placement was so satisfactory that the Loofbourrows tried to help his brothers as well. Their attempts to assist Charley were not successful, though their later efforts on behalf of Willie, the youngest child, were. When Willie Miller was twelve and it was time for him to the leave the asylum, Preston and Sarah requested him because they knew it would make "their Fred" happy. As teenagers, they would play together in Leonardville's brass band. Preston never considered Willie any match to Fred—he told the CAS that the youngest Miller was "better adapted to the farm" than to the print shop (a judgment about his spelling and writing) and that he had a "somewhat peculiar disposition and manner" (he liked to tell odd jokes and laugh boisterously). Yet Willie remained with the Loofbourrrows, accompanying them in 1894 to a new home in Willow Springs, Missouri. Both boys were raised by Mrs. Loofbourrow and treated as if they were her own sons. For Fred in particular, the unflagging loyalty of Preston and Sarah provided important emotional stability in the early 1890s, when Charley was in the national news for the terrible double murder. Even then, Sarah Loofbourrow told the CAS: "We still think everything of Fred."

<hr />

While Carrie, Fred, and Willie Miller were resilient and capable of responding successfully to the challenges posed by life after the loss of their parents, six-year-old Charley was not. In the asylum, he wet his bed, a behavior that was not easily ignored or excused after an initial period of adjustment, and as he matured. Wet sheets and nightclothes were an extra burden for the asylum laundress and offensive to caretakers who upheld middle-class expectations that children his age were supposed to control their bladders. They recognized that poor children accustomed to backyard outhouses had to be retrained to use water closets correctly, but Charley seemed unable to control himself even when he was reminded and awakened at night. For Charley, wet sheets were probably humiliating, and they led, eventually, to a cure that may have been traumatic.

For fastidious sanitarians such as the Dunlaps, Charley's bedwetting had to stop. They had no tolerance for the smell of stale urine, because they were always on guard for any odor that reflected badly on their management. They could make Charley wash his own sheets—a punishment based on the idea that humiliation was a good deterrent—but as long as Charley was small, he was unable to get the soaked bedding clean on his own. Despite asylum regulations, Superintendent Dunlap eventually turned to corporal punishment. When asked about his upbringing in the New York Orphan Asylum, Charley consistently told the same story: "I was whipped very often." When asked why, he replied: "Because I had a disease I couldn't stop it."

Charley's understanding of his bedwetting as a disease suggests that Dr. John Campbell got involved. Campbell understood that Charley's wet sheets were a symptom of a condition known as enuresis or involuntary incontinence, and he was disturbed that the boy's symptom continued even as he approached the age for placing out. Medical science proposed a wide variety of causes for *enuresis nocturna*, the kind that occurred during sleep: local irritations and infections; organic defects in the urethra, kidney, bladder, or penis; even the embarrassing business of onanism or masturbation, known then as "self-abuse."

Uncertain whether it was problematic plumbing or debased morals in Charley's case, Campbell probably turned to *Nocturnal Enuresis and Incontinence of Urine* (1869) by Dr. Frederick

Snelling. Here, in the definitive work on the disorder, he learned that Charley's problem was "one of the most loathsome and repulsive weaknesses that can befall a child." Snelling felt, however, that each case of enuresis was different, and that it was up to the attending physician to decide if the point of origin was principally organic or nervous (what we now call psychological). Snelling was generally not in favor of the scoldings, humiliations, and punishments that bedwetting traditionally generated, because, like most up-to-date doctors of his day, he assumed some biological cause that compromised Charley's self-control. When Dunlap's whipping did not work, Campbell must have agreed to step in, since Charley's bedwetting had been going on for a number of years.

Assuming that John Campbell read Snelling, it is likely that he began to look for a cause in Charley's maturing twelve-year-old body. This required a physical examination to determine if an organic defect or disease existed. Charley's genitals and rectum had to be checked, as well as the color, specific gravity, and organic ingredients of his urine. If Charley displayed "much nervous irritability" (what we call today attention-deficit hyperactivity disorder, or ADHD), Campbell might have tried a daily dose of a solution of morphine to tamp down his patient's rambunctiousness. More often, bedwetters were denied liquids at night and given a bland, soft diet in order to reduce irritating acidity in the urine.

Because Victorian medicine implicated self-abuse in bedwetting, Charley's genitals were a focus of Campbell's clinical probing. Masturbation in children was regarded with special horror because it was a form of precocious sexuality that violated middle-class notions of childhood innocence. Believed to be most prevalent in boys between the ages of eight and sixteen, masturbation was thought to deplete seminal reserves that needed to be saved for reproduction in the married state. Little girls were thought less likely to indulge, because—like their idealized mothers—they were believed to be more pure and less sexual than boys, no matter what their age.

Charley was now coming into puberty, the time of life that

psychologist G. Stanley Hall portrayed as a landmark in the development of masculinity. It was also a perilous stage, because the possibility of masturbation increased with sexual awakening. Almost everywhere—in popular treatises, advice to mothers, serious medical books—masturbation in youth was cast as a dangerous practice, carrying with it a sequence of physical and social ills including infertility, venereal disease, marital unhappiness, crime, insanity, and premature death. This kind of medical domino theory was not the invention of medical charlatans or crackpots. It was absolutely mainstream, and physicians with international reputations, such as Englishman Henry Maudsley, joined the war against it. Known for his pioneering work in classifying diseases of the mind, Maudsley reported that masturbation was common among the insane, a finding that many took to mean that it was causative in what came to be known as "masturbatory induced insanity."

Young men and adolescent boys in the nineteenth century internalized this fear of masturbation, so much so that any expression of autoeroticism caused them enormous guilt and anxiety. In newspapers and magazines they saw a myriad of worrisome advertisements for pills and nostrums claiming to help men resist the evils of the practice, also known as "the solitary vice." Theodore Dreiser, born in 1871—only three years before Charley Miller—regarded it all as "religious and moral piffle" when he was older, but he admitted that, in his youth, he was genuinely terrified by the prospect of sickness, brain trouble, and total physical collapse, all because he touched himself every two or three days, when he fantasized about the baker's daughter. The young Dreiser believed that if he managed to reach adulthood at all, he would end up an emaciated, sunken-eyed fellow, a pathetic victim of his own "youthful excess."

But as bad as masturbation was supposed to be, physicians in Campbell's generation were never really clear about its relationship to bedwetting. Some proposed that urine was passed involuntarily while masturbating in bed; others asserted that urination while sleeping caused discomfort and irritation, which then led to masturbation. A striking number of post–Civil War physicians, many of them well known and based in New York City and Philadelphia, posited that the prepuce, the foreskin of the penis, needed special scrutiny because it could be diseased, stimulate masturbation, and then generate a wide range of organic diseases including enuresis. Abraham Jacobi, the highly regarded president of the American Pediatric Society, advised that an irritated foreskin was the primary cause of masturbation; M. J. Moses, his colleague in New York City, was confident that a long prepuce contributed to masturbation. Although these Victorian doctors had no clear understanding of normal variation in the foreskin, their pervasive anxiety about sexuality and genitalia led them to perceive it as a site of enormous problems.

In the Miller case, Campbell suspected a condition known as phimosis, conceptualized as a type of strangulation of the male sex organ. In phimosis, the foreskin was elongated in such a way that it constricted the orifice of the penis and led to irritation. Joseph Howe, professor of clinical surgery at Bellevue Hospital Medical College and a fellow of the New York Academy of Medicine, reported that phimosis in children produced both incontinence and "a tendency to handle the parts." C. E. Nichols, a physician from Troy, New York, recommended a way to treat it. In the *Medical Record* for 1879, he explained that he had had good results with surgery on a fifteen-year-old with "an unusually long and somewhat thickened prepuce" who was unable to control himself day or night. Because examination for the condition was so painful, Nichols chloroformed his patient and then took the opportunity to remove surgically a liberal piece of his foreskin. After the circumcision, Nichols claimed that the Troy boy's enuresis disappeared totally, something that Dr. Campbell probably read with enormous interest, given his problems with Charley Miller.

As shocking as it may seem today, the decision to circumcise Charley at age twelve was a logical intervention based on the most progressive medical theory of the day. In both New York City and England there were physicians touting the idea that circumcision eliminated both bedwetting and masturbation. Jewish men were often proffered as proof of the claim. Dr. Moses, a Jew, claimed that, though masturbation was not "entirely absent" among his people, he had "never [seen] an instance in a Jewish child of very tender years" except where the organic condition of phimosis existed. Dr. Norman Chapman, a Kansas City Protestant, called for circumcision on broader hygienic grounds. "Moses was a good sanitarian," he explained in 1882. All of these ideas influenced John Campbell as he considered the recalcitrant case of the second-oldest Miller boy. In the end, he probably reasoned that, if circumcision did not cure Charley's chronic bedwetting, at least it was a sanitary precaution, a way to help him stay clean.

For cultural as well as scientific reasons, Charley was circumcised at the New York Orphan Asylum in a last-ditch effort to cure him of his "loathsome" habit. Except for American Jews, who maintained a ritual form of circumcision performed by a *mohel* at an event called a *bris*, the practice was still relatively unusual in the United States in the 1880s. Most babies were born at home, and most male infants remained uncircumcised until the early twentieth century, when the spread of hospitals and rigorous sanitary protocols normalized cutting the foreskin, making it a secular rather than a religious act. Well into the twentieth century, circumcision among non-Jews was confined to the carriage trades, while poor, working-class boys like Fred and Willie Miller grew into manhood with uncut foreskins.

Charley's penis never again looked like that of his brothers or most other boys in his social class and generation. His circumcision was a souvenir of the asylum that he always carried with him, although its exact meaning for him is hard to discern. If the procedure was done without chloroform, he probably experienced his surgery as a painful trauma, the memory of which lingered and festered. On the other hand, he may have been made "insensible" with an anesthetic, after Dr. Campbell explained to him that he was going to undergo a medical procedure that would make him better and take away his humiliating problem.

Today, we understand that, although recalcitrant bedwetting may be the result of organic problems, it is also a symptom of deep dependency needs associated with early loss, lack of sustained connection to a parent or caregiver, and profound trauma. Charley's caretakers at the asylum did what they thought was best for him, but their understanding of enuresis and child psychology was severely limited by their cultural preoccupations with order, personal hygiene, and control of sexuality in the young. The asylum physician found more hope in surgical treatments that altered the body than in any form of talking therapy that eased Charley's emotional anxieties or sense of abandonment. When Charley finally left the NYOA for good in 1887, his body had been changed, but his noxious habit persisted, and it continued to affect his life, making it less and less likely that he would ever share in the security and success his siblings were beginning to enjoy.

——◆——

Soon after his twelfth birthday, in December 1886, Charley was placed out in the home of Lyman Babcock, a thirty-one-year-old farmer who lived in the Kempsville district of Virginia's Princess Anne County. Babcock's need for extra labor was supposed to be Charley's big opportunity, but it was a bad match from the start. Babcock's household included his wife, Adelia, who was ten years his senior; their eight-year-old daughter, Minnie; and two older adolescent stepchildren from Adelia's first marriage. (The Babcocks also had some hired hands and at least one servant girl to help them with the backbreaking work of their successful 180-acre farm, most of it in apples and peaches, corn, sweet potatoes, and oats.) There were four horses requiring daily attention, as well as a milch cow, sheep, pigs, poultry, and bees, all perfect assignments for a young boy who was supposed to help fill the family larder, smokehouse, and table. But Charley was unfamiliar with this kind of work and ill-at-ease around farm animals. He never said much about his time at the Babcocks' except that it did not work out because of his "disease." He arrived from New York City in the midst of an uncharacteristically heavy snowstorm and was gone before the full bloom of a Virginia spring.

After a few months back in the asylum, Charley was placed out again. This time he was sent west on an orphan train much like the one that took his brother Fred to Kansas a year earlier. According to modern social-work protocols, Charley's next home placement should have been carefully investigated and precautions taken to ensure his success. But standards were different in the nineteenth century, and the boy's caretakers felt he was lucky to have any opportunity to start life afresh in a better physical environment. The CAS agent on Charley's particular train in March 1887 was probably Charles R. Fry, who in later years made his headquarters in the Palmer House in Chicago. As the society's "resident Western agent and superintendent of emigration" to the West, Fry was estimated to travel over thirty thousand miles a year, mostly by train, seeking out families and communities willing to take in needy orphans and indigent children, sometimes known as "street rats." Fry's reputation rested on the quantity of placements he made, not their quality.

At the end of March 1887, before the snow evaporated and the mud hardened, an orphan train bearing Charley Miller arrived in St. Charles, Winona County, Minnesota, a town of fewer than a thousand people serviced by the Winona and St. Peter line. (This line hooked up with the Chicago and Northwestern coming out of Chicago.) The trip from New York City with eighteen other boys and girls was grueling, and the distribution lengthy, because Agent Fry chose to speak about the CAS and its mission before turning to the drama of the selection. According to Charles Loring Brace, the very sight of the "worn faces" of the city children was always a call to action: "People who were childless came forward to adopt children; others who had not intended to take any into their families, were induced to apply for them; and many who really wanted the children's labor pressed forward to obtain it." In St. Charles that day, a family who fit the latter description had their eyes on Charley Miller. The boy's blue eyes and fair hair, inherited from his German parents, were an attraction in rural Minnesota, where a majority of the people were of German, Norwegian, and Swedish extraction.

Charley was taken home that Friday afternoon by William and Nancy Booth, a couple in their early fifties, who owned a 160-acre farm seven miles north of Chatfield in Olmsted County, southeast of Rochester, now the home of the Mayo Clinic. In the 1880s, Chatfield was a busy little agricultural town of about eleven hundred people, surrounded by a number of mills that harnessed the power of the Root River to grind local wheat. Farmers in the surrounding countryside also grew corn, oats, and barley, while their wives and daughters produced butter, still a barter commodity. Some of the locals had a vision of a grander, richer Chatfield. To that end, they experimented with a cooperative creamery to produce butter and cheese for sale, and they also began to build sidewalks, a sure way to draw in farm wives and their daughters to the local mercantile establishments.

On the drive there by wagon, a distance of twelve miles that took about three hours, Charley was surprised to learn that he would be alone with the Booths, because their six children were all grown. They said they needed a boy his age to help them bring in the wheat, oats, barley, and potatoes that were essential to their livelihood. And they openly lamented the fact that, the year before, in 1886, they had spent $150—a tenth of their total income—on hired hands to help them out. What they wanted now was a boy whom they did not have to pay cash wages. Their eldest son, Elmer, who lived with his own family nearby, came along to St. Charles to help his parents consider the pickings and make a good selection.

The Booths were exactly the kind of family that Charles Loring Brace predicted would be drawn to the possibility of acquiring free labor but also "doing good" at the same time. Nancy Booth was a longtime member of the United Brethren, a pietistic group with a church less than a mile from her farm. She wanted Charley to go to Sunday school there and mix with other farm boys his age who were upstanding and hardworking. William Booth told the new arrival that Chatfield could be his great opportunity, that he hoped he would "stay and be contented." Booth offered as an incentive "a good ranch or a farm" when Charley reached the age of twenty-one, but that kind of economic incentive was probably wasted on twelve-year-old Charley, who was tired and frightened by the strangeness of his new surroundings. The Booth farmhouse was a long way from the busy village, and Minnesota's wide-open landscape and its noticeable quiet felt unfamiliar, even foreboding, compared with the orphanage.

Charley's future depended on how he got along in the Booth household, and whether or not he fit in. Unfortunately, there was little time for pleasantries or emotional adjustment, because the demands of farm life were intense and the growing season was so short. Plowing, sowing, threshing, corn husking, and haying were always done with a sense of urgency, each stage so dependent on time and weather. Even in the winter, the Booths had to prepare for the next step in the agricultural cycle and also provide continuous care for their numerous work animals—both mules and horses—as well as sheep and pigs raised to be slaughtered for their own table and for sale. From four milch cows, Nancy Booth consistently churned three hundred pounds of butter a year, some of which she exchanged with neighboring families, some of which she sold.

Within days, Charley was thrown into a busy routine of farm labor that he never forgot. In every account thereafter, he claimed that he began plowing the Booths' farm almost immediately, "walking in a furrow behind the plow, morning until night." (The claim seems hyperbolic, since the ground in Minnesota was still frozen at the time of his arrival.) Charley plainly never liked the muck and mire of the barnyard, or the process of feeding and grooming animals. During his first summer at the Booths', outdoor work was particularly onerous because the weather was so hot and dry, and the chinch bugs so numerous that his face and eyes were covered with them. In *Son of the Middle Border*, an account of farm life in this era, Hamlin Garland captured how Charley must have felt after a day in the Booths' fields: "You can scarcely limp home to supper, and it seems you cannot possibly go on another day—but you do—at least I did."

Some adolescent boys enjoyed demanding farm labor because they gained a sense of responsibility from mastering jobs, such as driving a team of horses, usually reserved for adult men. But the orphan boy from Manhattan's West Side never found any pleasure in working the Booths' land or being with their valuable animals. Neither did he make any friends among the boys who lived on the adjacent McGuire and Halloran farms, and there is no evidence that he ever fished with them for bass on the Root River or had time to meander down the two streams that bisected the Booths' property. William did hire some extra farmhands after Charley's arrival, but their presence did not help. Charley still found life at the Booths' burdensome, emotionally harsh and socially isolated. He missed his brothers, and there seemed to be no one amusing to talk to. Charley also felt that he did not get to go to school enough, and that the Booths "used" him badly. When asked to specify the nature of the ill-treatment, he said: "Whipping me and didn't clothe me." When asked why he was whipped, Charley said again that it was his "disease."

Charley's wet sheets probably put the kybosh on any adoption plans, but it was also clear that he did not want to stay on the farm because of the work demands, the Booths' austerity, and William's harsh response to his bedwetting. Although a visit by agent Charles Fry reported back to New York that Charley was "a good boy" who was "doing well in an excellent home," trouble was brewing. Charley had already started writing to his brother Fred in Kansas with complaints that he was mistreated and poorly clothed. He mentioned that he would like to leave Chatfield and come stay with Fred in Leonardville, an indication of his deep connection to his older brother. At first, the Loofbourrows were uncertain what to make of these complaints, but the complaints kept coming, and they were eventually corroborated by a local teacher.

In the winter of 1888, when work at the Booths' was temporarily suspended because of the cold and snow, Charley—now thirteen—managed to attend a local school, a square frame building set down in an open field, less than a mile from the Booth farm. For two months, he mixed with approximately thirty other children, ranging in age from five to twenty-one, at School 57 in the Elmira Township, taught by a young woman who either boarded with a farm family or lived nearby. Although the name of the teacher at this one-room schoolhouse remains unknown, it is likely that she was unmarried, not more than twenty-five years of age, and a graduate of a high school or summer training institute, not the Winona State Normal School. (Winona's graduates were the *crème de la crème* of teachers in this area of the state, and they generally taught in towns, as opposed to rural schoolhouses.) Even rural teachers, however, were held to a certain standard in Minnesota: they had to take examinations, both written and oral, and they had to adhere to rules and responsibilities set out by the districts. In addition to being responsible for a daily curriculum and keeping the temperature in the schoolroom between sixty-five and seventy degrees (no small feat in a Minnesota winter), rural schoolteachers were supposed to keep records on each individual student. Unfortunately, no records from School 57 survive.

According to the superintendent of schools in Olmsted County, in the summer of 1885 eight people were qualified to teach in the county: Lucy Bowers, Carrie Armstrong, Phebe Sprague, Emma Outcolt, Anna Forster, Annie Tisdale, Mattie Forster, and Mary Dooley. Any one of these young women may have been Charley's angel, the person who verified his account of hard times and physical abuse in the home of William and Nancy Booth. Somehow, Charley managed to reach out to his teacher and tell her about his situation. He must have presented his story in a convincing manner—perhaps he showed her proof of his beatings—because the teacher became sufficiently sympathetic to write a number of letters on Charley's behalf to Preston Loofbourrow in Kansas. Although the letters do not survive, they validated Charley's unhappy story and prompted Fred's guardian to contact the Children's Aid Society in New York City to see what could be done to ease the boy's distress.

Charley had been with the Booths slightly more than a year, but it felt like an eternity to an unhappy thirteen-year-old hoping for a happy reunion with his older brother. In desperation, he tried to run away at least twice. Once he fled secretly to his teacher's home, but his whereabouts were uncovered by one of the Booths' married daughters, who saw him, as she drove by in her wagon, on the teacher's front porch. According to Charley, Booth's daughter "told the old man about it," and that prompted William and Elmer to come fetch him: "They didn't say anything until I got outside. They said they ought to take me and tie me to a tree and cowhide me." In order to avoid what they threatened, Charley agreed to return with them to the isolated farm.

A few days later, William Booth received a letter from the Children's Aid Society, advising him that he could not hold the New York orphan against his will. As a result, Booth abandoned whatever plans he once had to adopt Charley and quickly returned the youngster—much like an unsatisfactory purchase—to the place where he had gotten him. Without any explanation or even a backward glance, he left Charley alone at the St. Charles railroad depot, without any food or money, and without a train ticket home. It was an overwhelming and probably terrifying moment for a youngster who was accustomed to a modicum of security, daily food, a bed, and clothes that were warm enough. Even if Charley and his sheets were a constant problem for Booth and his wife, it was a harsh response, not in keeping with the vision of Charles Loring Brace. Booth's silent abandonment suggested that he felt no responsibility to nurture and protect Charley, and that, whatever value the boy might have had as a farm laborer, he was not worth the trouble.

Charley did what he needed to do in order to survive. "I started out in the country looking for work," Charley explained matter-of-factly about what it was like to be left totally on his own at the age of thirteen: "Met a farmer who asked me what I was crying about, and he gave me a job on his farm." His nameless savior was subject to periodic drinking binges, but he never touched the boy, and he also provided sufficient food while Charley waited, for months, hoping to get assistance from either Kansas or New York City. And then the long-awaited letter arrived: "I got a letter while I was there. It had $5 in it. It was the New York letter, and [it] told me to call at the depot and get a ticket." Janet T. Sherman, treasurer of the New York Orphan Society, a member of the committee that had originally admitted the four Miller children to the asylum, financed the arrangements that made Charley's departure and reunion with his brother possible. The two had not seen each other in more than two years, so Charley was raring to go. In October 1888, he arrived safely in Kansas, where, under Preston Loofbourrow's able direction, he wrote a polite letter to New York indicating that he was very "thankful for what the [Children's Aid] Society had done for him."

＞＊＜

Leonardville felt distinctly different from Chatfield, even though it was an even smaller agricultural center. There was still too much talk about weather and animals for Charley's taste, but he liked the fact that the house where he lived with the Loofbourrows was in the center of the village, just a stone's throw away from the busy post office and stores, and only a half-mile to the spot where the railroad stopped to bring in travelers. The print shop where the *Monitor* was produced was also centrally located, and open to daily visitors with stories and jokes to tell. Charley must have realized that his older brother had been much luckier than he: Fred didn't have to perform hard physical labor, and Mr. Loofbourrow was nothing like William Booth. Fred's situation seemed more like an apprenticeship, a chance to use his head, work alongside his guardian, but also have some fun. (At this point in 1888, eleven-year-old Willie was still at the New York Orphan Asylum.)

In Kansas, everyone expected things to improve for Charley, especially in the firm, competent hands of Preston Loofbourrow, who was having such success with Fred. Almost immediately Loofbourrow put Charley to work at the *Monitor*, but he also allowed the two brothers time to talk alone and to socialize with other young people. In November 1888, Charley turned fourteen with Fred at his side. After a few months, however, for reasons that were never entirely clear, the Loofbourrows arranged a change of residence for Charley, probably because they did not need his help and one of their friends did.

Charley was sent to live in the home of James and Mary Elizabeth Colt in Randolph, a tiny settlement on the Big Blue River, less than five miles away, a distance that would allow the brothers to remain in touch. (Charley could hop on the local trunk railroad to go back and forth.) James Colt was also a printer, but he had been in poor health for some time, and he also had a string of daughters living at home: Mary, Bertha, Florence, and Sadie. In theory, Charley was a valuable addition, because he could do things to assist in the shop that girls generally did not do. And if the unpleasant business of wet sheets intruded, Mrs. Colt had four daughters to help with the washing, whereas Sarah Loofbourrow had only one. In terms of the Colt family economy, Charley's new placement made good sense.

Colt, just like Loofbourrow, was a Republican newspaper editor and also the local postmaster. A graduate of Allegheny College in Meadville, Pennsylvania, he was a former minister in the Methodist Episcopal church, and someone who would provide Charley with an appropriate moral environment. Colt's newspaper, the *Enterprise*, was a county weekly, known for being a wholesome affair, the kind the family could read together around the dinner table or in the parlor: "It is a paper no parent need to be afraid to place in the hands of children, nothing tending to the slightest degree of impurity being admitted to its columns." At the *Enterprise*, Charley would have a chance to learn the printer's trade in much the same way as Fred. Loofbourrow clearly wanted the younger Miller boy to develop a marketable skill, a way to make a living, so that he might someday assist his older brother in a successful printing-and-jobbing operation, a likely pathway into the middle class.

To do the work, Charley had to be literate, focused, and able to take orders, none of which seemed out of his reach at this point. The Loofbourrows probably said good things about him to the

Colts, and the Colts trusted their judgment, since it was unlikely that someone like Preston Loofbourrow would try to pass off a worthless boy on a valuable friend and neighbor. Yet, after five months at the Colts', Charley was unable to cope and he ran away. In this case, there was no complaint about "whipping." Loofbourrow had made certain that the Colts were not the kind to abuse the boy physically even if he did wet his bed. Fred said that "his brother [had] behaved badly [at the Colts] and would not remain settled anywhere"; Loofbourrow thought the boy left Randolph because he was "restless and dissatisfied."

Charley's account was more explicit. When asked why he left his promising situation with the Randolph printer and preacher, Charley later said: "Because he did not clothe me." The issue seemed to be clothes that were attractive and well fitting, rather than clothes to keep him warm. Clothes were important to Charley, and they would figure prominently in his life as it unfolded. Whatever he was given as a wardrobe by the Colts felt sadly inadequate, causing him to become disgruntled. Because he was earning no wages, he knew that he would be unable to buy the kind of pants, jackets, and hats worn by the young men he had seen getting on and off the Union Pacific or advertised by smart haberdashers in the big-city newspapers that circulated in town. In small places like Leonardville and Randolph, advertisements were as interesting as the news, informing boys like Charley about what was in style and escalating their desire. At this point—Charley was now fourteen—his two old suits from the asylum were both tight and threadbare, because they were hand-me-downs to begin with. Angry with the Colts for their refusal to give him the clothes he wanted, Charley took his revenge in an adolescent way. He stole some shirts and a valise from the former preacher and hit the road, heading north on the Union Pacific to Omaha and Council Bluffs, larger cities where he hoped to find work in order to buy himself the kind of clothes that spoke of status and respectability.

On the way out of Randolph, the strong prairie winds blew open the valise and carried away nearly every stitch of clothing

Charley owned, including some of the stolen shirts. Despite this unlucky accident and the anger he felt toward the Colts and their penny-pinching ways, Kansas was planted indelibly in his mind. He would adopt the state and regard it as "home" no matter what happened, wherever he went. He would also continue to write to Fred, a sign of his steadfast commitment to the family of his birth. Although his childhood was essentially over, the fourteen-year-old remained strangely optimistic about his future as he made his way east on his own, this time to see what a reunion with his beloved sister, Carrie, might bring.

CHAPTER TWO

Becoming "Kansas Charley"

W ITH KANSAS behind him, Charley Miller immersed himself in a vastly different world, where he lived without adult supervision or protection. As he moved from place to place in search of food and shelter, he was on his own, although he had plenty of companionship in the tramping life. In the 1880s, transient unemployed workers were passing through American cities in large numbers as a result of periodic depressions that left many without work. Cities like Omaha, the place where Charley headed first, were large and anonymous (there were close to 140,000 people there), and they attracted homeless, unmarried men needing jobs and free passage on the railroad lines that spread out from that city like tentacles in all directions. In Omaha's "main stem," an area of dark, malodorous lodging houses and cheap saloons near the railroad yards, Charley had his first contacts with men who seemed brave and worldly in ways that Preston Loofbourrow and James Colt had not.

Charley quickly developed new skills in this predominantly male environment. One of the most basic was how to beat the railroad out of its required fares. (This was the basis for the familiar tramp expression "beating," which meant traveling by rail without paying a fare.) As he mastered the art of moving quickly and surreptitiously on the nation's railroads, he learned that his new lifestyle required flexibility and a degree of cunning. The tramp "never knows what is going to happen the next moment," explained writer Jack London, so "he lives only in the present." London, who spent thirty days in jail on a vagrancy charge in Erie County, New York, understood that those who survived by living in boxcars, working odd jobs, and begging meals at back doors needed to be artists and confidence men. Tramps had to be able to size up the person to be dunned, and then—in order to elicit food or money—deftly "conceive a tale that will hit home." London recalled the skills he developed when he was on the tramp in his youth: "There is a woman in the State of Nevada to whom I once lied, continually, shamelessly, for the matter of a couple of hours."

In all likelihood, Charley learned to lie, elaborately and inventively, as he made his way across the country. In the spring of 1889, a few weeks after his Kansas departure, he was picked up by a traveling salesman—a Mr. Cushing—who saw a "distressed looking German boy" in the railroad depot at Pacific Junction, Iowa, a tiny hamlet twenty miles south of Council Bluffs. Again, Charley's blond hair and blue eyes were assets that he used to his advantage. Hungry and penniless by now, he told Cushing selected parts of his biography—namely, that he was an orphan with training as a printer's helper—but he omitted the chapter about stealing from his former employer. Touched by the story, Cushing fed Charley, and then escorted him north to Glenwood, where he arranged for him to talk with William Robinson, the editor of yet another small-town newspaper. Although the Iowa Institution for Feeble Minded Children sat on the hills overlooking Glenwood and the Missouri River Valley, there was never any talk of placing Charley there, because he seemed so normal, even competent. As a result, the printer and his wife, Minnie, took him in, with the understanding that Charley would serve as William's helper. Robinson admitted later that his wife regarded the boy as "a chance for missionary work."

Glenwood, a quiet Iowa town of fewer than a thousand people, was Charley's last stand in terms of trying to adjust to middle-class family life. Though his work in the print shop was good— Robinson said he was "bright and a smart compositor"—his behavior at home became uncooperative and, finally, duplicitous. Mrs.

Robinson responded to his unpleasant nighttime bedwetting with some reasonable expectations, she thought: she made him bathe frequently and bought him a suit of new clothes on the promise that he would go to church and Sunday school regularly. Yet, in the two months he remained in Glenwood, Charley went to church only twice, and he categorically announced that Sunday school was "too pokey" for his taste.

Bored by religious schooling and small-town social life, Charley immersed himself instead in exciting dime novels, the inexpensive popular fiction of the 1880s that many regarded as a dangerous form of imaginative stimulation for boys. Perhaps these stories convinced him that he ought to hit the road in search of something more exciting; perhaps he tired of the Robinsons' efforts to socialize him into middle-class respectability; perhaps he left in order to avoid early-morning embarrassments. Whatever the reason—and it was likely to have been a combination—when Charley left the Robinsons', he took the store-bought suit and stole some of Minnie's hard-earned egg money right out of her kitchen. The Robinsons were deeply hurt by his dishonesty and had trouble understanding why he preferred the company of disreputable people to the good citizens of Glenwood, Iowa.

The tramping life had a deep attraction for Charley because he could now avoid the surveillance of adults and their behavioral expectations. When he was on the tramp, no one checked his fingernails for cleanliness or made him sit still to listen to boring lessons about God and Jesus. Tramping also made his disease seem less important, because few of the men he met now smelled any sweeter than he did.

In this new environment, Charley felt more like a man and less like a boy. Age distinctions were moot in a subculture where middle-class conventions were ignored, and a boy with a few dollars could buy all the privileges of adulthood: a drink, a smoke, even a woman. As a tramp, Charley felt that he was part of a larger fraternity of men, some with exciting lives akin to the characters in the books he read. Although tramps were considered disreputable among the middle class, in the inexpensive dime novels of the day they became heroes, transformed into millionaires, even royalty. Horatio Alger's *Tony the Tramp* and Frederick Whittaker's *Nemo: King of the Tramps* were just two of thousands of cheap books that boys like Charley could pick up in the 1880s, a moment when American publishing catered to the tastes of young working-class men.

Dime novels really were cheap. Some, like the titles in Beadle's Half Dime Library and the Five Cent Wide Awake Library, actually cost only five cents, and they were distributed in massive editions at newsstands and dry-goods stores, even in small towns. Young working-class men passed them around, traded them, and talked about the cowboys, hoboes, detectives, and outlaws who were the protagonists. Their lurid cover illustrations and the memorable names of their protagonists—Arizona Joe, Broadway Billy, Deadwood Dick, Fancy Frank, and Sure Shot Seth—promised exciting adventures, audacious confrontations, and bold escapes, all of which made for good conversation among one's peers. Although the plots were formulaic and the character development sparse, these cheap, portable books were enormously popular, because they provided boys with a vehicle for their fantasies, a way to try on masculine identities that were far more exciting than their lives in the factory, farm, or print shop.

Jesse James was especially popular among boys in Charley Miller's generation, largely because so many dime novels focused on the notorious outlaw. A Confederate raider who turned to robbing banks and trains in the 1870s and 1880s, James was shot dead in St. Joseph, Missouri, in April 1882, by Bob Ford, a member of his own gang, a development that prompted headlines, stories, and even drawings of the horrendous act of treachery. (In one of these, James was depicted standing on a straight-back chair adjusting and dusting a framed sampler that said "God Bless Our Home," much like the one Charley later hung in his Cheyenne jail cell.) A few weeks after his death, an auction of Jesse's belongings in St. Joe's attracted thousands of people who paid inflated prices for his washstand, his old dog, and the chair on which he was killed. In Chicago, crafty entrepreneurs sought permission to exhibit a piece of the blood-stained rag carpet from the room where Jesse died.

Charley Miller was only seven years old when Jesse took the bullet, but he grew up surrounded by songs and stories that fueled the James legend. "We used to read about him, Jesse James, Jesse James," was the first line in the chorus of one of many ballads about the bold, bad man known "from Seattle down to Birmingham" who generated so much print. Although there were a number of histories of James and his gang in the 1880s that claimed to be serious—"the truth and nothing but the truth," one author bragged—most boys in Charley Miller's generation took their image of James from dime novels and their larger-than-life accounts of the exploits of Jesse and his brother Frank. In books such as *The James Boys at Deadwood, Jesse James: The Midnight Horseman, The James Boys and the Mad Sheriff, Jesse James at Coney Island, Jesse James Among the Mormons*, even *Jesse James at the Stake*, young men with moderate reading ability found simple, easy-to-read stories that were veritable page-turners. Jesse's remarkable marksmanship, plus his superhuman ability to evade the law, were a staple of these tales. In real life the James brothers were violent, brutish, and cruel, but in the dime novels they were benevolent to the unfortunate, deferential to women, and, most of all, ingenious and brave.

Although Charley never had much extra money to spend on them, he admitted that he read dime novels whenever he could. Living independently, he had little adult guidance to make him put aside the so-called "vile literature" of his day for something more edifying. In Charley's situation, dime novels became a viable source of information—in effect, a guidebook for behavior worthy of imitation. As time passed, he modeled his own speech after the deadpan lingo of their tough male characters, and he idolized the figure of the outlaw because of his resistance to conventional laws and constraints, as well as his ability to escape when cornered or apprehended. Whether it was thick underbrush, a foreboding swamp, or a frigid wilderness, these fictive outlaws always got away, a scenario that appealed to a boy learning to steal rides on the railroad cars and avoid the law. On the basis of his reading, adolescent Charley concluded that it was not really a bad thing for a boy to be seen as somewhat dangerous, so he began to call himself "Kansas Charley."

Charley needed a special nickname of his own in order to be a part of the larger fraternity of vagabonds. Like his many traveling "brothers"—Pacific Slim, Troy Mickey, Buffalo Dan—he dropped his family name and took a place name instead. Logically, he should have become "New York Charley," to signify the place of his birth, but he chose to associate himself instead with the state where he had resided for only six months. The "Kansas" in his new moniker was probably a good way to remain connected to his brothers, both of whom were living now in Leonardville, playing in the local fife-and-drum band. (As soon as Willie was twelve, he was placed out with the Loofbourrows at their request.) When asked on the road what "Kansas Charley" stood for, Miller could always say, "I have brothers there," and feel as if he had a family, a home, a place to return to.

Charley used his moniker in ways that were commonplace in the subculture of tramps. He wrote "Kansas Charley" inside his stiff-rim black Stetson hat, and on a pair of gloves he picked up along the road. Whenever he passed through a community, he sur-reptitiously carved or scratched his nickname, sometimes with date and destination, under bridges or on viaducts and water towers. (He later told the Cheyenne court, "I register on the water tanks as other bums do.") According to Jack London, water tanks served as "tramp directories," because they were so often covered with hobo nicknames or "noms de rail." The water towers also provided criti-cal tips for tramps arriving in town: "Main drag fair." "Bulls not hostile." "Round House good for kipping." "North bound trains no good." Cryptic information like this signaled that the business district was okay for handouts, that the local police did not enforce vagrancy laws, that there was a decent place for a good night's sleep, and that traveling without paying was more difficult in one direction than the other.

As Kansas Charley headed north from Iowa to Chicago, he experimented with his new identity, watching and listening attentively to those who knew the ropes. In addition to the special lingo, he learned that, on a daily basis, most tramps needed to accomplish a "set down," an opportunity to get inside a house, wash up, and eat a full meal sitting down. "Tramps love to throw their legs under a table," London quipped. Backdoor benevolence was a pervasive feature of middle-class life in post–Civil War America, and it was treated in some places with acceptance, even wry humor. According to a report from St. Charles, Minnesota, in 1887: "A tramp who had hidden all of the way from Winona in a snug corner of a box car loaded with lumber crawled out at the depot at Sleepy Eye a few days ago and worked a benevolent housewife for a free lunch, while the train was switching in the yard. When the train pulled out, the tramp resumed his quarters in the box car bound for Dakota. He said he had not heard of the interstate commerce law, but did not think it interfered with his method of free transportation." Police could be tolerant of tramps: some simply looked the other way when they trolled kitchen doors; others provided a bed in the municipal jail when the temperature dropped.

Yet, in many other locations, the police and the local citizenry were more antagonistic than kind, believing that men on the tramp threatened social stability, set a bad example for workers, and generated crime. Some states, such as New Jersey, New York, and Pennsylvania, responded to these fears with special legislation known as "Tramp Acts" which criminalized vagrancy to a new degree. In big cities, like Chicago, there were reports that tramps watched the papers for the death notices of men "in good circumstances," and then besieged the widows with "piteous stories of poverty and large families, winding up by begging for the deceased husband's clothes." Tramps were also suspect because they raised the specter of homosexuality or "perversion"—much like men in prison or at sea, two other notably womanless groups. There was always the risk of arrest in the kind of backdoor begging that Charley had to do in order to survive without stopping to take a job. "Some people gave me something to eat and others would not," was all Charley had to say about the economics of beating hunger on the road.

The railroads themselves provided a challenge to tramps in the form of their own security police, known as "bulls," hired to keep freeloaders off the cars. The bulls could be brutal and, when they worked in close cooperation with local law enforcement, the effects were hard on tramps. Jack London made it clear that Cheyenne, Wyoming, had a national reputation for being "horstile" to homeless men and boys due in part to a man named Jeff Carr, a sheriff, who "manhandled hoboes" when they were unlucky enough to cross his path or be turned in by Union Pacific bulls. Jack Black, who also documented tramp life in the West, called Carr "bum simple"—simple-minded on the subject of killing bums. "If you run, he'll shoot you; if you stand he'll get you six months, and he'd rather have you run." In some locales, when a bull pulled in a tramp on vagrancy charges it meant six months on a chain gang or time in jail. As a result, it was important that new recruits to tramping learn how to avoid detection, run swiftly, and jump adroitly between (and off) moving cars. As he beat his way to Chicago, Kansas Charley saw some crippled tramps who had suffered unlucky accidents in their attempted escape from the law. These men, with stumps where they used to have arms and legs, were a powerful symbol of both the bravery and the brutality embedded in his unsupervised new life.

<hr />

Charley's game plan was to get to Chicago and then to Rochester, New York, where he hoped to be reunited with his older sister, Carrie, now a young woman of seventeen. In Leonardville, Fred and Charley had talked about Carrie, and they both remembered the difficult day when the family from Ilion came to take her away from the asylum. Carrie was only ten at the time, and her younger brothers all hated to see her leave. Now she was grown-up, and her letters to Fred suggested that she was well situated in a house in Rochester with the same people, the Weavers, who continued to treat her well.

Rochester held the promise of work as well as reunion. A bustling city located east of Buffalo on the Erie Canal, Rochester had nearly a hundred thousand people—half of whom were under the age of twenty-five—and a reputation for its many successful printing establishments, places where Charley thought he could find a job with wages sufficient to buy himself the kind of wardrobe he desperately wanted. When he got to Chicago, he dawdled for a few weeks in and around the railroad yards, collecting information about how best to get to Rochester. There were railroads heading east, but also steamship lines that carried passengers through the great interior ocean of Lakes Michigan, Huron, and Erie, ending up in Buffalo. Charley did not have the kind of money that a passenger ship required, and being a stowaway seemed more dangerous than traveling by rail. But traveling the lakes seemed like a great adventure, so he waited for work to become available as a deckhand on a commercial freighter carrying grain and flour to Buffalo. Although the voyage was rougher than he anticipated, there were some benefits. At the end of the trip, when he collected his wages—fifty cents a day—he had enough to stake himself for a while when he got to Rochester. In Buffalo, Charley headed for the railroad yards and easily beat his way another fifty miles eastward to Rochester, where he found Carrie, doing well, living in the heart of a respectable middle-class neighborhood immediately adjacent to East Avenue, the most splendid residential boulevard in the city.

Charley knew from conversation with Fred that Carrie had moved with George and Esther Weaver from Ilion to Rochester earlier that year, but he could not have anticipated the ways in which his sister's surrogate father would figure in his life. In 1888,

George Weaver had sold his interest in the *Citizen* and said good-bye to Ilion forever. Weaver got his big opportunity in Rochester because of the reputation he had made in Ilion as a progressive printer, one with an eye to new technology and the ways it could improve profits. From the start of his career in Ilion in 1881, Weaver had been aggressive about increasing advertising and readership. He was successful in both, all the while tinkering at home. (He eventually held at least a dozen U.S. patents.) Then, in 1884, Weaver and some other local inventors, George Lee and John L. McMillan, began to experiment with electricity as a way to run the press at the the *Citizen*.

One day when steam power to the shop was temporarily stopped, Weaver and Lee made their move. They ran two electrical wires from a Parker dynamo (used for lighting the local armory) over buildings and alleys into the newspaper office where a Remington electric motor waited. Lee adjusted one wire to the motor, the other to the three cylinder presses. The current of charged particles immediately began to do its work, the presses turned, and printing began. Within the year, John McMillan, Weaver's cousin, devised a machine to set type, and the two innovations together made it possible for the the *Citizen* in Ilion—not the *New York Herald* or the *San Francisco Chronicle*—to become the first newspaper in the world to be composed mechanically and printed by electric power.

The historic event was of enormous interest to nineteenth-century Americans convinced of electricity's power to transform and improve human life. There were admiring announcements in the *New York Evening Herald* and the *New York Journal*, and important verification from *Electrical World*, a journal for inventors, scientists, and many others infatuated with the promise of "harnessed lighting." *Electrical World* officially confirmed on March 14, 1884, that "the Ilion, New York, *Citizen* printed 3000 copies by electricity, using an electric motor, deriving current from a ten light dynamo 15 rods away." Weaver's successful experiment with electricity put the town on the map and boosted his own celebrity.

There were requests for the historic March 14 editions for their value as keepsakes and for collections in museums.

In Rochester, there were men with ideas and capital who sought out George Weaver for his particular blend of business experience and printing know-how. They called themselves the Lawyers Cooperative Publishing Company (LCPC), and they revolutionized the study of law in the United States within a few decades. By the 1880s, lawyers and courts throughout the country needed more and more law books—such as the yearly proceedings of state and federal courts—but the cost, often as much as five hundred dollars to purchase a set, was prohibitive for most attorneys. In addition, many valuable law books were simply unavailable, because their initial print runs were too small. Two Newark, New York, attorneys, James and William Briggs (a father and son), found this situation troublesome, particularly when they had to travel thirty-five miles to Rochester to get to a law library with the kind of texts they needed to represent big clients, such as the Ontario Southern Railroad. As a result, they hatched a plan, along with their partner, Ernest Hitchcock, to reproduce, print, and sell important law books and digests by subscription.

In 1882, while Weaver was still in Ilion, LCPC sent out its first direct-mail flyer, offering to reprint 103 volumes of the United States Supreme Court reports for only one dollar a volume, *if* twenty-five hundred lawyers would agree *in advance* to buy them. The initial circular described cooperative marketing as a "revolution" that would put the most important American legal decisions within reach of every lawyer and student. The organizers of the new venture were flooded with positive responses from members of a profession eager to reduce its research time and appreciative of the way the LCPC added annotations that served as a citation index. In addition to U.S. Supreme Court reports, LCPC soon expanded to offer digests of commercial and chancery laws, interstate-commerce reports, and compilations of the laws of New York, as well as a dozen other states in the East and Midwest. According to the *New York Herald*, LCPC publications were a model of accuracy, "certified to be a correct and complete transcript of the records of the court." Within a few years, the company accumulated almost three hundred thousand dollars in capital and added to its editorial staff "some of the ablest lawyers in the country if not in the world."

In 1888, Weaver was tapped for a managerial position with the LCPC, headquartered by this time on Main Street, in the center of Rochester's commercial district, overlooking activity on the busy Erie Canal. Two years later, at the age of thirty-five, Weaver became secretary of this lucrative publishing adventure, with responsibility for both printing and financial operations. Although he was not an attorney and he had no control over the actual content of the volumes, Weaver still mixed easily with the editorial staff, prominent lawyers with contacts in the New York State legislature and the United States Congress. Weaver's position at the LCPC thrust him into a much larger pool of men and ideas, who proved to be important resources when he and his wife had to deal with the problems associated with Carrie Miller's younger brother.

In August 1889, soon after the birth of a new child, the Weaver family arrived in Rochester at their new residence on a green, leafy street where a canopy of tall oaks moderated the summer sun. The house at 32 Rowley Street was modest, but it had some up-to-date new plumbing as well as a fine side porch. There were now four children—Joe, seven; George, five; Reuben, two; and Marion Esther, an infant, less than two months old. Carrie Miller, finished with formal schooling, stayed at home to assist Esther Weaver in running the house and caring for this demanding brood. For George Weaver, the move to Rochester meant a more sophisticated life filled with symbols of bourgeois success. He left home every day to work in the central business district; his family mixed with other prosperous families at the Presbyterian church; and his wife was able to shop at Fahy's or Sibley, Lindsay & Curr, grand department stores that were far more fashionable than any they had frequented back in Ilion. Rochester was a progressive city, and Weaver, who looked to the future with boundless optimism, seemed temperamentally suited to the spirit of his new home.

There is no record of what was actually said when Kansas

Charley arrived unannounced at the Weavers' front door, but he was not taken in. For Carrie, a young woman on the brink of adulthood—perhaps with a beau and the hope of making a respectable marriage—having a brother who was a tramp must have been something of a liability. It is not clear how often she saw him, or if Esther Weaver considered him "missionary work" the way Minnie Robinson did. But in all likelihood, the Weavers made some effort to assist him, because they were charitable Christian people. George's web of local contacts probably helped Charley land a job as a galley boy at the *Union & Advertiser*, one of the city's leading newspapers.

Rochester provided Charley with an interlude of relative security in proximity to his sister and her resources. Although the *Union & Advertiser* was a union shop with a fixed number of journeymen and apprentices organized by the International Typographical Union, Charley found a niche. He hung around the newspaper shop, making from three to six dollars a week, an amount that enabled him to pay $2.50 a week for his room and meals at an East Avenue boarding house only a few minutes from Carrie and close to Rochester's commercial center. When the weather was warm, he actually made more money, because the typesetters went to baseball games, leaving him to distribute type on his own. Charley was the only young boy living among a group of single, older men, but the fact that he had his own room relieved his anxiety about bedwetting, which apparently continued to plague him.

Life in Rochester had its pleasures, however. Charley had enough money to buy a ten-cent ticket for the grandstand at the ballpark on Culver Road, or a fifteen-cent admission to roller-skate at the popular Washington Rink. Sometimes, he even had a bit extra to dip into Power's Gallery of Art to see the "French art novelties," photographs of scantily clad women, raved about by the older men. And because of his connections at the newspaper, he had an exciting new opportunity to step out and be entertained in a way that brought him into contact with hundreds of other Rochesterians. "I received two tickets every week to [H. R.] Jacobs Academy from Manager Curtis," Charley remembered fondly about his time in Rochester. Since the theatrical productions at the Jacobs Academy came from New York City and stayed for a run of a few weeks, playing both matinees and evenings, Charley probably saw many "entertainments" more than once, providing him with an opportunity to familiarize himself with certain actors and dramatic roles.

Through the largesse of J. Wendell Curtis, his boss at the *Union & Advertiser*, Charley tasted the pleasures of melodrama and comic opera, and thrilled to the excitement of variety shows including acrobats, animal acts, dancers, musicians, and stand-up comics. Even in Rochester—an inland city at some distance from New York—theatrical productions were lavish in this era. A paying audience expected moving scenery, elaborate costumes, curtains of steam, and marching choruses of substantial size. Part of the excitement was always in the promotion. When *The Arabian Nights* came to the academy, the posters proclaimed: "The Scenery, Acting and Mechanical Effects Applauded to the Echo." A few months later, when Miss Fanny Louise Buckingham arrived with her "celebrated steed" for a three-week run in *Mazeppa*, a "great equestrian drama," Charley and countless others marveled at her wondrous performance, the fine horse, and the bold and extravagant tournament scene.

Exposure to the theater and its audiences, to the ball park and the skating rink, and to the downtown arcades and department stores all meant that Charley spent more time than he ever had before thinking about what he looked like. In Rochester, he was "out and about," both looking and being seen. His heightened concern about his appearance was, in part, a function of his age: adolescents are notoriously self-centered, and he turned fifteen in November 1889 while he was in Rochester. Yet some of his new concern about appearance was the result of the situation in which he found himself. Like countless other urban youths in this era, Charley's desire for stylish clothing was stimulated by the exciting crush of well-dressed people on the street and in the theater, as well as the bountiful, seductive display of ready-made clothing in the downtown stores. Rochester was a city where clothing was important—it was manufactured there, and the garment trades employed a sizable portion of immigrant workers—but it was also widely promoted and hawked, often in a crude, aggressive way that was hard to ignore: "Willie's Pants Get Rusty! All Pants Get Rusty! If you want first-class trousers that will always be stylish, neat fitting and pretty go at once to Quinn's." In addition to the unabashed competition for shoppers, there was the push to stimu-late material desire. A haberdashery advised: "You always want extra pants."

At the moment when Charley Miller was cruising the streets of Rochester, wardrobes across America were being elaborated and critiqued in all kinds of ways. In addition to promoting the need for more clothes, especially pants and shirts, local stores presented a dazzling array of choices that fed the idea that style was an impor-tant expression of individual identity. In Rochester, Charley could select among trousers of worsted, Scotch goods, stripes, checks, and different seasonal weights; he could try on hats of "foreign and domestic styles"; and he could ogle hundreds of winter overcoats available in all kinds of materials—melton cloth, chinchilla, beaver, corkscrew and wide-wale worsted, cashmere with or with-out silk facing, and ribbed kersey—all from three to fifteen dollars. Choices like this were mouth-watering for a boy like Charley, whose earliest concerns about clothing had been simply to have enough.

In this new milieu, Charley wanted some assurance that he looked "decent," especially among people his own age, the kind he wanted to impress. The more he saw of Rochester, the more his tastes escalated, and he began to feel that he needed more money in order to improve his wardrobe beyond the basics. "Style"—a concept that became so central to the merchandising of clothes in the late nineteenth century—became a deep personal concern for him, and this was reflected in his attention to the kind of hat, trousers, collar, or watch worn by others of his sex. Rochester always stood out in Charley's mind not as a safe haven offering a modicum of emotional comfort and safety but as a landmark for haberdashery. When asked what he remembered most about his time in that city, he said very simply: "When there I had good clothes to wear. It was the only suit I ever had that was whole." Charley's anxiety about the status of his own clothes and those of others stayed with him, hardening into a permanent feature of his mental landscape, one that would be activated again when he met the young men he eventually murdered.

Despite the benefits that Rochester afforded him, Charley took off again in mid-June 1890, after only eight months. He told Carrie that he was headed out west to become a cowboy, like the ones he read about in books. In reality, he went south to New York City, where he hoped to connect with a friend of his father's who, he believed, held an unclaimed family legacy for him. Whatever plans he was concocting for an adventure in the West, they were foiled by problems almost immediately. After Rochester, Charley became increasingly vulnerable to the dangers embedded in an environment where he had neither protectors nor advocates.

In June 1890, Charley barely escaped arrest for robbery in Lyons, New York, a stop along the Erie Canal, just thirty miles east of Rochester. However anxious he was to get back to the metropolis where he was born, he was diverted by another stint as a printer's helper, this time in the shop of Nelson Mirrick, editor of the *Courant*, the local Lyons newspaper. Again, Charley presented himself in such a way that he appeared both earnest and sufficiently skilled to merit a job. But the wages were not enough for him to board on his own. Instead, he arranged for lodgings in the home of Rosa Pohl, a German immigrant widow, who lived near the print shop with her four adolescent children—two boys and two girls—ranging in age from fifteen to twenty. In a number of ways, the Pohls mimicked Charley's family of origin.

Nevertheless, one week after his arrival at the Pohls', Charley went downstairs in the middle of the night and stole two gold pocket watches that were sitting on the mantel. Perhaps his experience in the asylum—where there were so few things for an orphan to call his own—made these items too tantalizing to ignore. After hiding one watch outside the house, he kept the other and returned to his bed. The next morning, Rosa Pohl noticed the missing watches and alerted her children before confronting Charley. When he made an attempt to flee, he was caught and searched by the family, who found one of the missing watches in his back pocket rolled up in a handkerchief. Although the Pohls intended to turn him over to the local police, when they heard Charley's pleas for forgiveness they softened, took their watches back, and sent him on his way with his meager belongings and some dime novels. The Pohls kept the story of their thieving boarder to themselves until he became famous, when it seemed safe to admit that they had been badly duped by one of their own who "went bad."

By beating, begging, and probably pilfering, Charley got himself to New York City, where he hoped to raise money from people connected to his early life. First he tried George Holz, his father's friend, a man he called "uncle," but Holz was not forthcoming with any of the funds that Charley thought were his due. Still, he lived with Holz for at least two weeks above the very saloon where his father used to drink. On June 17, 1890, Charley sought assistance at the Children's Aid Society, but he was referred back to the New York Orphan Asylum, considered his home institution from the perspective of a charitable system anxious to avoid duplication of effort. "Charles calls in today," reported the CAS agent keeping their books: "Told him to call on Miss Sherman [the treasurer] at OA."

Charley was seeking money in order to get a new start in life, but Janet Sherman, the woman who had bailed him out of the awful situation in Minnesota, failed to come to his rescue this time. Perhaps she hesitated because Charley's problems were beginning to accumulate, he was older now, and he bore some personal responsibility for his continued wandering and failure to settle down. Turned down by the asylum, his alma mater, Charley now severed all contacts with the welfare system that had brought him up. Within weeks, he left New York City for a job advertised in the *New York World*, again with a printer, this time in Orange, New Jersey. He lasted, however, only three days and then went on the tramp, having scored only a shirt, five dollars, and a leather match safe from his "Uncle" George. The match holder—Charley's only real inheritance from his father—had the name "Muller" or "Miller" (it was hard to discern which) scratched into the leather.

First Charley retraced his steps back into New York City, where he met a fellow at the Brooklyn Bridge. Together they decided on a plan of action: after jumping a ferry back to New Jersey, they boarded a Pennsylvania Railroad car bound for Philadelphia and filled with dry goods, a convenient cargo for comfortable sleeping and hiding. As they entered the city, however, something went dreadfully wrong. All that summer, the Philadelphia police had been doing battle with a gang of boys, billed locally as "The Dirty Dozen," who were robbing freight cars. As a result, the municipal and railroad police were on heightened alert, looking for illegal travelers, tramps and hoboes, as well as the celebrated gang.

According to the Pennsylvania Tramp Act of 1879, persons with no fixed place of residence or lawful occupation who were engaged in "beggary and vagrancy" were guilty of a misdemeanor and subject to confinement by a local magistrate in the county jail or workhouse for up to a year. Although the same law exempted females and male minors under the age of sixteen, when fifteen-year-old Charley Miller was picked up by the bulls and handed over to the local Philadelphia authorities, he was treated as an adult. "Entering RR car with intent to steal," was a common charge in vagrancy cases, although Charley always denied any theft: "Nothing was touched of the goods. We were only stealing a ride." Charley had no lawyer to challenge the sentence; there was no court-appointed social worker to pose questions about the whereabouts of his family, how long he had been riding the rails, or why he had

"Kansas Charley" written on his hat and gloves. Instead, the young tramp was dispatched on July 2, 1890, for a six-week sentence at the House of Corrections in Holmesburg, Pennsylvania. This was Charley's first and only experience with incarceration before Cheyenne.

The House of Corrections was a county jail outside the city of Philadelphia run by the Philadelphia Bureau of Charities. It was distinct from the Holmesburg Prison, a facility opened later for more serious crimes and longer sentences. Of the nearly one thousand inmates at the House of Corrections when Charley entered in 1890, most were men between the ages of twenty-one and forty confined because of vagrancy and "habitual drunkenness." More than 50 percent were of Irish or German descent; most had been laborers, waiters, and teamsters, although the roster of their occupations on the outside ranged widely from actors to weavers. Charley was a special inmate from the start because of his age, and the fact that his term was shorter than the average, normally three to six months. Inmates slept in barrackslike quarters and spent their days doing agricultural work on the prison farm, quarrying and breaking stone, grading and repairing macadam roads, digging trenches for lines that carried gas to private homes in the area, and also making and repairing shoes, all of which brought in money to support the institution and the city of Philadelphia.

Life at Holmesburg was designed to be hard, physically demanding, and routinized in order to bring about the moral reclamation of its disreputable inmates. However, according to Thomas Kirkpatrick, the institution's "Moral Instructor," Holmesburg also provided a library, a night school, regular religious services with music, and a stream of ministers and charitable women who "visited and delighted" inmates with their "kind and loving words." In 1890, when Charley was under his supervision, Kirkpatrick claimed that he took "special notice" of the youths, bragging of his success in "returning many of them to anxious and loving parents, with a promise of obedience and a better life in the future." Kansas Charley received no special attention, however, and there was no treatment plan to redirect his peripatetic, unsupervised life. Instead, he returned to his tramping ways in August 1890. When he left the Philadelphia area, he had only a pittance, earned from raising vegetables at the prison farm.

In a jail like Holmesburg, Charley was intimately exposed to older men, many of whom had lived outside the law. He heard them balk at the tight supervision, the dreary food, and the absence of women and sex. Even though these inmates were not violent or homicidal, their conversation served as a short course for Charley in a wide range of adult male behaviors. Six weeks in the House of Corrections probably hardened Charley, and it may have fueled his bravado, causing him to take even greater risks, because he now considered himself knowledgeable about the ways of criminals and outlaws. After the interlude at Holmesburg, he could claim some real kinship with those who had been arrested, and he could talk authentically about "doing time," adding another notch in the belt of Kansas Charley.

———◆———

As he moved west again, in search of his cowboy dream, Charley fell prey to sexual predators in the boxcars that were now his home. Although he never gave a specific location or date, somewhere between Pittsburgh and Kansas City, tramp culture turned on him. Instead of fellowship and camaraderie, he was brutalized by fellow tramps in a manner approximating a gang rape. Today, we regard this as horrific and pathological, but in the late nineteenth century, it was not uncommon for sailors and other groups of womanless men to have sex with younger men and boys, and they indulged in these sex acts without losing their claim to manhood or being pathologized. When Charley talked about the event, he made it clear that the abuse was not one on one, that it involved intimidation by more than a single individual. "Bums" and "Parties I met on a freight train" were his most explicit identification of those who had attacked him.

Charley never said much about the incident, because he was

neither psychologically nor culturally equipped to do so on the basis of his life experience. For most adolescents, coercive sex is shocking, confusing, and traumatic, but some individuals have more support and better emotional outlets for understanding it, especially today, in our therapeutic culture. In the 1890s, there was no broad understanding of what happened to Charley, and little language to explore it. In Charley's case, involuntary penetration by bums—most likely in full view of others—would have felt first and foremost like an act of ridicule constituting a brutal physical assault. But it is hard to tell from a modern vantage point what involuntary sodomy meant for the psyche of an adolescent boy in that era. At trial, it became apparent that he was unable to give a name to the act. It is likely that the experience left him confused and anxious about issues of sexual identity and sexual pleasure. For as long as he could remember, his body and his "private parts" had been problematic, a source of stress and anxiety in the asylum and beyond. The gang rape in the boxcar only added to the problem of his psychosexual development as he approached adulthood. And it undoubtedly left him suspicious, hostile, even furious, in ways that he had not been before.

Demoralized by the incident, and scared that it could happen again, Kansas Charley became more protective as he tried to keep hunger at bay. In Kansas City, where he worked as a dishwasher, he bought himself a pistol—a secondhand .32-caliber revolver made by the Hood Arms Company. In a city as big and bustling as this one, Charley had a wide range of sources for guns, but he chose a friendly pawnshop because it was probably the least costly path to ownership. Charley paid $1.25 for his gun—more than half his weekly wage—but he considered it necessary in order to protect himself from bums.

With the memory of the attack still fresh, day-to-day life became insufferable for the boy who continued to call himself Kansas Charley. He managed to survive by stealing scraps from the unwashed plates of hotel patrons, but the kitchen where he worked long hours was tense and unnerving because of a demanding boss:

"The man was all the time at me to hurry with the dishes. I was not fast enough." Unhappy and angry with just about everything, Charley did what he usually did in order to cope: he ran away on a freight train, heading again to Omaha, the railroad hub that was the best launching point for trains to the West. When he got to Omaha, he heard that there were jobs—riding horses and tending sheep—at Gleason's Ranch, just outside Cheyenne, Wyoming, about five hundred miles away. Known as "The Magic City of the Plains," Cheyenne was rumored to be a fine place, a bustling town of cattle millionaires where oysters and champagne arrived every day on the Union Pacific. If Charley heard about the bum-busting terrors of Jeff Carr, it did not faze him. Cheyenne became the focus of the fanciful dreams he chased even in the face of mounting stress.

By this time—it was September 1890—Charley's basic needs for food, shelter, and safety were no longer being met. The longer he spent on the road without any stable connections or support, the greater the likelihood that he would be touched again by the violence and betrayal that were part of tramp culture. Periodic letters to his brothers in Kansas, or to Carrie in Rochester, did not substitute for the emotional bonds that Charley was denied by the peripatetic pattern of his life, especially after the boxcar attack, which left him anxious and fearful in some profound new ways. As he left Omaha, Kansas Charley was hungry and fragile but also armed. From a psychological and social perspective, he was poised for a violent encounter rather than a career as a cowboy.

CHAPTER THREE

"Where Is My Wandering Boy Tonight?"

As Charley Miller made plans to make his way west to the fabled city of Cheyenne, two other young men heading for Denver said their last goodbyes to family and friends in St. Joseph, Missouri. One was fair-haired Waldo Emerson, just nineteen; the other, a tall, dark-haired fellow, Ross Fishbaugh, who was almost twenty. At 130 pounds each, they were taller and broader than Charley Miller, who at this point was slightly over five feet and weighed only about one hundred pounds. The difference in their builds captured the economic and social chasm between them: Charley Miller represented the world of scarcity; Emerson and Fishbaugh, the upbeat world of American economic opportunity. No one knew then that the three were on a violent collision course; and no one ever understood completely how and why their encounter exploded as it did. But what happened to them in a Union Pacific boxcar over a century ago still stands as an unsettling example of what the culture of boys can deliver when deprivation and affluence clash in the company of alcohol and guns.

Although Horace Greeley, the well-known New York City newspaper editor, gave currency to the idea that young men should deliberately uproot themselves in order to make a better life, many American parents were understandably apprehensive when a son announced that he was following Greeley's advice. "Go west, young man; go west, young man," was a fine promotional slogan for stimulating interest in the settlement of the region and in the construction of a transcontinental railroad to the Pacific, but it did little to ease the anxiety of parents when their children started packing their suitcases, as Emerson and Fishbaugh did in September 1890.

A popular hymn written thirteen years earlier expressed the sentiment of all the American parents who had already seen their boys walk out the door for the great adventure in the West. In church pews across the nation, they stood up to sing about a good, pure boy who left his family home: "Where is my wandering boy tonight?/Go search for him where you will./But bring him to me *with all his blight.*/And tell him I love him still." Although the blight was never specified and the boy in the song did return, the lyrics acknowledged that something could go wrong, that there was reason to be concerned about the way American boys were being lured westward by both real opportunities and also vague, unrealistic dreams about making a pile.

What Greeley claimed was the right and natural thing for American boys to do was emotionally difficult for mothers and fathers, and it was also laced with dangers that tempered the enthusiasm of even the most supportive, forward-looking parents. They were rightly uneasy because of patterns of adolescent male aggression and risk-taking embedded in the culture of even normal boys. In St. Joseph, Fishbaugh and Emerson packed their suitcases with the optimism of youth; their parents would review it all later, in tears, wishing they could have turned the clock back.

———◆———

Waldo Emerson and Ross Fishbaugh were relatively new friends, not boys who had grown up together. Ross was the only child of a widowed mother, whom he helped to support after the two moved together from Ohio to Missouri just a few years earlier. Waldo lived with both parents and a younger brother, in a modest frame home in a pleasant neighborhood. John Owen Emerson, his father, was a longtime Missourian, a saddler and a foreman, employed at Wyeth Hardware and Manufacturing Company, where he earned enough to own his own house and buy his son a silver pocket watch and chain when the boy left school at the age of fifteen. (In choosing their eldest son's name, the family almost certainly intended to honor America's most vigorous literary proponent of self-reliance, Ralph Waldo Emerson.)

Both Waldo Emerson and Ross Fishbaugh had successful work experience in St. Joseph, known as St. Joe, a busy town of over fifty thousand people, the third-largest city in the state, located just east of the Kansas border. After he finished his schooling, Waldo worked first as a "bundle boy," carrying garments at a local shirt-making establishment. By the time he was eighteen, he had moved up to a clerk's job at the R. G. Dun Mercantile Company, a branch of the respected New York City agency that established credit ratings. In St. Joe, as in fifty other American cities and numerous foreign capitals, R. G. Dun, the precursor of Dun & Bradstreet, billed itself as a promoter of "capital, capacity, and character." At Dun's, Waldo learned that there were many ways to make money in late-nineteenth-century America, and he began to socialize in town with other young men looking for ways to seize the main chance and profit from what the economy had to offer them.

Ross Fishbaugh was employed as a billing clerk in one of the city's largest grain dealers, R. T. Davis Milling Company, located just a few blocks away from Waldo's office. In 1889, the Davis company began to package a ready-mixed, self-rising pancake flour, a novel idea at the time. Randolph Truct Davis named the pancake mix "Aunt Jemima" for a catchy vaudeville tune sung by a woman in blackface with a bandana wrapped around her head. The song and the image were so popular in St. Joe that Davis began to look for a real Negro woman to employ as a living trademark. (He eventually found fifty-nine-year-old Nancy Green in Chicago, where she worked as a domestic servant in the home of a judge.) Filled with schemes for promoting his pancakes, Davis brought his own son back to St. Joe to assist in the business, but he dismissed Ross Fishbaugh in the process, in order to keep expenses down.

After losing his job, Ross began to talk about leaving for the West, Denver specifically, and he encouraged his new friend Waldo Emerson to join him. Davis, the man who made pancakes in America into a year-round, eat-anytime food, considered Fishbaugh such a promising fellow that he provided him with a glowing letter of recommendation to carry on his journey. Both boys already had some money saved, so Fishbaugh's plan seemed doable. Whenever they talked about it, Ross always promised that it would be a lark as well as financially rewarding. He was always the more aggressive of the two, ostensibly older and wiser about the ways of the world beyond St. Joe.

Waldo Emerson told his family that he was about to quit Dun's and head west only a few nights before he left. "His intention was to go to Denver, and I consented," his father remembered. Waldo presented the plan in a positive, rational manner, emphasizing the ways in which the move would improve his economic future. "If you think you can better your condition," his father told him in earnest, "you can go of course and it may do you some good." John Emerson and his wife were not entirely pleased about the scheme, and they felt some natural hesitancy because they did not know Ross Fishbaugh at all. But they were willing to help their son financially, the way loving parents often do. "I asked him if he had money enough," the concerned father recalled. "He said yes. I didn't ask him how much he had got. [But] I put my hand in my pocket and gave him ten dollars." John Emerson understood the impulse for adventure that drove so many boys westward—"They wanted to see the country," he explained—but he and his wife still expected confirmation of their son's whereabouts, in the form of letters and cards, mailed along the road.

There were certain aspects of the plan that the boys never told their parents, because they knew that adults would disapprove. They did not admit, for example, that they intended to save money and have an adventure by beating their way west rather than paying for their fare. This decision meant that they would travel, at least part of the time, with men and boys who were real hoboes and tramps. The appeal of this experience was not something that John

Emerson understood. "My impression was [Waldo] was going to take a first-class passage on the railroad," his naïve father later admitted. Another thing the boys forgot to mention was that Fishbaugh would carry a .38-caliber Smith & Wesson pistol just in case they needed it.

In the last few days at home, both boys were excited as they shopped for new clothes and fantasized about the adventure that lay ahead. Although Waldo sewed his diamond collar studs into the pocket of a pair of pants—probably to protect himself from being an easy mark—he went out and bought some flashy new garments as well as a five-dollar pair of gaiters with stylish stitching on the outside. Likewise, Ross purchased a good-looking light-brown overcoat. Both left St. Joe wearing well-tailored new suits and sporting the kind of felt hats popular with men their age. Ross's was brown and soft; Waldo's black and stiff.

For a brief moment, the departing adventurers had celebrity status among their peers in St. Joe. They knew they looked good, and they felt empowered by the cash in their pockets. On the night before they left, at a gambling house on Third Street, they talked about their common purse and actually showed off a roll of bills. Those who saw the display verified later that Emerson had about forty dollars; Fishbaugh, they thought, carried close to a hundred dollars, won in a crap shoot that evening. Expectant and raring to go, the two youths headed west to try their hands at tramping, a way of life that was already taking its toll on fifteen-year-old Charley Miller.

Kansas Charley first laid eyes on Waldo Emerson and Ross Fishbaugh in Nebraska as he traveled westward on the Union Pacific from Omaha. The tall, solid boys in the trendy felt hats had paid for their initial passage on the smaller St. Joseph and Grand Island line running north and west out of Missouri into Kansas and Nebraska, and then they hooked up with the Union Pacific at Grand Island, midway across Nebraska. Within the first two days, they sent postal cards home from Alda and Grand Island indicating that all was well, and that they had met up with another, unnamed fellow from St. Joe, who was also heading west. Their cards did not say that at Grand Island they began to travel without paying their way, riding surreptitiously in Union Pacific boxcars that moved day and night through the Platte River Valley, across the prairie toward the Rocky Mountains. At Julesburg, a stop on the Union Pacific about a hundred miles east of the Wyoming border where the train line dipped briefly into northern Colorado, the two clerks braved an overnight in a hobo camp where Charley Miller also slept. The next morning, all three boarded the same freight train, headed due west for Sidney, Nebraska, and then Wyoming.

Sidney, a town of fifteen hundred people, was named for Sidney Dillon, the original New York solicitor for the Union Pacific Railroad, who went on to become a fabulously wealthy railroad magnate. When gold was discovered in the Black Hills in the 1870s, Sidney became a popular jumping-off place for prospectors, gamblers, and many others lured by the hope of getting rich quickly. The settlement was so wild and lawless, filled with saloons and thieves, that the Union Pacific did not stop there regularly unless it was necessary. (When it did, it allegedly kept the car doors locked.) By the 1880s, Sidney had calmed down, the town and the railroad had built a handsome stone depot in the Queen Anne style, and railroad officials regularly patrolled the cars to keep out freeloaders and suspicious riffraff. On the afternoon of September 26, 1890, as the number 23 train made its regular stop and then began to edge its way slowly out of the depot toward the West, William Carley, a conscientious Union Pacific brakeman, came upon some boys who should not have been on his train: "I put them off because they had no right to ride. They were not paying their way."

Although incidents like this were common, the brakeman recalled something unusual about the young men he threw off the train that Friday afternoon. There were three illegals, but they were not all riding together. Surprisingly, he reported that Miller and

Fishbaugh were in one car while Emerson was just "a few cars ahead." When the brakeman approached Miller and Fishbaugh to tell them to leave, Charley Miller was willing to get off but Ross Fishbaugh was not. In fact, the young man with the soft brown hat countered by saying that he wanted to continue riding just as they were, and then he offered the brakeman fifty cents to let them all stay. William Carley rejected the bribe and exhorted them again to leave the car, which they finally did. As the three young men walked back east toward Sidney together, the same cheeky one who had tried to bribe him brandished a gun and waved it in the air. "He didn't point it at anyone," Carley explained—he was just showing off, the way boys often do in front of friends.

The brakeman had no way of knowing that Emerson and Fishbaugh were friends, and that Charley Miller had made their acquaintance only recently. On the walk back into town, the boys took each other's measure. Perhaps they talked about the fact that the two older youths hailed from St. Joe, the place where Jesse James was killed, which was less than 120 miles from Leonardville as the crow flies. Charley was impressed that Emerson and Fishbaugh were tramping the same way he was, despite their fashionable clothing. Both were exuberant about their journey and nonchalant about life in general. Both talked about the kind of well-paying jobs they expected to get in Denver, after they had seen Cheyenne and its parade of millionaires. Charley couldn't help noticing that Fishbaugh seemed the more adventurous of the two, and that Emerson occasionally checked the time on a good-looking silver pocket watch. In the six weeks since his release from the prison in Pennsylvania, Charley had not fared well, and he was sensitive to the ways in which his appearance compared with that of the natty young men from Missouri. Dirty and without any money, he hadn't had a "set down" since Omaha, three days before. Still, given his history on the rails, he thought he could probably offer these less experienced fellows some ideas about how to ride the next portion of the trip free, right into the center of Cheyenne.

On that particular September day in Sidney, there were many ways for three youths to keep busy as they waited for another train.

It was the last day of the county fair, an annual event promoted for weeks beforehand by the *Telegraph*, the town's only newspaper. Although the summer of 1890 had been so hot and dry that the harvest was skimpier than usual, the fair was still a not-to-be-missed event: "The fair next week promises to afford an abundance of sport even if there is a failure in crops. It will be well to take a couple of days off and enjoy what there is to see." In fact, the isolated Nebraska town was overrun with people, all there to enjoy a wide variety of activities, ranging from the decorous to the exuberant. In the new agricultural hall, there were the usual prize-winning Holsteins, mules, sour pickles, and jars of choke-cherry butter. Despite the drought, one local farmer still managed to bring in cabbages that weighed twenty pounds each. And among the exciting "entertainments" there was a fine-arts display arranged by the town's female elite, band music, and horse racing, a major attraction. A week beforehand, the *Telegraph* described all the different running and trotting races along with their purses, a few as grand as one hundred dollars.

Waldo, Ross, and Charley sensed the festive atmosphere, but the relationship between them soured as the afternoon progressed. In Sidney, the two young men who were playing at tramping had no use for the real tramp, who quickly became an unattractive, smelly nuisance rather than a chum. Emerson and Fishbaugh wanted Charley to scram, and their attitude made for an unhappy afternoon for the boy with the torn trousers and deepening hunger in his belly. Somewhere near the fairgrounds, the two clerks suggested to Charley that they break up the troika, that he "take one road and they would take another." And when that didn't work, they used one of the oldest ploys in the game: they told Charley to wait for them on a certain street corner in Sidney, but they never showed up to meet him.

Instead, Emerson and Fishbaugh headed to a popular lunch counter that adjoined the billiard hall on Sidney's busy Front Street. Recognized as strangers in town, they spoke easily and confidently with the owner and local patrons as they ordered, ate, and paid for two whole meals. They also played some pool and, in the

course of the next few hours, dipped into the Court, a popular saloon owned by the local sheriff and located just four or five feet
away from the billiard hall, across a narrow alley. While they were
there, Charley entered the saloon looking for them. Fishbaugh
treated him to a drink but made something of a show about it.
After pulling a ten-dollar bill from his pocket, he bragged in a loud
voice: "That's nothing. That's the second one I busted today." In
addition to the beer they consumed that afternoon, Waldo and
Ross bought some whiskey to carry with them on the train, as well
as five bullets for Ross's gun, a purchase Charley shrewdly noted.

As his friends ate and drank on the town's main drag, Charley
followed the smell of baking bread to the back door of Hugh Mc-
Fadden, the local baker. McFadden, who had seen many beggar
boys before, explained his policy regarding handouts: "Anyone
who comes into my place and asks for something to eat, I generally
study for a few minutes before I say yes or no." McFadden apparently had some doubts about this particular boy because of the way
he looked. There was something about his face and disreputable
clothing that made the baker stall. He sent Charley up the road to
fetch coal in payment for the food he would give him, and then
held off the food for a while longer. He explained his reluctance
later: "I thought he was of the Jewish race when he first spoke and
afterwards I was convinced he was not. It was on account of his
nose." So much depended on looks, but this time Charley's face
was misread, setting off an anti-Semitic alarm at a time when Jews
were vilified both in the United States and in Europe.

McFadden and his wife never invited Charley in for a set
down, but they did provide some bread, a piece of cheese, and two
pieces of pie, all in a paper sack. The hungry youngster ate the
bread and cheese immediately and then wandered back through
town with the pie, feeling somewhat better, at least for the moment. When the three youths met up again, Charley gave the pie
to the fellows from St. Joe, despite their rejection of him earlier in
the day. ("I thought they were hungry too," he later explained to
his lawyer.) The gift was a simple act of generosity on the part of a

ragged fifteen-year-old hoping to be accepted by boys who were older and more successful. He probably also expected the boys to return the favor, but, unfortunately, they never did.

———◆———

About nine-thirty the same evening, Charley noticed that there was another Union Pacific freight train at the Sidney depot being prepared for departure to Cheyenne. This particular freight carried mostly coal and cattle and offered thirty-eight cars to choose from. Charley climbed alone into one of the open livestock cars, covered himself with hay, and fell asleep before the train even pulled out. When it shuddered to a stop to take on water, probably at Potter or Kimball, Nebraska, he awoke and realized that he needed a better, more secretive hiding place, away from cows and their excrement. He carefully jumped to the ground with the load of hay that served as his bed and began to sneak from boxcar to boxcar, looking for an open door. As he threw the hay into one of the cars and boosted himself up onto the hard metal floor, Charley heard a familiar voice ring out—"Hey, kid"—and he knew at once that he had reconnected with the fellows from St. Joe.

The three slept together for a while as the train crossed the border into Wyoming. There was no reason for Emerson and Fishbaugh to fear sleeping with Charley Miller: he seemed to be more of a nuisance than a danger. Unlike Fishbaugh, who was a braggart, Charley deliberately kept his gun out of sight. The boxcar they shared, the fifteenth behind the engine, was filled with wooden railroad ties piled so high at each end of the car that they almost touched the ceiling. In the middle, the ties were stacked much lower, providing an open space where the boys talked and smoked cigarettes. At Pine Bluffs, a town in Wyoming only three-quarters of a mile across the state line, the train stopped again in order to take on some coal, meet other trains, and make some transfers of goods. Although three youths were seen stretching their legs, only two ventured into the local eatery while the train sat in the station for the long layover. According to Amanda Kauffman, the proprietor, it was about 6 A.M. when Waldo Emerson and Ross Fishbaugh entered her dining room and downed a hearty breakfast, before the trainmen came in for theirs. Afterward, they hightailed it back to their "private car," where Charley remained curled up and hungry in his bed of straw. Waldo and Ross obviously had no intention of returning Charley's favor, the gift of the pie.

At 8 A.M., the three young men left Pine Bluffs together, but at some point during the next three hours—before the train came to the tiny settlement of Hillsdale—the boxcar they shared became the scene of a horrific double murder. While Emerson and Fishbaugh slept with full stomachs on top of the stacked railroad ties, Charley remained below, in the middle, agitated and unhappy, maybe even rethinking what he had done with his last food. The contented clerks removed their shoes as well as their cardboard collars and cuff links, setting them out neatly on the lower pile of ties as if it were a bedroom dresser. Next to their belongings, in full view, there was a whiskey bottle still containing enough for a few stiff drinks. As the older boys slept soundly in the darkness of the moving boxcar, Charley Miller began to drink on an empty stomach.

What happened next was brutal, unforgivable, and never really explained by the boy who did it. Charley climbed deliberately (and quietly) up the pile of ties and shot Waldo Emerson at close range directly in his head, through his right temple. When Fishbaugh stirred from the noise of the gun, Charley shot him too, in almost the same spot. Unlike Emerson, who died instantly, Fishbaugh rose up and struggled for a moment before he fell from the top of the pile to the platform below in a face-down, spread-eagle position.

Charley rifled the bodies looking for money and valuables, but he was less than systematic, because he had never done anything like this before, and he was beginning to panic. He reached into his victims' pants but totally forgot about their coats. From Waldo Emerson, he took a knife and the silver pocket watch, but he dropped its chain and never found the diamond collar studs that

Waldo had hidden so carefully before he left home. From Ross Fishbaugh, still alive and frothing at the mouth, he stole forty-five dollars in paper money, two silver dollars, a knife, and the .38 revolver he had seen in Sidney. Because that pistol was so much better than his own, Charley left the actual murder weapon, the old .32 purchased in Kansas City for protection, tucked beneath Emerson's bloody body.

By the time the train pulled into Hillsdale, slightly after 11 A.M., Kansas Charley's protective instincts had kicked in. He left the boxcar unnoticed, carrying the stolen booty, but he was uncertain what to do next. Instead of being a tramp and an imaginary ruffian, he was now a real criminal, afraid and on the run. Charley felt confused. What he did in the Union Pacific boxcar had happened so quickly, and it seemed to transform everything.

❦

As the train with the dead bodies sat in the station at Hillsdale taking on water, Charley Miller went out boldly in search of food. He headed immediately for the section house, a small sod building inhabited by John Brooks, a pump engineer who lived there with his wife. He glibly told Mrs. Brooks that he had been traveling days and nights from New York City and that he was tired and needed a "fill up." Although the boy looked poor—his clothes were ripped and patched—he was able to pay twenty-five cents for a meal.

Since it was getting close to the noon dinner hour, Mrs. Brooks called her husband to stop his home-improvement project and come eat with the hungry young traveler. "I was calcimining [whitewashing] a room," the dutiful spouse explained, "and my wife asked me to come and have lunch with him. I sat on one side of the table and he on the other." Since the boy seemed to be moving west, Brooks asked him "why he didn't beat this train [the one in the station] and he said he was tired of riding and wanted something to eat." Brooks noted that the kid actually ate very little, and that he nervously consulted a silver pocket watch without a chain, as if he were in a hurry. At the time, Brooks made no connection

between the boy's anxious behavior and what was going on outside his kitchen window as they ate the midday meal.

George W. Mannifee, head brakeman on the train, had just
discovered the bodies of two boys in car number 15, one that was
dead, the other barely alive. He put straw under the head of the
one whose groans caught his attention, but there was not much
else anyone could do in tiny Hillsdale, and there was no time to do
any real examination. On the platform outside the Brookses' window, Mannifee huddled with William Hubbard, conductor of the
waiting Cheyenne-bound train, and Frederick McGuire, the
Union Pacific ticket agent. The train had been stopped for only
twenty minutes, and the water was not yet fully pumped, but Hubbard wanted to get moving as quickly as possible for the run into
Cheyenne, still almost two hours away. Before the train left,
McGuire helped Hubbard telegraph Cheyenne officials about the
grisly cargo that would arrive later that afternoon.

Charley was relieved by the departure of the train but fearful of
being caught with any of the dead men's possessions. He cut
across the tracks and hid the stolen gun and knives under a loose
board at the end of the platform. Then he came back across the
tracks to the Union Pacific office to see about buying a ticket.
Agent McGuire later remembered that soon after Hubbard's train
left the station at Hillsdale a boy appeared, as if out of nowhere,
asking about the cost of a fare to Manhattan, Kansas. When the
agent responded that he wasn't entirely sure and would need a
minute to "hunt it up," the young man backed off, saying that the
trip did not have to be specifically to Manhattan, just to Kansas.
McGuire indicated that the second request was much easier, but
within a split second, the youngster changed his mind again and
bought a ticket to Cheyenne. Just a half-hour later, Charley Miller
boarded the smoking car of the next train bound for the capital of
Wyoming. He arrived only a few hours after the train carrying his
victims, and by that time, the story of "the boxcar murder" was on
everyone's lips.

When Hubbard's train came into the Cheyenne station with

the bodies about one-thirty that Saturday afternoon, it was met by a crowd of a few hundred people. According to the *Cheyenne Daily Leader*, "a hundred stories of the affair swept over the town like cholera" that day. Rumors about the cause of death were rampant, and the newspapers late that evening offered the most current speculations. Some thought that the two youths had been accidentally crushed by an avalanche of railroad ties set in motion by an emergency stop of the train. Others found it equally plausible that the unidentified bodies belonged to two young lads whose foolish fantasies about the West led to the disaster. One of them allegedly leveled a gun playfully at his companion in imitation of the gun battles they expected to see everywhere in Wyoming. But the hammer on the pistol fell accidentally, firing a fatal bullet, killing his best friend. The inadvertent murderer, stricken with remorse, became so terrified about proving his innocence that he killed himself. It was an overwrought scenario, to be sure, but it reflected people's suspicions that violence among young men could erupt from foolish, confused motives.

Once the local doctors in Cheyenne got a look, they could tell from the neat, similar head wounds they knew that something more sinister had transpired. The bodies were taken immediately by wagon to Hoyt's Drug Store, on the main street, where Albert Hoyt, a town commissioner, ordered the corpse of Waldo Emerson to be sent on to the morgue at the Warren Funeral Home for examination by Henry Maynard, a local surgeon. Ross Fishbaugh—still breathing but essentially comatose—was conveyed to the county hospital, to be met there by William A. Wyman, another local doctor. By late afternoon, he was nearly dead, and the business of establishing the strangers' identities became the top priority.

Papers in Ross Fishbaugh's pockets explained who he was and provided the people of Cheyenne with their first impression of the social status and character of the two victims. The coroner found a small leather case holding business cards imprinted with his name, as well as a receipt for luggage to be claimed at the railroad station in Denver. These items indicated a person on the rise with serious intentions, an identity confirmed by two letters of recommendation from former employers found on Fishbaugh's still-breathing body. Both letters were printed in the Cheyenne paper in their entirety, and both were exuberant in their praise of the young man who finally died about 6 P.M. in the Cheyenne hospital.

The pancake entrepreneur, Randolph T. Davis, called Ross Fishbaugh a "very excellent young man with good habits," and he recommended him without reservation: "Anyone needing a good bill clerk could not do better than give him a trial." Fishbaugh knew how to figure and write a good hand, and he was tidy. "He did not leave us on account of any misconduct," assured Davis, "but solely from the fact that we did not need his services at present." Charles W. Gregg, a grain dealer, who had been Ross's employer for two years before Davis, added to the boy's luster, calling him "competent, honest and apt." Although Waldo Emerson's corpse revealed no such credentials—he was identified by the name written on the underside of a flap on his shirt—he was cast also as an "exemplary citizen" looking for commercial work in the West. The first reports of the bodies noted the quality of the travelers' clothing: "Fishbaugh, tall, strong, dark, lately shaven clean, wore such clothes as a young man roughing it would choose from a fair wardrobe." Emerson was described as well dressed, in a suit of fine fabric and a good fit, someone with "soft white hands," a marker suggesting he was not a member of the laboring class. The *Leader*, attentive to the same sartorial details that usually caught Charley Miller's attention, ran the headline: "Well Dressed, the Dead and Dying Were Not Ordinary Tramps."

Because of the letter found in Fishbaugh's pocket, Cheyenne officials immediately wired Randolph Davis about the situation. After receiving the first communiqué with its ghastly news that Emerson was dead and Fishbaugh in desperate condition, Davis telegraphed back to confirm that both boys were from good families and that he personally wanted Fishbaugh to be well cared for. Davis then brought Ross's widowed mother, Maria, to his home to await further developments, and he took on the difficult business of informing the Emersons that their son was no more. Waldo's mother was, understandably, "prostrated with grief," and unable to accept the idea that her boy would never return. According to the *St. Joseph Gazette*, she hoped at first that some mistake had been made and refused to believe that her son was dead until details were received. Davis, acting as counselor to both families, was the bearer of these unfortunate details as they came out of Cheyenne. Later that day, he had to tell Maria Fishbaugh that her beloved Ross was also dead, and he directed Cheyenne officials to send the bodies home, Waldo's to his father and Ross's directly to him.

In both cities, ideas began to percolate that a third (or even a fourth) party was responsible for the deaths of the two young men. In response to questions sent by wire about his son, John Emerson told the Cheyenne authorities that at Grand Island Waldo met up with someone from St. Joe who began to travel with them. "Suspect third party," the grieving father telegraphed, but the postcards home offered no name to tell the authorities. At the Coroner's Inquest in Cheyenne on Sunday morning, Union Pacific employees from Pine Bluffs recalled seeing the murdered boys early Saturday morning, along with a number of other young tramps who jumped off the same train. (Fishbaugh and Emerson looked different, they noted.) The agent at Hillsdale gave suggestive testimony about a boy who had popped into his office after the train pulled out, asking confused questions about getting to Kansas, but then bought a high-priced ticket into Cheyenne.

Clues began to emerge as boxcar number 15 was searched carefully and the railroad ties removed. In addition to finding the murder weapon (which revealed that only two shots were fired), inspectors located a silver watch chain, sleeve buttons, a worn leather match safe with an illegible name scratched on it, a bottle containing a trace of whiskey, and a soiled finger "wrapper," like a Band-Aid. Late on Sunday, in St. Joe, Randolph Davis received a message from County Prosecutor Walter Stoll in Cheyenne with a set of questions indicating that the Wyoming authorities were trying to run down all the material evidence: "Did Emerson or Fishbaugh have a pistol, if so what kind? Did either have money, how much and what kind? Did they have watches? Did either have cloth [wrapped] about a finger? Were they enemies or friends?"

Since neither Emerson nor Fishbaugh had any sores or marks on their hands, the discovery of the wrapper set a rumor in motion about a tramp seen in Cheyenne with a bandage on his hand only hours after the bodies arrived. Simultaneously, a story emerged in St. Joe that the murderer was Lee Frazell, a ne'er-do-well already under indictment there for larceny. Allegedly it was Frazell who had met the boys at Grand Island and then stalked and killed them for the common purse they bragged about before leaving town. The deputy sheriff in St. Joe had yet another hypothesis: he thought Waldo and Ross were the victims of a notorious criminal gang in the Missouri, Indiana, and Illinois tristate region. One of the suspects he had in mind was an expert thief, the other a counterfeiter, and their departure from St. Joe coincided with that of the two boys, now affectionately known as the "amateur tramps."

For the parents of the amateur tramps, theorizing about the crime was only one piece of the sad and dismal process of coping with what had happened to their sons. On Monday evening, only two days after the tragedy, the Emersons and Maria Fishbaugh went to the railroad depot in St. Joe to receive the dead bodies of their boys, arriving on the same line that had carried them west less than a week before. When she heard the initial news on Saturday, Maria Fishbaugh wanted to rush to her son's bedside in Cheyenne, but there was never any real chance that Ross would survive. Now she joined the Emersons, relatives, and friends for a final look inside the handsome metal caskets after they were removed from the train to the baggage room for a medical check and final viewing.

As the local surgeon made a brief examination of the wounds, the parents had to deal with the hard facts of what they saw. Their boys were cold and still. They were wearing the new clothes they had purchased in the heady days of planning before the trip, a time filled with youthful idealism. But each now bore an undisguised, lethal head wound that mocked their optimism. In Ross's case, the wound was especially unsightly, creating a horrible assault on the emotions of his widowed mother, who struggled to contain her sobs.

When the caskets were finally closed, Maria Fishbaugh made arrangements to send her son's body to Litchfield, Ohio, to be buried next to his father. She did not accompany Ross on his final passage and chose to grieve now in private, out of the sight of local reporters and the curious. Waldo Emerson's mortal remains were removed to Heaton's, a well-known local undertaker, and then to his parents' home at 423 North Seventh Street, where the family received many sad and supportive visitors. According to the *St. Joseph Gazette*, the funeral the next day was "largely attended" and included many of Waldo's peers, anxious to show their respect for their departed companion. Eight of these young men, fellow clerks and workers, served as pallbearers, carrying their friend's casket for internment at Mount Mora Cemetery.

It was a sad and shocking end to what should have been Waldo Emerson's most excellent adventure. Everyone wondered what had actually transpired in the boxcar, and whether Waldo and Ross were shot by a stranger or betrayed by someone they knew and considered a friend. For young men their age, the boxcar murder was particularly upsetting because it was so disillusioning. It suggested that enthusiasms had to be tempered. It meant that danger lurked almost everywhere—even in situations, and among people, that seemed to be harmless or amusing.

For the Emersons, the slow walk to their son's newly dug grave was painful in a very different way. Brokenhearted but also aggrieved, they considered how things might have been different if they had only kept their son at home under their protective wing. They thought also about the questions they could have asked, or the advice they might have proffered about avoiding certain kinds of risks and suspicious people. Though the funeral brought some degree of finality, only a week later the families learned that authorities in both cities had forgotten to ascertain whether the lethal bullets had come from a .38 or a .32 pistol. The gruesome request to exhume the bodies, coupled with the investigation's unfulfilled promise of an arrest, caused the parents yet another hurt as they struggled with the unbearable loss of their wandering boys. The "amateur tramps" were not just "blighted" like the boy in the hymn—they came home dead, and no one was certain why.

CHAPTER FOUR

Attention, at Last

O N SEPTEMBER 27, when Charley Miller finally arrived in Cheyenne, the community of fifteen thousand people was abuzz with news of the cargo carried in on the Union Pacific earlier that day. As the town talked, the young murderer spent his stolen funds on a hearty meal, a new shirt with a black silk handkerchief, and a haircut with a spritz of tonic. He also struck up an acquaintance with Henry Howland, a young fellow from Grover, Colorado, and the two made their way out to nearby Lake Minnehaha, where they spent the evening and shared accommodations at Kimme's, a saloon and brewery. Howland later remembered that the boy he befriended said he was from New York City, and that he was looking for work as a cowboy on a ranch.

Charley never got the glamorous work he dreamed of, because he knew little about how to ride and care for horses, and he was not particularly strong. Instead, he hired on with some sheepherders heading south by foot to Grover. Along the way, out of fear that he might get caught with incriminating goods, he threw Waldo Emerson's silver graduation watch into a gopher hole. When he reached Grover, tired out from the physical labor that herding required, he made the decision to hightail it back to Kansas, forsaking further outdoor adventure for the safety of a place and people he knew. Only four days later—on Monday, October 6—he arrived in Leonardville to be reunited with Fred and Willie, now living together under the roof of Preston Loofbourrow.

The following Sunday morning, as he sat in the privy outside the Loofbourrows' farmhouse, Charley had a crisis of conscience. It was provoked by reading an article about his crime in the *St. Joseph Ballot*, a report that was, by then, three weeks old. An enormous headline—"IS IT MURDER?"— accompanied a ghoulish description of his victims' bodies as well as speculation about a "traveling companion," all of which shook Charley to the bone. In the 1880s, old newspapers were often stacked in outhouses for use as toilet paper, but instead of tearing it up for his personal use, Charley grabbed the relevant sheet and carried it to Fred, suggesting that they take a walk together, alone. Charley showed Fred the graphic story and then admitted: "I was the boy who murdered Emerson and Fishbaugh." He also said that the "terrible deed so preyed on his mind that he could not keep it [a secret]." Shocked and frightened by his brother's admission, Fred told him earnestly that "the best thing to do was to tell all and give yourself up." Although Charley respected Fred, he was uncertain as to what he should do. He repeated that he felt terrible about what he had done, yet, in the next breath, he indicated that he planned to flee.

Trusting in his foster parents, Fred ran back to the house and unburdened himself to Sarah Loofbourrow, who immediately told her husband. Preston, always inclined to see the best in young people, was incredulous and figured that Fred's brother was fibbing and only imagining himself a murderer because of the kind of ghoulish reading boys usually did: "I could hardly believe that Charley had told the truth, rather surmising that he was trying to build up a sort of James' boy reputation among the [other] boys."

There was no sign of Charley as Fred, Willie, Preston, and Sarah anxiously considered what they should do if the story was really true. Finally, late the following day, Charley showed up again, asking to talk with Fred alone. This time, he told his older brother that he would give himself up but that he wanted to have Preston Loofbourrow go with him to state his case, an arrangement that Fred's guardian accepted. At that moment, Fred realized "the enormity of the crime" and started to cry, as did the anguished young murderer. Charley had his opportunity to run, but he did not take it, perhaps because he thought that if he said "I did it" he would be treated more leniently than if he were tracked down and found guilty; perhaps he was contrite because of the moral environment of the Loofbourrow home. In either case, he never denied his atrocious misbehavior, and he displayed an honesty that was in sharp contrast to the demonized boy murderer who would now emerge in the national press.

———&—

Three days after divulging his awful secret, Charley traveled to Manhattan, Kansas, to turn himself in to an officer at the Riley County Jail. This Manhattan was diminutive compared with the island he had known as a small boy. Manhattan, Kansas, only had about twenty-five hundred residents in the late 1880s, but it was the home of the burgeoning Kansas State Agricultural College, founded in 1863 as a result of the Morrill Land Grant Act. Along Poyntz Avenue, the town's wide but unpaved thoroughfare, industrious college students, faculty, and local farm families supported a cluster of well-provisioned general stores, banks, and a livery stable. Manhattan also boasted a roller-skating rink, an opera house, and a number of imposing residences, built from bricks made of local limestone.

Charley was accompanied to Manhattan, as promised, by Preston Loofbourrow. When they arrived at the jail, it was not a total surprise to Sheriff Joseph Meyers, who had already been warned by telegram from Cheyenne that a suspect in the boxcar murders was likely to be in Kansas. In that message, John A. Martin, sheriff of Laramie County, told his counterpart in Manhattan that the murderer could be the boy with a "silver watch without a chain," the one who "inquired the fare from Hillsdale, Wyoming, to your place." Sheriff Martin admitted: "We cannot find him in Cheyenne. Look out for him, arrest him if he comes there and let me know by telegraph at my expense."

Charley's voluntary surrender made Sheriff Meyers's job relatively easy. All he had to do now was listen to the confession and
convey what he heard to the authorities in Cheyenne. Charley's
initial statement probably reflected some prior coaching by Preston Loofbourrow, who remained at his side. Sitting with the two
adults in the sheriff's front parlor, a sitting room attached to the
county jail, Charley outlined what he had done and dutifully indicated his remorse: "My crime has been a great burden to me and I
concluded to give myself up to the officers." Trained to ask for
proof, Meyers wanted some way to validate the awful story, so
Charley told him about the gun and knives he had hidden at the
Hillsdale depot. Meyers immediately sent a telegram to Martin:
"The murderer is named Chas. Miller. He will come without req-
uisition. Confessed to shooting two men in a box car close to
Cheyenne. Says he left a revolver in the [box]car, also a match safe
with the name 'Charley' on it. Look under west side of depot, at
Hillsdale and you will find a revolver. Miller's brother lives here.
He is right man sure." On the other end, an excited Sheriff Martin
wired up to Hillsdale with information about where the gun could
be found and then left for Manhattan, on the next train, in order to
bring the boy back to Wyoming for speedy indictment.

Confident that he had the right person, Sheriff Meyers booked
Charley into the Riley County Jail and sent Preston Loofbourrow
back home to Leonardville. Whatever goodbyes were said between them were never a matter of record. Loofbourrow had seen
the boy cry and he had heard an authentic statement of remorse.
An avuncular figure with a commitment to the idea of moral rehabilitation, he must have offered Charley assurance that he had
done the right thing by confessing to the crime rather than being
haunted forever. "Honesty is the best policy," was the kind of
aphorism that guided Loofbourrow's life, and which he tried to
teach to Fred and then Willie. As worried as he was about
Charley's future and the effects of all the publicity on the boys in
his home, he probably never thought to warn Charley about the
need to be guarded, to hold his tongue, in case he was approached
by journalists seeking grizzly details for their true-life crime stories.

The morning after Charley's first night alone in jail, Sheriff Meyers moved him from his cell back into the parlor and arranged for him to have an extended personal interview with Albert A. Stewart, publisher and editor of the *Daily Republic*, a leading newspaper in the Riley County capital. Stewart, a native of Wisconsin, entered the printing trade at the age of twelve, and by 1876, the year he turned eighteen, he was made foreman of the *Register* in Oswego, Kansas. Only a few months later, he was appointed superintendent of printing at the Kansas State Agricultural College, allegedly the first institution of higher learning in the country to establish a printing department. Stewart remained at the college for almost eight years, and then left for bigger pastures: foreman of the jobbing department at the *Capital* in Topeka. He returned to Manhattan, however, when he was appointed postmaster of the town by President Chester A. Arthur in 1884, and he remained in that position until the Democrats won control in 1886, at which point he took charge of the *Daily Republic*, a fiercely partisan paper that represented both the Republican and the temperance point of view. In his youth, Stewart helped to organize a division of the Sons of Temperance in Manhattan, and he later served the organization as their grand scribe.

At the time he met Charley Miller in the autumn of 1890, thirty-two-year-old Stewart was deeply involved in promoting Republican candidates in a gubernatorial election year in which both Democrats and the new People's Party offered a serious challenge to Republican hegemony in Kansas. Stewart's columns during the campaign were avidly pro-temperance, and intended to stimulate moral fervor about the issue of "demon rum." "Since the territory was organized," he wrote, "Kansas has been the battle ground of every great moral question," a reference, of course, to the bloody period in the 1850s when free-soilers and slaveholders clashed over the future of the "peculiar institution." By 1890, there was a different kind of moral emergency, according to Stewart, in the form of a prohibition referendum on the upcoming November ballot. Readers of the *Daily Republic* knew exactly where their editor stood, because his paper was filled with all kinds of warnings about the

ways in which inebriation defiled family and community life and
also stimulated crime. "Every home in Kansas is in danger, and so
has a vital interest in the mighty issue of this campaign," he wrote.
"Arouse, ye temperance men, without regard to party and rally to
the standard of prohibition. Rum never sleeps."

As involved as he was in partisan politics that October, Stewart
was willing to switch gears to a different kind of journalism when
there was a homicide to report. Although he always claimed that
the sheriff invited him to the parlor that day, the opportunity to talk
with a boy murderer clearly served Stewart's professional self-
interest and his political goals. He wanted to be the first newspaper
man to break the story because of the cachet it would carry in the
world of competitive journalism. The boy had already admitted his
guilt, he reasoned, so why shouldn't the public know the full story,
told in Miller's own words? As he heard more of it, he also recognized that this particular homicide, with its cast of young men on
the tramp, provided a powerful example of alcohol-related may-
hem that was good for the temperance and Republican cause.

Neither the misguided sheriff nor the enterprising editor
stopped to consider the implications for Charley's future legal defense or the issue of fairness, as we must today. In the 1890s, the
Fourteenth Amendment to the Constitution of the United States
had not yet been interpreted to provide pretrial rights, such as the
right to remain silent or the right to an attorney. (These rights were
not articulated by the Supreme Court until the 1960s, in landmark
cases like *Miranda v. Arizona* and *Gideon v. Wainwright*.) There
was no attorney at Charley Miller's side in that Manhattan parlor,
and he probably was unaware that he did not have to answer the
questions posed by the sheriff and the editor. From a contemporary standpoint, the two-on-one setup during the process of custodial interrogation eviscerated Charley's Fifth Amendment rights
against self-incrimination, but in the late nineteenth century this
kind of pretrial cooperation between a local sheriff and an enterprising editor was not unusual at all.

Despite the unfairness in the situation, Stewart's cordial interest probably felt flattering to a boy who had never had much positive attention from adults. He started to "ask me everything," and he also wrote a great deal on his "tab[let]," Charley remembered. Over the course of the interview, Charley provided a comprehensive account of his life, from the New York tenement to Leonardville, Kansas, and points in between. Stewart drew the boy out about the dreary economic circumstances of his early childhood (including his saloon-keeping, beer-drinking father) and probably also talked with him about their mutual experiences in the printing trade. Then Stewart worked his way into the murder, the real reason for the interview. According to Stewart, it was all cordial and noncoercive: "[Miller] sat down by the table [in Sheriff Meyers's office] and talked freely and frankly about the deed which has caused him so much trouble of mind since its commission, and concerning which he could have no peace until he had made a full confession." Like many youthful offenders today, Charley may have tailored his confession to what he thought the adults wanted to hear; some boys in his situation will say almost anything, in the hopes that they will get to go home or simply stop the painful questioning.

In his first confession, when Sheriff Meyers asked why he had killed Emerson and Fishbaugh, Charley was uncommunicative, saying only that he "did not know." But in the newspaper confession, a confession seduced, orchestrated, and reported by Albert Stewart, a motivation was crisply articulated for the first time. "I killed them for their money," he allegedly told Stewart as Meyers listened, and then he added: "I was penniless, hungry and desperate." Then Miller admitted something that Stewart really wanted to hear: he was drinking immediately before the murder. Details like this were sweet music to the ears of the Kansas editor, because they made for a human-interest story that conveniently confirmed the evils of alcohol, his pet political issue. He was anxious to tell the Kansas reading audience that there were partly emptied liquor bottles found in the boxcar, something that may have been an exaggeration.

Stewart's journalistic coup was picked up and transmitted in condensed form on the wires of the Western Associated Press to hundreds of newspapers, including, of course, those in Cheyenne and St. Joe, where interest in the story was most intense. In a brief transmission that blanketed the region and the nation, the son of the miserable Frederick Muller made his first entrance on the national scene: "Manhattan, Kas. Oct. 16—Chas. Miller, a 15 year old boy, of Leonardville, Kas. has confessed that he is the murderer of Fishbaugh and Emerson, two young men from St. Joseph, found dead in a box car at Cheyenne, Wyo. Sept 27. He was beating his way on a freight train with them and killed them while they were asleep for their money."

The Manhattan confession hit Cheyenne in the form of a special dispatch two days later. In it, the people of Cheyenne learned the sad details of the murderer's early life and read a description of what he looked like. In an era before the widespread use of photographs in newspapers, Stewart's "pen picture" of the boy was much discussed: "Miller is about five feet and four inches high, light complexion and hair, prominent features and full gray eyes. Shows plainly his German descent. He appears like a peaceable, well-disposed boy, but looks as if he has seen a hard life with lots of trouble." The description was inconsistent, however, on whether or not Charley Miller actually looked sinister. At one point, Stewart said: "No one would judge [him] from his looks and actions to be a murderer." At another, he stated that the boy "has a kind of cat eye, which betrays a dangerous character when aroused or angered." Images like these increased the curiosity of readers, making them anxious to see for themselves if the tramp from New York looked sneaky or mean.

In Cheyenne and elsewhere, the Manhattan confession was capped with oversized headlines that acknowledged the young murderer's social status and the frame of mind that led him to confess: "THE BOY WAS COLD, HUNGRY, PENNILESS AND DESPERATE" and "TERRORIZED BY HIS SECRET HE TOLD THE STORY TO HIS BROTHER." Because Miller was likely to stand trial in Cheyenne, the editorials there focused on the serendipitous way in which the three young men ended up together in Wyoming, and how the murderer was able to pass so boldly among the citizenry without detection. Despite Stewart's emphasis on "liquor bottles," nothing at all was said in the Cheyenne papers about the issue of alcohol, suggesting that local editors cut this part of Stewart's story because there was nothing unusual about young men drinking in a town where there was a saloon on nearly every corner. Instead, the people of Cheyenne were riveted by the narrative conveyed by Albert Stewart: "The story of the killing and subsequent flight of the murderer is marvelous. Every circumstance seemed to conspire to aid his escape and shield him from detection."

A few days later, as the dust began to settle, and the city realized that it was faced with a *boy* murderer instead of a grown man, an editorial in the *Leader* speculated on the larger issues involved in the emerging story of Charley Miller: "It seems strange that the nineteenth century and a country like this should develop the conditions which led to the perpetration of such a crime. The case is an interesting one for the philanthropist and the social reformer, but while everyone decides that the boy should suffer for the crime (and justly too) aren't the impelling circumstances which led him into a commission of the crime just the same a reflection upon society as it is present[ly] constituted?" Regardless of where one stood on the issue of societal responsibility, after the Manhattan confession everyone in Cheyenne was keen to see Charley in the flesh, to take his measure.

Back in Manhattan, Stewart was afraid that the boy might change his tune when he got to Cheyenne. For that reason, he made a point of seeing him off as he left Kansas under the control of Sheriff Martin for the two-day trip to Wyoming. The apprehensive editor reportedly told him as he stepped onto the wagon that would carry him to his train: "Charley, you have told everyone about this. Now when you get to Cheyenne don't let anyone persuade you to contradict this, but throw yourself on the mercy of the court." Fred Miller, who was also there to say goodbye, answered for his brother with a clear vote of confidence: "Charley wouldn't do that. He has told me this and he will tell the same thing there."

Across Kansas and Wyoming, the press reveled in stories about the Miller case, because it made for such vigorous sales. As the people in Cheyenne waited for his arrival, the two leading dailies published every scrap of information they could obtain, including the texts of mundane telegrams sent back and forth between the two cooperating sheriffs. Because the time of the train's arrival was well known, people checked their watches on October 18 to note the moment of the strange delivery. It was no surprise, then, that more than two thousand people showed up at the Union Pacific depot that day to catch sight of the boy murderer as he disembarked from the train with the sheriff who had gone to fetch him from Manhattan. Despite a rumor that some roughnecks might attempt a lynching, the shackled fifteen-year-old was conveyed without incident to the Laramie County Jail, smack in the middle of town, to await a preliminary hearing. Charley was finally at the center of many people's attention.

———◆·◆———

When he was on the tramp, Charley Miller dreamed of the day when he would finally reach Cheyenne, the magic city where he intended to make his fortune. In Kansas City and in Omaha, he had heard stories about the lucrative seasonal work he could get as a cowboy in Wyoming, and how a fellow could "ride the grubline" from ranch to ranch when the weather turned bad. As he traveled with other men and boys, he listened to stories about the huge fortunes being made from cattle in the West, and the way that some men—without any prior experience or even a great deal of effort—were able to multiply a single beef cow into a herd of thousands. Books like *The Beef Bonanza, or How to Get Rich on the Plains* (1881), and *Cattle Raising on the Plains of North America* (1885) made it seem as if anyone could become a cattle baron, since the required natural resources—land, grasses, and water—were abundant and free to everyone who settled in Wyoming.

In reality, Wyoming was less than an equal-opportunity state, although it was the first state in the nation to give women the right to vote. Wyoming had a sparse population in a vast area—just under twenty-one thousand people in ninety-eight thousand square miles—but it was not the open society that this ratio implied. By the autumn of 1890, when Charley Miller arrived in Cheyenne, there were deep class divisions which would eventually have an impact on his case. Political power in Wyoming was located in a ruling class of cattle barons who had made vast fortunes in the 1870s and 1880s based on borrowed capital and free access to all territorial land. This elite, centered in Cheyenne, regarded free grazing on the range as their inalienable right. When Ethelburt Talbot went west to Wyoming as an Episcopal bishop in 1887, he later remembered, he was told by a senior official in the church: "My young brother, Cheyenne is the richest town of its size in the whole world today." (In 1886, per-capita assets in Cheyenne did make it the wealthiest city in the world.)

By the late 1880s, the cattle barons were increasingly uneasy, however, about the encroachment of smaller homesteader-ranchers who also had cows on the range, but in far lesser numbers. Some of the biggest Wyoming operators owned five or six thousand head of cattle, compared with a cowpunching farmer, who typically had a herd of between fifty and a hundred animals, and also raised a crop of hay. The big operators were represented by the Wyoming Stockgrowers Association (WSGA), a powerful lobbying group that controlled the territorial legislature and shaped the development of agricultural, mineral, and water resources in ways favorable to their interests. In addition to the assumption that their livestock should be able to graze public lands absolutely free without restriction, the WSGA battled for decades with the small ranchers over the issue of mavericks—unbranded, motherless calves of uncertain ownership who got lost or strayed. Mavericks were a normal part of everyday life on the range, and the problem of how to handle them should have been worked out in a manner that represented both large and small stockgrowers. But mavericks became an obsession with the big operators, who tended to perceive the small ranchers as thieves and rustlers looking for ways to steal their cows. (Anxious to discourage cattle ownership among these small ranchers, the WSGA blacklisted any employees who owned cattle themselves, a policy that suggested that small operators could not possibly own their animals honestly.)

Then, in 1884, the territorial legislature passed a maverick law that gave the cattle barons even more power and resources: instead of putting control of the maverick issue in a public body representing both small and large stockgrowers (as was done in other cattle states), the WSGA was empowered to organize all roundups in the territory and, most important, claim all mavericks on behalf of their association. Mavericks were branded on the neck with an "M" by WSGA foremen, and then sold at auction every ten days. The proceeds went directly into the WSGA coffers, ostensibly for an inspection fund. But there was no public accountability, and rumor had it that the money raised at auction really went into the coffers of the lavish Cheyenne Club, an exclusive, by-invitation-only hangout where cattle barons mixed with the state's political elite, currying favors and smoking expensive cigars. The maverick law of 1884 was grossly unfair, and the auction process that went with it an outrage, because it gave all kinds of advantages to the big operators, who drove up prices, virtually excluding the little guys. It was no wonder that the *Laramie Boomerang* proclaimed: "The Association [Wyoming Stockgrowers] is stronger in Wyoming than the press, the courts, and even the legislature." (Although a territorial livestock commission did replace the WSGA as the official livestock authority in 1889, according to all reports the new body was "dominated by the same individuals and the same interests merely wearing different hats.")

The WSGA was still a dominant force in Wyoming politics when the territory finally became a state in July 1890. Despite significant financial losses to the cattle industry as a result of the brutal winter of 1886–87 and a subsequent drop in membership, the power of the WSGA never really waned, and cattle wealth remained concentrated in the hands of a small coterie of rich men who made Cheyenne their business center and playground. In

1890, there were somewhere between thirty-five hundred and five thousand cattle-owning taxpayers in the new state, but 85 to 90 percent of the state's cattle was still owned by a handful of WSGA members. Although the WSGA never formally promoted statehood, most big ranchers were in favor of it. In fact, the Republicans who carried the statehood banner—notably Joseph M. Carey and Francis E. Warren, who became the first U.S. senators from Wyoming—were members and former officers of the association. By 1890, the WSGA not only controlled the state legislature, it now had its own men in Washington and a friend in the White House, Republican President Benjamin Harrison.

By October 1890, when Charley Miller arrived in Cheyenne, Wyoming's cattle machine looked to the new state government to preserve and protect a status quo that gave them a clear economic advantage. The big operators generally supported a law-and-order position on any issue that would help them dominate the upstart rancher-settlers, who challenged their property and their way of doing business. As always, they wanted more muscle from the state in the matter of mavericking, and the control and ownership of those troublesome motherless calves, which were a symbol of the deep-seated conflict between the haves and the have-nots.

Everyone knew what the cattle barons wanted when it came to motherless cows. It was less clear what the local elite wanted for the future of the motherless boy now incarcerated in their midst. In the days after Charley's arrival, this powerful clique said little in public, although they were surely reading the newspapers and monitoring the story, waiting to see, as they usually did, how their own self-interest could be served in the upcoming case of *Wyoming v. Charles Miller.*

———≈·≈———

As the boy murderer adjusted to the routine of life in the Laramie County Jail, his future was the subject of speculation both within and outside Cheyenne. Locally, procedures were set in motion to call the grand jury that would indict him, only ten days before his sixteenth birthday, on two counts of assault and two counts of murder, for "feloniously, unlawfully, purposefully, maliciously, willfully, deliberately, premeditatively and of his own malice and aforethought" killing Waldo Emerson and Ross Fishbaugh. It was, essentially, an indictment for murder in the first degree, an offense that could carry the death penalty.

For the ten citizens on the all-male grand jury, the state's presentation was sufficiently compelling to convince them that Charles Miller should stand trial regardless of his age. Wyoming had only recently moved from territorial status to statehood, and the state criminal code made no special provision for minors accused of a felony. Wyoming was not unusual in its lack of protections for minors: in 1890, only Texas prohibited the execution of those under seventeen; a few other states, such as Kansas, outlawed the death penalty entirely. Still, there were plenty of people—both within and outside Wyoming—sympathetic to the idea that Charley's age should entitle him to special treatment, especially since he had come forth with a voluntary confession. Many saw the case as a test of the social and judicial environment of the new state, and whether or not its courts would mandate, and its people tolerate, the execution of a boy. In the 1890s, some Americans still regarded a fifteen-year-old as a functioning adult; others, especially among the better educated, considered a fifteen-year-old a child, worthy of protection and requiring moral guidance and adult supervision. In anticipation of a trial that would say as much about Wyoming as it did about the young defendant, those who cared about Miller's fate participated in a pretrial war of words designed to influence public opinion.

The first shot was fired by Preston Loofbourrow from Manhattan only a week after he helped Charley turn himself in. Loofbourrow's statement on behalf of the orphan boy appeared first as an unsigned column in his own newspaper, the *Monitor*, but it was reprinted the next day, as a letter above his signature, in both Cheyenne and St. Joe. Loofbourrow explained that he and his wife were the guardians of the "industrious, faithful and upright" Fred, a brother to Charles, and this connection made them familiar with the history of the Miller boy. Admitting that the crime was absolutely awful and that it should not go unpunished, the letter nevertheless argued that "justice be tempered with mercy" on the grounds of the "extenuating" and "palliating" circumstances in the youngster's life.

Using the collective "we," Preston spoke for himself and Sarah in a passionate but carefully constructed statement of the environmental argument embraced by those who feared that Charley Miller might hang. The Kansas couple depicted Charley as an unfortunate child—a "homeless, fatherless, motherless boy"—who had never had a single advantage. In words intended to pluck the heartstrings of readers, the Loofbourrows explained that Charley had never known a mother's love or the benefit of her "watchful care," nor was he ever exposed to a father's "counsel and restraining authority." Deprived of both love and discipline, he endured harsh, unfair treatment in the home of an unfeeling Minnesota farmer; then, as a mere child, he went out on his own, living hand-to-mouth, wandering aimlessly, without benefit of consistent guidance from kind, responsible adults.

Despite these deprivations, the Loofbourrows still found characteristics to admire in this sad, unfortunate orphan. In their letter, they offered an interpretation of Charley's psychological state at the time of the murders, and also some thoughts about his basic character. At the time of the awful crime, they said he was in a "frenzy of despair" brought on by painful hunger, and also anxiety about his traveling companions, who seemed not to like him and were carrying a loaded gun. They admitted this fear might have been imaginary, a moment of paranoia, but it was "none the less tormenting" and explained his turn to violence. They made no mention of alcohol, probably because they were teetotalers themselves, and they wanted to present Charley in as pure a light as possible.

To his credit, they felt, Charley was guilt-ridden about his behavior: "From that fatal moment the boy has been scourged by the lashings of conscience and tortured by pangs of remorse." When he fled back into the arms of his stable older brother in order to speak the truth, Charley demonstrated that he was, in his heart of hearts, a moral youngster anxious to atone: "He told Fred that he would rather hang then suffer the mental agony he had to endure continually. He said that whenever he shut his eyes to sleep the murdered boys stood before him and he could not rid himself of their presence." Once Miller came to grips with his crime, he did not "falter or swerve from his purpose, but went manfully to the sheriff's office." The Loofbourrows agreed that there should be consequences for the boy—"Not that his crime is in any sense justifiable; not that he should go unpunished or that the penalty should be made a nominal one"—but they hoped that the better impulses of human nature would prevail, and Charley would receive some appropriate but merciful punishment for his mistake. Because of their earnest commitment to the Christian ideal of saving souls, they believed the self-confessed, remorseful adolescent deserved a chance to repent, and reclaim a life "blighted" so sadly in its "early bloom."

Two days after the publication of the Loofbourrows' appeal for mercy and rehabilitation, the still-grieving parents of the victims—both the Emersons and the widowed Maria Fishbaugh—wrote collectively to Cheyenne with a sharp response that captured the depth of their anger about the callous murder of their sons. After thanking the local authorities and the citizens of Cheyenne for their humane handling of the bodies, they drew a portrait of a depraved, deliberate killer rather than a deprived, remorseful orphan. On the issue of Miller's impoverished family background, the parents of the victims cut their boys' murderer no slack. They claimed that statistics from the very New York City asylum where Miller was reared "prove[d] that the training and influence there [were] equal if not superior to that of the best homes." Charley's advantages were "ample for him to grow up a good citizen," asserted the understandably angry parents.

In their eyes, Charley was not to be pitied, he was to be reviled. It was his rotten character—not hunger, heartbreak, or humiliation—that accounted for his barbaric behavior, a "dastardly crime." The Emersons felt that Charley's inherent immorality was apparent from an early age, and that it resulted in his choice of a wandering, rootless way of life. The murder of two sleeping, innocent boys was an uncommonly vicious crime, the parents said, one of "the worst in recorded history."

In a lengthy retelling of the crime story—scripted for the people of Cheyenne, where Miller was likely to stand trial—the inconsolable parents elevated Waldo and Ross to the pantheon of boys who acted morally and generously even in the face of temptation and the well-known snares of young manhood. Their version of what happened in the hours before the murder was intended to remove any taint of irregularity or "demon rum" from the reputation of their sons; it was also designed to undermine the notion that Charley Miller's crime was caused by hunger in his belly or aggressive behavior on the part of Waldo or Ross. To make their case, they relied on second- and third-hand information, actually hearsay, provided by the private detective they hired to follow the boys' trail during the last days of September.

According to the parents' script, on the critical afternoon in Sidney before the murder, Waldo and Ross were led by Charley into a busy saloon on Front Street. "It is presumed our two boys mistook it for a lunch counter," the parents asserted in a classic act of self-delusion. In their sanitized version, their sons left the place immediately while Charley stayed behind to drink alcohol and ridicule his teetotaling friends. "They do the eating and I do the drinking," the impecunious boy tramp allegedly boasted. The parents also claimed that in Pine Bluffs, early the next morning, the abstemious duo acted righteously again when they performed an act of kindness, treating Miller to breakfast, thereby alleviating his hunger. "The three took breakfast together," the parents assured, "one paying for the three, so that it was not hunger that drove him to desperation." In their final hours, their benevolent, gentle sons failed, unfortunately, to recognize the wolf in their midst: "They evidently had confidence enough in this friend to lie down in his presence and go to sleep. Little could they have known of [Miller's] character."

The grieving parents never swayed from their message: Waldo and Ross were pure, good, and unsuspicious; Miller was malevolent, not miserable. By denying that there was booze in the boxcar, they alerted the people of Cheyenne to the way they intended to uphold the impeccable character of the dead boys even if there was evidence to the contrary. By portraying their sons as paragons of middle-class virtue, they helped themselves feel better, and they also counteracted those who might write off the entire affair as just "one bum killing another." The victims' parents were adamant about what price the murderer should pay for his hideous, unforgivable deed: "He is plenty old enough to bear the punishment to the *fullest extent of the law.*" Regardless of his age or what the Loofbourrows had to say about mercy as an expression of society's best instincts, they weighed in for the death penalty, because they were absolutely convinced that a boy who killed like a grown man should be punished as one.

Before Charley even went to trial, the people of Cheyenne were already educated by the press on the fault lines that defined a pro-Miller or an anti-Miller position. The calm, decidedly religious sentiments of Preston and Sarah Loofbourrow drew the approval of those who believed in the ideal of moral rehabilitation and compassionate punishment for those whose bad start in life constituted a mitigating circumstance for their crimes. The angry, more demanding voice of the victims' parents spoke to those who felt Miller was a bloodthirsty fiend who should be hanged for deliberately savaging the lives of two perfectly respectable boys. Unfortunately for Charley, the parents' push for retribution dovetailed with the sentiments of many vested interests—large stockgrowers, legislators, merchants, and professionals—who wanted to see the law applied firmly, as a counter to the vigilantism that had characterized Wyoming in the territorial period. By the autumn of 1890, there had been no legal hanging in Wyoming for over twenty

years, although there had been numerous unsolved murders and illegal lynchings.

On the streets and in parlors, Cheyennites argued about the
options—prison or hanging—without knowing a great deal about
the youngster who was at the center of the controversy. Charley
Miller remained something of an enigma, despite the early reports in
the newspapers and bits and pieces of information leaking out of the
county jail. Because the trial would show what kind of boy he really
was, people on both sides of the great divide—rehabilitation versus
retribution—awaited the opening gavel with enormous interest.

PART TWO

CHAPTER FIVE

In Court

O N DECEMBER 7, 1890, Charley Miller left his cell in the county jail for the short walk to the Laramie County Courthouse, where he would stand trial for murder. Despite the icy winds blowing off the prairie, there was a crowd of gawkers to stare at the shackled boy. When Charley entered the warm courtroom, he was visibly embarrassed at the attention he attracted. He must have noted the preponderance of local women in the visitors' gallery, as well as two individuals whose eyes were coldly fixed on him in an especially intense way. They were the mother and father of Waldo Emerson, and they had come to town the day before in order to attend the trial of their son's killer. Maria Fishbaugh was not in attendance. The local paper announced where the Emersons were staying—the posh Inter Ocean Hotel— and reported how pleased they were with the friendly interest and attentions of the people of Cheyenne.

At his first appearance in court, Miller was perceived as slightly pale and not very strong, even though he had filled out a bit as a result of regular meals over the time he had spent—almost two months—in the Laramie County Jail. Still, his physique was slight—he was small for sixteen—and that made him an unusually diminutive defendant. Charley was seated next to his attorney, Frank Darwin Taggart, who was appointed to represent him and paid by the District Court and Laramie County. Each jurisdiction contributed fifty dollars, making a hefty sum.

Despite his client's well-known public confession, Frank Taggart advised Miller to plead not guilty. If there had been a decent plea offer from the state—such as confinement in the Wyoming Penitentiary at Laramie in exchange for Charley's pleading guilty—Taggart might have taken the offer for his client, because confinement usually left open the possibility of parole. But there was no reason for the state to bargain: the Wyoming courts were not clogged with cases, and this particular case seemed like an easy one for the prosecution to win, since the boy had already confessed. Because there was no satisfactory offer from the state, Taggart probably chose to go to trial with the not-guilty plea because any offer the state made was no better than the worst result Charley might get at trial—namely, murder in the first degree.

The not-guilty plea ensured that there would be a trial, at which the state had the responsibility of proving the murder charge beyond a reasonable doubt. If there was a trial, Taggart might be able to discredit the Manhattan confession or gain the jury's sympathy for Charley by proving that there were mitigating circumstances that reduced his criminal responsibility. If Taggart got lucky, Walter Stoll, the able, well-respected Laramie County prosecutor, or the presiding judge, Richard H. Scott, might do something wrong procedurally, something that would facilitate an effective appeal later on. It was a gamble for the defense, to be sure, but if it worked, Miller might get a conviction short of first-degree murder, and Frank Taggart would make his reputation in Wyoming for having stood up to one of the sharpest prosecutorial guns in the region.

⊰⦿⊱

Charley Miller did not know that his lawyer was a greenhorn, although others in town surely did. Frank Taggart had no experience in capital cases, and only a limited acquaintance with the courts of Wyoming. Although he was a partner in the Cheyenne law firm of Armstrong, Breckons and Taggart, he had not yet been admitted to the Wyoming bar at the time the Miller trial began—he gained formal admission nearly a year later, in October 1891. In the territorial

era, the bar in Wyoming was fairly casual about checking credentials of people seeking to appear before them as lawyers, so Taggart's situation was not that unusual. Before coming to Cheyenne,
he had been admitted to the bar in Nebraska, but he rarely made
law his full-time occupation when he was living there. Instead, he
had the kind of peripatetic professional career that was characteristic of many educated young men in nineteenth-century America.

Born in Orrville, Ohio, in 1857, Taggart attended public schools
there and actually taught school himself as a teenager before ma-
triculating at nearby Wooster University, a liberal Presbyterian institution that admitted women as well as a few "colored" men. As a
student, Taggart took prizes in Greek and Latin, joined the Beta
Theta Pi fraternity, and was a star debater for Athenea, a literary
society. He was popular enough to be elected vice president of the
Class Day activities in his senior year, a jovial moment when he
boasted in a school publication that girls were his "favorite study"
and pie his "besetting sin." After graduation in 1880, he was associated with the Normal School in Millersburg, Ohio, but he soon
left his home state for life farther west, on the "middle border,"
where he began to study law in the Hastings, Nebraska, firm of
James Laird and Benjamin Smith.

Taggart was admitted to the bar in short order—his training
took less than two years—but life in Hastings involved more than
legal practice. Taggart managed the Kerr Opera House, founded a
newspaper, and was elected in 1888 on the Republican ticket as a
state senator representing the 27th District. In the last year of his
two-year term, he sponsored a law against trusts that provided
penalties and punishments for any person or corporation obstruct-
ing free competition in the state. He was best known, however, for
casting the decisive vote when the Nebraska state legislature split
over the issue of temperance in early 1889. Taggart was absent
when the debate began, but he was brought back by train to Lincoln, the state capital, by those who assumed he was friendly to
temperance. The former collegiate debater then gave a lengthy
speech summarizing the arguments on both sides, but finally voted

no, killing the hotly contested bill, and angering the popular and highly organized Women's Christian Temperance Union in the state.

In April 1889, soon after his pedantic performance in the legislature, Taggart married Louise (Lula) Bostwick Williams, a Massachusetts native, in Lincoln, Nebraska. They moved together to Cheyenne with their infant daughter, Beatrice, in the summer of 1890, only a few months before Charley Miller arrived in Sheriff Martin's custody. Taggart hung out his shingle and attempted to establish his own legal practice; when that did not work, he quickly joined Armstrong and Breckons. At the moment when the Laramie County Court needed someone to represent the poor orphan from New York, the "dapper" and "energetic" Taggart was on the spot, ready to serve as counsel to the down-and-out youngster. He probably saw the Miller case as an opportunity to do good, establish his reputation in the West, and, along the way, make some decent money to help support his charitable, stylish wife and their little girl. When he went to visit Charley in his cell, Taggart occasionally took Lula along, because she felt kindly to the motherless boy, the way many Cheyenne women did.

Taggart's adversary before the bench was Walter R. Stoll, the Laramie County prosecutor re-elected in 1888 for a second term because of his success in bringing lawbreakers to justice. Although the defense attorney and the prosecutor were almost the same age, they had little else in common. Walter Stoll was born in 1858 to a prominent family in Deckerstown, New Jersey, and he graduated from the U.S. Military Academy at West Point in 1881. He made his way west with the army, serving at Fort McKinney and Fort Russell, both in the Wyoming Territory, before resigning his commission in 1886, at the age of twenty-seven. While in the army, he took up the study of law on his own, and over the next few years was admitted to the Wyoming bar to practice in the 3rd Judicial Circuit. The practice he started in Cheyenne quickly became so large and lucrative that he ran for prosecuting attorney on the Democratic ticket and was elected for the first time in 1886. The

West Point graduate was known for studying cases "with the greatest care," for "preparing his legal papers with the most scrupulous exactness," and for deep familiarity with all "the devious details of practice." When he appeared in court to prosecute Charley Miller, he already had a reputation as an ace in Wyoming legal circles.

Outside the courtroom, Stoll's life was also vastly different from Taggart's modest, hand-to-mouth professional existence. Described as "affable," "courteous," and "attractive," Stoll maintained a substantial Victorian home for himself and his wife on "Cattlemen's Row"—they had no children—and he socialized with other civic-minded men in fraternal orders such as the Masons, in which he attained a 32nd Degree in the Scottish Rite, and also the Benevolent Order of Elks. (Throughout the territorial period, key political figures from both political parties in Wyoming were involved in Freemasonry.) But the real jewel in Stoll's social crown was membership in the Cheyenne Club, the city's elite, all-male association, where high-status professionals, wealthy businessmen, state and federal legislators, and prominent cattle-growers socialized and did business at the same time. Although the articles of incorporation stated that the organization's purpose was strictly social, people in the know openly acknowledged that the Club was also a business center, the kind of place where "many a bottle of fizz paved the way for a big deal."

Located in a two-story brick building with central heating, an elevator, and an elaborate cupola, the Club provided members with an elegant refuge from children and family life. In addition to six private sleeping rooms decorated with Oriental carpets, walnut beds, and marble-top commodes, there was a smoking room provisioned with the best Havana cheroots, and a library stocked with practical as well as literary reading—newspapers from New York and Boston, *The Atlantic Monthly*, *Harper's*, and *The Drovers Journal*, a weekly publication for the livestock industry printed in Chicago. Because the Club was renowned for having the best cuisine west of the Mississippi, its oak-paneled dining room was usually full, acting as a magnet for men like Andrew Carnegie whenever they came to town. There was a chef trained in Europe, a wine vault filled with prime vintages, and a staff of "perfectly trained" servants who delivered complicated multi-course meals with grace and aplomb. Some Cheyenne women understandably wanted access to the delicacies their husbands enjoyed at the Club—fine olives and fresh oysters, Roquefort cheese, and Swiss chocolates—but an initiative to develop a special restaurant for them was voted down by the membership, keeping it a male preserve except on special evenings. Outside this lavish home away from home, there were nineteen hitching posts to accommodate a range of fine horses as well as the phaetons, traps, landaus, and broughams, all carriages of varying cost and complexity, which made the establishment's yard a Victorian version of a contemporary country-club parking lot.

Walter Stoll was invited to be a member in 1889. The Club provided him with more than an opportunity to eat oysters and smoke cigars. As the territory made its transition into statehood, membership meant that he had access to Wyoming's most important and influential men, including U.S. Senators Joseph M. Carey and Frank E. Warren, Acting Governor Amos Barber, State Attorney General Charles A. Potter, State Supreme Court Justices Herman Groesbeck and Homer Merrell, and also opinion-makers J. F. Carroll and E. A. Slack, editors of Cheyenne's two daily newspapers. In dining room and library, Stoll also mixed with the formidable cattle barons, whose economic interests set the pace in Wyoming politics.

As he broke bread with the Wyoming elite, Stoll became familiar with what these men wanted and expected from the legislature, the local government, and the courts. Just like everyone else in Cheyenne in December 1890, the cattle barons followed the flamboyant Miller case, and most shared a common point of view. Because of their increasing edginess about settlement on public lands and rustling of their cattle, big-livestock men generally wanted the new state to punish the young ne'er-do-well who had entered their territory and caused trouble, much like a stray calf.

The law-and-order position made good sense to Stoll, and the support of his fellow Club members stoked his determination to be especially meticulous as he built the case against the confessed boy murderer and his upstart attorney. The prosecutor had more on his side, however, than experience, enthusiastic Club support, and the Manhattan confession. To his added advantage, the new presiding judge in the 1st Judicial District, Richard H. Scott, was a man of his ilk. Scott also had a military career before coming to the bar (Annapolis instead of West Point), and he was a fellow Mason, high up in the hierarchy of the Cheyenne lodge. In terms of Cheyenne's social geography, the prosecutor and the judge lived in virtually the same neighborhood, a fact of life that Frank Taggart must have considered as he began the uphill struggle in the defense of the Miller boy.

<hr />

In order to ask for the most severe verdict—murder in the first degree—Walter Stoll had to prove *every* element in the indictment—namely, that Charles Miller killed Waldo Emerson and Ross Fishbaugh with premeditation and malice, deliberately and willfully, beyond reasonable doubt. If the prosecution could substantiate all these accusations, Charley could receive the death penalty. If the crime came off as the impulsive act of a starving boy, he would be proved guilty of a lesser offense, such as second-degree murder or manslaughter, for which he would not receive the death penalty. In the event that Taggart put forth evidence suggesting that he had acted entirely in self-defense, Charley Miller might even be acquitted.

In the opening session, the prosecution crafted a picture of Miller as a deliberate and intentional killer by deftly re-creating the narrative of people, places, and events that led to the boxcar murders. As Stoll called his witnesses—twenty-two on the first day—he unveiled each piece of evidence as if he were constructing a puzzle, carefully fitting one piece next to another in order to establish a definitive chronology of the crime. There were two critical points that the prosecution had to firm up immediately: first, that

Miller was on the Union Pacific train with the victims at the approximate time of their deaths, and, second, that the boys from St. Joe were still alive when they crossed the border from Nebraska into Wyoming. This was an important geographical distinction, a question of venue, essential to upholding Wyoming's jurisdiction in the Miller case. Stoll needed to prove that the murders occurred in Wyoming because if he did not the defense would try to remove the case to Nebraska, where the legal and social climate might be less punitive and the boy might get off.

Stoll began by calling as witnesses those railroad men who first found and examined the dead bodies in Hillsdale and Cheyenne. Then he worked backward in time to those who remembered seeing the three boys alive at different points along the way from Sidney (in Nebraska) to Pine Bluffs and Hillsdale (in Wyoming). Because of the jurisdictional issue, much of the testimony focused on the timing of the Union Pacific train as it moved westward that particular day, carrying the three boys. Stoll called conductors, brakemen, and agents to testify to the hour when the train arrived in Pine Bluffs, Wyoming, how long it stayed, and whether or not there was anything unusual about the schedule on September 27. The prosecution wanted to establish that the train arrived there between 5 and 6 A.M., a time that meant the double homicide occurred later that morning, after the victims ate their breakfast, and at some point before arrival in Hillsdale, around 11 A.M.

The defense, on the contrary, wanted to confound the witnesses whenever it could, in order to undermine the prosecution's timeline. In a lengthy cross-examination of George W. Mannifee, the brakeman who discovered the still-warm bodies, Taggart acted incredulous when the witness was not absolutely precise about the time, and then suggested that he had been lax in the performance of his job. "You have no facts in your mind by which you can fix the arrival of the train within an hour or two?" Taggart asked skeptically, in response to Mannifee's statement that he did not remember the exact arrival time. "You would not be willing to swear within two hours?" And then he ridiculed the witness: "Were you asleep part of the way coming up from Sidney?"

Taggart also tried to disrupt the prosecution's presentation of physical evidence related to the double homicide. On the first day, he objected to nearly every piece of material evidence submitted by Stoll on the grounds that it was either irrelevant, incompetent, or both. Taggart's objections were intended to head off any incriminating evidence, but they also suggested his intent to take Charley's case on to a higher court, if need be, since objections laid the groundwork for appeal by establishing that the court was acting improperly. Taggart was consistently overruled, however, and at one point Judge Scott chided him for his behavior with some annoyance: "The question is answered. You should object before the answer is made."

Despite Taggart's persistent interruptions, the prosecution still managed by the end of the first day to introduce a powerful trail of material exhibits, including a photograph of one of the victims, the murder weapon (a .32 pistol from which two shots had been fired), a watch chain, diamond collar studs, and an overcoat belonging to Waldo Emerson. The most incriminating piece of all was a match safe found among the hardwood ties at the scene of the crime. Stoll asked John Chaffin, the Laramie County coroner, if there was anything special about that object, and Chaffin replied: "I could see some name was scratched on it but was unable to see what it was. The most I could make out is 'Miller' but my eye sight is very poor." To ensure the full impact of this incriminating calling card, Stoll told the coroner, "Please point out to the jury on this match box the place where the name was"—and Chaffin did exactly that, putting Charley's "monogrammed" match safe into the hands of the jury foreman, William Phillips, who then passed it to the other men for their careful scrutiny.

When John Emerson, Waldo's father, came to the stand as a prosecution witness, the defense was outmaneuvered. John Emerson was called, ostensibly, to provide a photograph of his son at age fifteen to be used to help others identify his boy. But the testimony that Stoll artfully extracted from the victim's father provided important emotional ammunition for the prosecution. No one could miss the heartache in John Emerson as he looked at the picture and described the sandy hair, dark-hazel eyes, and soft skin of his dead youngster's face before he had sprouted any beard. And it was perfectly tragic to see him identify the silver watch chain that he had given his son as a celebratory gift for graduation just a few years before. But no one would ever forget the gruesome moment when John Emerson handed over a small souvenir, the lethal bullet extracted from Waldo's head by the St. Joe coroner. (Unfortunately, the photograph and all the other evidence provided at the trial have not survived.)

Given the emotional content of this testimony, Frank Taggart had to navigate delicately. Whenever he interrupted Emerson's solemn testimony with an objection, it seemed frivolous, if not nasty. In cross-examination, there was no polite, risk-free way for him to dislodge the father's deeply held belief in his son's superlative character. In the newspapers, the father had disavowed the idea that Waldo knowingly patronized saloons, and in court he repeated that his boy never rode the Union Pacific without paying. Taggart asked other witnesses if the boys from St. Joe were riding illegally or if they were sober, but he never asked John Emerson these questions, because to do so would have seemed unkind, particularly with a grieving father who seemed to merit a modicum of kindness.

Although the original report out of Manhattan claimed that the bodies of the dead boys were surrounded by empty bottles, Frank Taggart never made any real attempt to portray the boxcar murders as an alcohol-related crime, the way Albert Stewart had. Perhaps Taggart felt that alcohol was not an effective issue in wide-open Cheyenne, where saloons were a way of life and young men learned to drink early and hard. Perhaps, he was personally unsympathetic to temperance, given his controversial vote back in Nebraska, earlier in his career. A more skilled attorney might have tried to suggest that the boys from St. Joe were roughnecks, or that Ross, the older and more adventurous of the two, led Waldo into risky activities that he would never have undertaken on his own. But Taggart did neither. Whatever his reasons, the decision to ignore the influence of alcohol empowered the prosecution. By failing to suggest that the victims were impudent young lawbreakers stoked by the liquor they had been drinking all day, Taggart allowed the prosecution to hold the moral high ground. From the very first morning when John Emerson testified until the end of the trial, Waldo and Ross were cast as good boys while Charley Miller was demonized.

Taggart did his best, however, to undermine the prosecution's evidence by resorting to the limp argument that the murder weapon was so old that it probably did not work. But as often as he tried to raise objections to material evidence, discredit the memories of witnesses, and label incriminating testimony hearsay, there was little he could do to challenge the thick fabric of detail that Stoll wove together to place Charley Miller in the boxcar with the murdered victims. Mrs. Amanda Kauffman, the hotel owner in Pine Bluffs, testified with absolute confidence that she served an early-morning breakfast to a hungry pair, Emerson and Fishbaugh, after they had crossed the state line. Her detailed account supported Wyoming's authority in the case, but it contradicted the claims of the Emersons, whose story hinged on the notion that the three boys had breakfast together. Nevertheless, by the end of the first day, Stoll had most of the major elements of the prosecution case in place: the boys from St. Joe were alive and well when they entered Wyoming, Charley was definitely with them, and, shortly after the murders, he turned up in Hillsdale sporting a watch that belonged to one of the victims. When the court adjourned at 6 P.M., Stoll had only two pieces missing: "What actually happened? And why did the boy do it?"

Whatever Taggart lacked in criminal-trial experience, he tried to compensate for with raw energy on Charley's behalf. Even before any witnesses were called on the first morning, he attempted to have the court disallow any use by the prosecution of the Manhattan confession. During the pretrial-motion hearing to suppress

Miller's statement to Stewart, Taggart argued that the circumstances surrounding the confession required the court to put aside
the incriminating document, but Judge Scott was not convinced.
As a result, when the court reconvened at 9 A.M. for the second
day, Taggart was primed to attack Albert Stewart's testimony on
the stand. If he could undermine the credibility of the Kansas
newspaperman, Charley Miller might be saved.

Mindful of the tremendous power of a pretrial confession, the
prosecution knew that Albert Stewart was a critical witness, because he was the person who took down the admission of guilt in
the boy's own words. Stewart could substantiate what Miller had
said about the crime before there was an attorney at his side advising him what not to say. Stoll also knew from the original newspaper story, as well as conversation with his star witness once he
got to Cheyenne, that the Kansas editor would confirm the adverbs
necessary for substantiating the charge of murder in the first degree. Stewart was the person who claimed to hear Charley say that
he had murdered for money, and that he had had a conception or
plan of action before firing his gun, both proof of premeditation.

Taggart's strategy was to undermine the Manhattan confession
by painting Albert Stewart as a wily newspaperman who seduced
information from an unsuspecting youngster and then fabricated a
statement. Immediately after Stewart was called by the prosecution, and at first mention of the meeting in the sheriff's parlor, Taggart fired off a series of objections aimed to derail the prosecution's
line of inquiry and discredit Stewart's claim that he had provided
an accurate and responsible report of the interview. Taggart was
successful in the short term: the court allowed him to cross-
examine Stewart to determine if he was competent to testify on the
subject. Taggart hoped to suggest that the editor was "incompetent," meaning, in this case, that he was self-interested, biased, and
not credible.

Taggart tried first to cast doubt on the circumstances that surrounded the interview between Stewart and his client on October
16, 1890. Through his questioning, he revealed that Charley Miller

had been alone with the sheriff and the newspaperman, and that the boy had had no idea that he did not have to answer the editor's questions. He also suggested that Charley did not understand Stewart's intentions to publish his answers in any newspaper. And then he implied that Miller's tongue was loosened by pressure and "inducements" that Stewart did not want to admit. Judge Scott was especially careful on this second point. In order to avoid being overturned by a higher court, he asked the witness himself: "Do you know whether or not it was through fear that he made the confession?" Stewart's answer seemed reassuring enough for the judge: "I don't think it was. He talked without any reserve at all."

The defense, however, refused to acknowledge that there was a confession, referring always to a "conversation" or a "discussion" instead. "We object to the introduction of any conversation that will [in]criminate this defendant," Taggart asserted as he struggled to demonstrate that Stewart was not just a self-interested witness, but also the wrong person to call on the issue of how the boy initially explained his own behavior. Taggart argued that Albert Stewart was not actually the first person Charley ever told about his crime. He probed Stewart about this: "You don't know how many people Mr. Miller had talked with previous to his conversation with you in regard to the same subject matter of the conversation he had with you?" When Stewart answered that he was "not certain," Taggart suggested that, before the court heard Stewart's testimony, it really should call as a witness the very first person "to whom any conversation purporting to be a confession was made." (This could have been a ploy on Taggart's part to get the court to pay to bring Fred Miller or Preston Loofbourrow from Kansas to testify, since they were the first to hear the boy say that he had done it.) When the judge asked the defense if he had any precedent on the point, Taggart responded: "I have not at this moment but I understand that the authorities will bear me out." Judge Scott then called a thirty-minute recess—enough time, he thought, for Taggart to dig up some precedent. Yet, when the trial resumed, the newly-minted criminal attorney had nothing more to say on the issue of first confessions. He was unable to turn up the relevant citations quickly enough (a common problem for trial lawyers in the era before Lexis and Westlaw, both electronic search engines), and his failure to do so doomed his strategy to block the jury from hearing about the Manhattan confession.

When the prosecution went on to the redirect, Stoll got Stewart to say almost everything that Taggart did not want the jury to hear. In a graceful and efficient manner, he asked the Kansas newspaperman about the circumstances that had led to the confession the defense wanted to deny. Stoll's questions (and Stewart's answers) were meant to assure the court that the editor had done nothing improper: he was never alone with the boy, there was no element of coercion, and the youngster was handled with the utmost consideration. With these issues resolved, the prosecutor asked his witness to describe the substance of his conversation with Charley Miller, but on the first pass, Stewart said only: "He told me first his name. Second his trip to Wyoming and the West." Immediately, Taggart injected, "We would like to have the exact words," and the judge actually agreed with him this time. Editor Stewart then took out his reportorial notebook and explained: "This is the little tab I used the morning I had the conversation with him." Stoll promptly established that the notes his witness would use were taken in October and that they had not been changed, an assertion designed to establish their authority with the jury.

The introduction of the reporter's notebook provided Taggart with an opening to develop the idea that Albert Stewart had misrepresented Charley Miller by putting words in his mouth. At first sight of the tab, the defense rose to ask three important questions: "I would like to ask if you made them [the notes] in the language of the defendant at the time? Or did you use it to draw up the newspaper report for publication, drawing your own conclusions as to some facts, and stating it in your own language? To what extent did you rely on the language of the defendant?" Taggart was raising issues essential to the practice of responsible investigative journalism (as well as Charley Miller's future), but his pithy questions were put aside by Stoll, who came back with a point of law about the reliability of notes taken at some prior date: "A witness in detailing conversation is always permitted to refer to entries or memoranda that he made at the time for the purpose of aiding his memory. As to whether he varies them or not is a matter to be brought out on cross examination." Judge Scott then gave his approval for Stewart to read directly and authoritatively from his notes, a directive that meant that the pretrial confession would now effectively dominate all other evidence.

With notebook in hand, reading slowly and deliberately in order to give the boy's very words, Stewart retold the story as he said Miller had told it back in the Manhattan parlor. This testimony allowed him to describe what Charley had said about his early life, and also the details of the hours leading up to the gruesome double murder and robbery. In response to probing by Stoll—"Did you put any inquiry to him at any time as to when he first thought of getting their money?"—Stewart articulated words that were key to establishing the defendant's motivation: "[Charley] said when he sat in the [box]car and thought they were asleep he conceived of the idea of killing them for their money." These two expressions about motivation and premeditation—"he conceived of the idea of killing them for their money" and he had "a conception of the killing"—became the prosecution's mantra, stated by Stewart in response to Stoll's deft questioning at least a dozen times that day. Neither "conceived" or "conception" was an expression that had appeared in Stewart's initial news story, and neither was a word that Charley Miller was likely to have used— he simply did not speak that way. But they were both allowed to stand in the hot air of the overcrowded courtroom, pointing to an act of premeditation.

Taggart was now in a difficult bind. The court had enabled Stewart to read verbatim from his notes, as if they were a complete and accurate transcript simply because he had written them down in Manhattan that October day. The defense needed to alert the jury that how a reporter took notes and told a story from them was not an entirely objective activity. There was also the delicate issue of whether or not Stewart was tailoring the whole story of the confession to Stoll's purposes. Through a series of cross-examination questions, Taggart tried to debunk the authority of Stewart's notes by suggesting that certain words and phrases used to describe Miller's behavior and frame of mind at the time of the murder were actually Stewart's words and interpretation, not Charley's, but he was unsuccessful despite his persistence. Over and over he asked questions meant to suggest that there could be errors of memory, transcription, and even intent in Albert Stewart's account: "Did you take down the exact words of the defendant on that point?" "Was it all in your memoranda, taken in the exact words as they fell from his lips?" "Then you didn't take it all down, all the words of the conversation? So things you deemed immaterial you did not take [down]?"

The struggle over what Charley Miller did or did not say in the sheriff's parlor went on for the rest of the morning and well into the afternoon, but the stakes became higher when the words in question related to the critical issues of motivation and premeditation. More than once, Stoll had Stewart state that the boy said that he "conceived" of the idea of murder in order to get money; Taggart, working a variety of angles, tried to trip Stewart up on the issue of what he had actually asked Charley, and what the boy said on his own without prompting. "Do you remember the form of the question in regard to motivation?" Taggart queried. Stewart, unwilling to tie himself to any one question, temporized: "No. I don't believe I can tell. I don't remember." The editor stuck to the prosecution mantra that the boy had said he killed "for money"—money that he knew his victims carried because he had seen it earlier that day, in Sidney. The stalking scenario, like everything else in the prosecution's armory, was intended to suggest a premeditated rather than an impulsive killing.

Taggart was never able to get Stewart to admit that Charley Miller had told him he was lonely, frightened, and famished in the Union Pacific boxcar. In fact, the defense and prosecution spent a good deal of time sparring over exactly what the boy had said about being hungry on the day of the murder. According to Stewart's first testimony for the prosecution, Charley said only that "he was hungry and did not have any money," a statement that suggested ordinary, garden-variety hunger. Taggart tried to get Stewart to confirm that the boy was ravenous, that he told Meyers and Stewart explicitly that he had not eaten since Omaha, and that he was "nearly starving" when he reached Pine Bluffs, but the editor would never do so.

Stoll may have been lying in wait, knowing that Stewart's memory about the hunger discussion could make a critical point—namely, that Charley was insincere. The jury, of course, had already heard from the baker in Sidney, who said that he had given Charley a decent lunch the afternoon before the murder. Now Stoll asked Albert Stewart to explain how the subject of hunger had come up in the first place. Surprisingly, his witness offered an answer that confirmed Taggart's earlier suggestions that someone had put words in Charley's mouth: "After he [Charley] finished the statement of the shooting and he spoke of having killed them for their money, we [Sheriff Meyers and I] suggested to him that [his being] hungry might have had something to do with it [the murder]." Stoll then asked for clarification: "State whether or not the question was asked him or he suggested the idea of hunger himself." Stewart acknowledged: "I am not sure he suggested it at all. My best recollection is that Sheriff Meyers asked him if his being hungry was not one cause of it."

Under cross-examination, the editor went even further to suggest that Charley's claim to hunger was not his own: "I know that I didn't [suggest hunger] and I don't think that Charley did, but he endorsed what we said about it." When Taggart asked him directly who first mentioned hunger as a motive, Stewart dropped the collective "we," and pointed his finger at the man who had made the Manhattan confession possible: "If I should undertake to say, I should say Sheriff Meyers." The newspaperman then added his own interpretation of why this had happened, giving a new twist to the dynamics in the parlor that day: "The sheriff seemed to be a good deal interested in the boy and disposed to make light of the confession and action as [best] he could." Meyers was not in court to confirm or deny Stewart's statements, because he was back in Manhattan, too ill to make the trip to appear as a witness.

To have Stewart agree that Charley Miller's expression of hunger came from Sheriff Meyers and not the boy himself was a Pyrrhic victory for the defense. Though it confirmed Taggart's larger point that some of the words attributed to Charley Miller were not his, it also discredited the idea that his hunger was genuine, and that it contributed to his violent behavior. At this juncture in the trial, the lengthy discussion about who said what in Manhattan was going nowhere for the defense; in fact, Walter Stoll had turned it against the boy, so that some jurors probably now assumed that Charley's hunger was just a fiction, the invention of a softhearted sheriff hoping to explain away the youngster's ugly crime.

Although he tried valiantly, Taggart was never able to undermine the Manhattan confession and the central fact that his client had admitted to killing the two boys in the Union Pacific boxcar. There was enormous authority in the words read from Albert Stewart's reportorial notebook, and Walter Stoll used the Kansas editor to best advantage, emphasizing his reliability and avoiding any discussion about alcohol use by the victims. By the afternoon of the second day, the prosecution had mapped the crime and provided the jury with a narrative account of the murder derived from the defendant's own admission of guilt. Albert Stewart's surprising revelation about how the "hunger" issue had evolved was just icing on the prosecution's cake, but it cast suspicion on the sincerity of the boy whose future would now rest on his ability to convince the jury that his awful crime was the unhappy result of a deprived life.

Frank Taggart must have realized at this stage that the prosecution had scored some very important points in the effort to prove a premeditated act of homicide. As a result, he was willing to take the risk of putting Charley on the stand, hoping that the jury would see how pathetic and unthreatening the boy really was. To be sure, it was a gamble, like the trial itself, but if Miller did not testify on his own behalf, the jury would never buy a sympathetic story about the ways in which his life experience had provided the mitigating circumstances that explained his violence. A great deal now rested on how Charley Miller represented himself in the most crucial performance of his life.

CHAPTER SIX
Boys Don't Cry

THE COURTROOM was thronged when Charley Miller finally came to the stand that afternoon to testify. Extra seats were placed within the bar to accommodate the many Cheyenne women there to hear the young boy tell a story expected to be a heartbreaker. In the back of the courtroom, a score of rough-looking men stood together, craning their necks and straining their ears to see and hear what the accused young murderer would have to say for himself.

When Charley entered, under the supervision of Sheriff Kelley, there was a noticeable buzz, as people turned to one another to comment on what they saw. He was wearing a three-piece suit and a tie, an altogether conventional outfit provided by the sheriff with the help of some benevolent Cheyenne matrons. But clothing was not the focus of the crowd's interest. The boy's head and face were what people wanted to see most, particularly the slope of his forehead and his expression, since these were regarded as telling indicators of character by nineteenth-century Americans. No one in the courtroom, not even the official reporters, felt any embarrassment about evaluating the appearance of the self-confessed boy criminal, and the journalists' "pen pictures" commented cruelly, and without apology, on how physically unattractive he was.

Even the *Leader*, the local newspaper most sympathetic to Miller, described him as "immature and undeveloped," a "little, round shouldered, hollow-chested" fellow whose appearance reflected "a mother who died of consumption." The *Cheyenne Daily*

Sun, less tolerant and eager for speedy punishment, told its readers: "Get in front of him and you have a telling glimpse of an eye that scarcely invites confidence. The blonde hair is down over the imperfect forehead. At a distance, Miller's face doesn't seem as bad, but a close study reveals an expression of fiendishness." There was frequent mention of the nose that had led Charley to be mistaken for a Jew in Sidney. In the excited atmosphere of the courtroom, many a neck was strained to see the defendant's face without obstructions, but it was tough, as the *Sun* explained: "The best a spectator can do is secure a view of his peculiar profile with the long sharp nose and hanging lips." Some stated that the diminutive murderer wore an "idiotic expression," but there was never any serious suggestion that Miller's mental abilities were compromised. Most people agreed that, though he looked "peculiar," Charley displayed absolutely ordinary intelligence.

⇒◆◅

Until this point, Charley had said almost nothing, so there was intense interest in what he would say, and what he would sound like, when he finally took the stand. Frank Taggart had done some coaching beforehand—he probably spelled out some of the questions he would ask and then reviewed the answers Charley would give—but with a young defendant there was no way to really know how he would respond either to public scrutiny or to interrogation by someone as adept as Walter Stoll.

In the effort to portray his client as a pathetic youngster engaged in a struggle for survival, Taggart began his examination with a review of the defendant's early life. He covered many important facets in the first few minutes—Charley's loss of both parents by the time he was six, the impersonal orphanage in New York City, separation from his older sister and brother, ill-treatment at the hands of adults who were supposed to provide safety and security. When asked if he remembered his father in the time after his mother's death, Charley said briefly: "Only he drank hard and always mentioned that he was going to kill himself." Taggart did not dwell on the father's alcoholism or his mental health, and he did not ask the modern follow-up question: "How did that make you feel?" Instead, he instructed Charley to "tell what took place after your father died." The boy answered efficiently but not effectively: "Four of us were taken to a home in New York City. Stayed there until we were twelve years old and then were sent West."

Charley spoke in plain, unsophisticated language, typical of a boy of his social class and experience. He delivered his pitiful autobiography with almost no affect, and Frank Taggart did little to draw him out. The defense missed some golden opportunities— such as the moment when he asked Charley how he was treated when he was sent west to Minnesota at the age of twelve. The boy answered flatly, "He would whip me in many ways," but Taggart never pushed him to describe the painful details of the beatings he had received from the cruel farmer. Neither did Taggart dig into the reservoir of fraternal sentiment represented by Charley's short, raw response when asked about why he went to Kansas in the first place: "I wanted to get by my brother." Charley's affection for his older brother was one of his more endearing, sympathetic qualities, but his attorney never emphasized his deep attachment to Fred or his inability to lie to his older brother.

Taggart tried to illuminate Charley's experience, and there were a few moments when his client's laconic answers provided compelling evidence that his childhood had been truncated by both hardship and bad luck. But the defense attorney was not adept in the kind of socially conscious digging for motivation that is part of a modern defense strategy, rooted in our understanding that perpetrators can also be victims. Taggart did try to present Charley as a serious worker. He queried him repeatedly about why he had left one place for another, and Charley always replied the same way: "I went there to look for work." The defense then asked, "What did you want to get work for?" and the young defendant responded in a serious manner: "So I could live." These terse words underscored the fact that Charley had no adults to lean on, and that he was amazingly self-reliant for someone so young. Taggart's questioning was intended to establish that he lived hand-to-mouth like a workingman, and that he never had any extra money. "You spent it as you got it?" he asked, and Charley responded: "I never had any to lay aside."

As Charley's testimony moved into its second hour, Taggart focused on the immediate circumstances leading to the crime. When asked what had happened in Sidney on the way to Cheyenne, Charley said: "Only that I met these two young fellows." Taggart responded, "Who do you mean by these young fellows?" and Charley uttered the words that all the people in the courtroom had been waiting to hear for themselves: "The ones that I killed."

This chilly, seemingly nonchalant admission was a setback for the defense, and it reinforced the defendant's responsibility for the murders, forcing his lawyer into a new line of inquiry about motivation. Taggart asked first whether or not there had been any unkind words or threats between Charley and his victims, but the boy denied that with a firm "No, sir," a response that ruled out any claim to self-defense as a motive. Taggart then suggested that the older fellows might have behaved unkindly to Charley. He got his client to tell how Waldo and Ross had tried to shake him in Sidney because of his scruffy appearance. "They were afraid they would get arrested [for tramping] because I was ragged," Charley explained. "Did they tell you that?" Taggart asked, and Charley answered knowingly: "No, sir. I knew it was that from the way they looked at my clothes." Taggart never pursued the ways in which Charley had been excluded by the older boys that day in Sidney, and he never articulated the idea that his client might have been bullied, belittled, or frightened by them. The omission—that there were bad feelings between the boys—was surprising, because most people were familiar with the aggression of boys and they understood, from firsthand experience, how even innocent play could erupt into violence in short order. The notion that "boys will be boys"—disorderly, aggressive, wild—would not have been alien to the twelve men who sat in judgment of the youthful murderer in Cheyenne.

Instead of playing the age-and-gender card, Taggart naïvely returned to the issue of hunger as motivation, trying to establish that Charley had been ravenous by the time he got to Pine Bluffs, the spot where Waldo and Ross ate breakfast. He put a series of detailed questions to his client designed to demonstrate the meagerness of the handout he obtained at the back door of the Sidney baker. "What did he give you?" Taggart asked, and Charley enumerated every item in the paper sack: "Bread and butter and cheese and two pieces of pie." The defense attorney then queried him on how many pieces of bread he was given (only two), whether or not the bread was buttered (it was), and the size of the piece of cheese. Charley responded to the inquiry about the cheese by holding up his hand and using his fingers to approximate the morsel: "About the size of that, I guess—two inches." "Were you hungry at the time?" asked Taggart, and the boy replied with a bland understatement, "I could have eaten some more if I had had it."

The meal in Sidney clearly was no feast. Taggart managed to demonstrate that, but he did not let the issue of food rest there. In order to demonstrate that his client was not all bad, he led him through the story of how he had given away his pie to Waldo and Ross, even though these fellows had shoved him aside in Sidney and he was hungry himself. (This story must have piqued the Emersons, whose earlier letter to the people of Cheyenne claimed that Waldo and Ross were the good Samaritans.) If the food in Sidney was really only a snack and not a satisfying meal, Taggart asked, why had he given any of it away? Charley explained, "I thought they had just got off the train and were hungry too"—suggesting again that his offer was an earnest attempt to make friends in the way men and boys did in the tramping fraternity. Anxious to make the most of this small act of youthful generosity, Taggart asked the defendant to tell the court when he had last had a real meal before that afternoon in Sidney. Charley answered impassively, "I hadn't had a square one since Omaha," a trip the jury knew had taken him at least three days.

Being hungry was not enough to absolve Charley Miller of his homicidal behavior, however. A really effective defense—one that could beat back the first-degree-murder charge—needed to paint a picture of a desperate, impulsive act of violence that involved no premeditation or forethought. "I swung [the gun] over my head and did it as quick as I could fire the revolver," Miller told the court, but that sounded more like melodrama from a dime novel then a truthful explanation of how the bullets had ended up in the heads of his two victims. Fortunately, Albert Stewart had told Taggart earlier under oath that it took Charley "a very short time" to carry out the crime, an idea the defense now tried to develop further. When asked how much time elapsed between the moment when he first thought of killing his victims and the act itself, Charley said: "It was done right after I got up there [in the boxcar]. I got into the car and went to lay down and got right up. I never slept at all. It was done all in a minute." The same question, asked again, but amended this time by Taggart's plea—"Just tell the truth, Charley"—yielded an even better answer: "I cannot remember ever thinking of it," he said, hammering home the point that he had no prior conception of the deed at all, that he did not know why he had done it.

That was exactly what Taggart wanted the jury to hear. In order to convince them that Charley had never had murder on his mind, the defense reviewed the purchase of the murder weapon produced by the prosecution on the first day. The defendant's testimony affirmed that he had purchased the gun in Kansas City, but only as a form of self-protection. The defense then asked Charley a series of crucial questions about his past behavior, intended to show him off as a first-time offender: "Had you ever thought in your life of killing anyone before? Had you ever in your life aimed a revolver at anyone before?" In both cases, the youngster who liked to swagger to ballads and books about the James boys admitted that he had not.

Because Miller's frame of mind at the time of the crime was key to undermining the charge of premeditation, Taggart carefully reopened this subject. Although Charley consistently denied that he had had any hard feelings toward the boys from St. Joe, he did tell the court that he was scared of them: "I knew they had a revolver because I saw them buy five shots in Sidney and put them in the gun, and I supposed that when they left me on the corner they were making out some scheme for me, and when I was in the [box]car I was afraid they were going to do something to me then."

Taggart failed to dig any deeper into what Charley had thought they might do to him. Was he afraid that the boys from St. Joe would call him a filthy street waif or say something else that was mean? Or was there something in their attitude or behavior that frightened him by bringing up memories of the time he had been attacked in the boxcar by the older men? Today, the idea that Miller may have experienced "homosexual panic" as a result of his prior sexual abuse would be part of the arsenal of a savvy defense lawyer. But in 1890, a fellow like Frank Taggart would not have known much about psychological theory, and his understanding of the sexuality of male youth was constrained by conventional Victorian morality. He did, however, push the boy to explain what had been on his mind as he fired the revolver. To that question, Charley produced a reprise that he would offer many times: "I thought I was far away from my folks and I wanted to get back and didn't know how and was all ragged, and cold weather coming, and nothing to eat and no money and I didn't know what to do."

This ill-phrased, awkward statement of the boy's misery was not as solid a motive as self-defense, but at least it gave the jury something sorrowful to remember when they got to the business of evaluating why Charley Miller had committed the murders. Taggart also wanted to leave the jury with a portrait of what the boy actually felt and did *after* he pulled the trigger and the boys were dead. "How did you feel after you had shot them?" Taggart asked, hoping for a convincing statement of contrition, but his taciturn witness said only: "I realized what I had done then." Looking for a strong statement of remorse, Taggart probed again: "Can you tell the jury how you felt at the time?" Charley's phlegmatic style still failed to deliver anything even close to heartrending: "I felt pretty bad, that's all." Taggart must have been disappointed. Drawing emotion from Charley Miller was as hard as wringing water from a stone.

Over the next half-hour, Taggart tried to demolish the idea that his client had killed and robbed in a methodical manner like a professional criminal. In answer to the question "What did you do immediately after you shot them?" Charley said only, "I took the money from them." Taggart wanted more detail: "Did you go through their pockets?" Charley answered, "Yes. Through one or two that is all." Recognizing that this was an opportunity to make the argument that the boy was a less-than-calculating thief, Taggart began another detailed inquiry, this time about the pilfered pockets. How many pockets did each victim have? Whose pockets did he put his hands into first? Was it the inside or outside pockets of the jacket or the pockets in the pants that he stole from?

Although Charley answered, "I never noticed," to a number of these questions, he did specify that he stole forty-five dollars in bills, two silver dollars, and the watch, knife, and revolver. However, he firmly maintained that he had rifled only one pant pocket and one hip pocket on each of his victims before he stopped. The defense then asked for an explanation—"Why did you stop going through their pockets? Why didn't you go through all their pockets?"—and the witness finally gave a helpful answer: "Because I had enough money to get my breakfast with and something to eat." This was exactly what the defense attorney wanted the jury to hear. If Miller stole only enough money to feed himself, he was neither a hardened criminal nor a vicious street boy.

Hoping to clinch the point that Charley was confused and pitiable rather than scheming and fierce, Taggart finally revisited the Manhattan confession and asked his client what had transpired when he met Sheriff Meyers for the very first time. "Sheriff Meyers asked me what I killed them for," Charley reported, "and I told him I didn't know." The next day, Mr. Stewart appeared on the scene and asked again why he had done it. Charley said under oath that Stewart was introduced as the sheriff's friend, and that he was totally unaware of any publication plans: "I didn't know he was a reporter, he said printer was his business." "Did they ask you any questions about the money at the time?" Taggart inquired, in the hope of insinuating again that Stewart had invented the money motive himself. "He [Stewart] asked me what I killed them for and I didn't know what to say," Charley explained once more: "I kept saying, 'I don't know.' " Taggart pushed Miller as to his veracity on this point: "Did you feel that you were telling the truth when you said you didn't know why you killed them?" To this Charley answered firmly, "Yes, sir," and then the defense rested, hoping that the jury understood that it was hunger and confusion—not calculated thievery—that motivated the awful crime.

◆◆◆

When Walter Stoll began his cross-examination, he was polite and gentle with the young defendant, who had been on the stand now for a number of hours. In the first few minutes, he covered much the same ground as Taggart, but with a very different slant. Stoll intended to show that Charley Miller's early experiences were actually not that grim, and that the vagabond from New York failed to take advantage of a number of significant opportunities in his life. Stoll, a hard-edged realist, wanted the jury to recognize some critical facts about American life in the 1890s: many American boys Charley's age had to work, and among those who were unlucky enough to become orphans, few ever became murderers like Charley.

Stoll never asked Charley a single question about the death of his parents, beginning the boy's biography instead at the moment when the Miller children were brought under the care of the New York Orphan Asylum. Stoll asked Charley to describe how his siblings were placed out of the orphanage into families where, he pointed out, they had remained "ever since." No one could miss Stoll's intent in his reiteration of that phrase: the sister in Rochester and the two boys in Kansas had adjusted successfully, despite the same unfortunate beginning and nearly identical asylum experiences. It was misplaced sympathy, Stoll suggested, to link Charley's crime to childhood deprivation or mistreatment. Charley was simply a bad apple, who fell close to the tree of his suicidal father.

Stoll's cross-examination about life within the New York Orphan Asylum painted that experience as favorable instead of traumatic or even difficult. "When there, you were or [you were] not, treated the same as the rest of the children?" To this, Charley answered: "I was whipped often. I had a disease and couldn't stop it." For the moment, the issue of the disease went untouched, but Stoll used subsequent questions to make the point that whipping was relatively normal in the asylum, and that Charley was not singled out for harsh treatment. He got the boy to confirm that at least ten other children were punished for the very same thing, and he asked Charley to make an important comparative judgment on his own: "How did your whippings compare with the whippings you say the other children got?" Charley acknowledged that they were the same and that he didn't get any more than any of the rest. The institution that emerged from Stoll's cross-examination was a responsible, cordial place where poor children learned to read and write, study the Bible, and play with friends, all under sound moral leadership. Miller's early life was not, then, so deprived; in fact, it was improved by the kindness of others, kindness that he did not appreciate.

The prosecution put a similar spin on Charley's experiences with the Booths of Chatfield. Questions such as "Did you live in a neighborhood with other children?" and "Were there other children working on the farm?" elicited affirmative answers that made it seem as if nothing abnormal had happened at the Booths'. Instead of endorsing Charley's picture of himself as being chained to a plow like a draft animal, Stoll got the boy to say that there were many young people in the Chatfield area performing exactly the same kind of labor that he found so offensive. And in the winter, after the crops were harvested, he acknowledged that he and his peers were given an opportunity to go to school together for a number of months. At Stoll's prompting, Charley described how, in the winter of 1888, he had been instructed the same as other children in reading, writing, ciphering, and geography, and how when he left he could actually read and write "pretty well." When he complained about going to school that year for only two months, Stoll used an astute question to suggest that Charley was a malcontent: "Was it not the custom in that country for farmers' sons and daughters to go to school in the winter and stay until it was time to begin spring work? Isn't that the way farmers do it?" Charley had to answer yes because it was true, but that response gave strength to the prosecution's idea that he was a presumptuous, cheeky kid who had no right to expect a hardworking farmer to give him special opportunities and better treatment than other children in the town.

When Stoll got to the business of Charley's tramping life, the prosecutor began to show off his legendary interrogation skills. First he tried to rattle the witness about his imprecision with respect to the chronology of his solo trip from Kansas to the East and back again. On one occasion he quipped: "You can't tell whether it was summer or winter, is that right?" On another: "You couldn't state whether it was two weeks or two months?" The boy never kept a journal, and his lawyer had not prepared him well for this line of interrogation. As a result, Charley seemed to be withholding facts about his movement around the country. Stoll used this weakness, along with the boy's tendency to be sullen and tight-lipped, to suggest that the witness was deliberately evasive, if not lying.

Stoll was also intent on undermining the popular idea that Miller was completely down-and-out. To do this, he exploited one of Charley's deepest fantasies: the idea that he had a guardian in New York who held in trust for him money and property left by his alcoholic, immigrant father. This personal tidbit was probably conveyed to Stoll by someone who hung around the jail talking and listening to the boy. "You have a guardian in New York?" Stoll in-

quired in an ingratiating manner without supplying any name.
"And your father left a little property—a little real estate did he?
You will have one fourth of the property your father left whatever
that will be?" Although Frank Taggart must have known that there
were no such family resources, he let these powerful suggestions
stand, leaving Charley to answer, "He left money I think." Stoll
then proposed the following: "And when you come of age—twenty
one, you expect to get your share of the money altogether with
whatever interest has accumulated?" The naïve boy, with little idea
of what it meant to accumulate interest on capital, answered yes, a
reply that left the jury with the impression that he might well be a
future property-holder with an inheritance.

In Stoll's hands, Charley Miller not only became a mini-
capitalist, he was also an inveterate shirker, a thoughtless, lazy boy,
who rejected sound, long-term employment opportunities in the
print shop for an unsupervised, licentious life on the road. The
prosecution's version of his tramping life was unrelenting in its
demonstration of his defective character rather than the wretched-
ness of his hand-to-mouth existence. Stoll suggested that the defendant spent whatever money he did have on "lurid" novels, and
that he enjoyed living off the largesse of others even though he had
resources of his own. "You depended upon the charity of people
along the way?" Stoll queried, and Charley answered honestly, yes.
Because the incident involving the pie showed Miller to be generous, Stoll attempted to demolish that story with the suggestion that
Charley only gave the food away because he didn't like it. "You
gave them the pie because you did not like the pie? Was that it?"
he queried. Charley responded that he liked pie "pretty fair," and
he was insistent about his motive: "I gave [the pie] to them as I
would anything else. Gave it to them friendly. [I] have always
shared with any other bum I ever met." Stoll let this response go,
but he was zealous about trying to intimate that the boy was proud
of his crime rather than guilt-ridden. In Stoll's version of things,
Miller took on the nickname "Kansas Charley" only *after* the murders, as a way to brag about his bloodthirsty deed. Charley again

corrected the prosecutor, explaining that he had used the moniker long before September 27: "I always put it everywhere before that."

In the final hour of the cross-examination, things got worse for Charley as Cheyenne's favorite prosecutor moved in for the kill, berating the boy for his stupidity and implying that his explanations for his crime were ludicrous and dishonest. Stoll's interrogation relied on proposing alternative courses of action at a number of crucial moments in the story, such as the now familiar stop in Pine Bluffs, when Charley claimed to be desperately hungry and Waldo and Ross were eating at Mrs. Kauffman's place. After Charley admitted that he knew the two boys were carrying plenty of money, Stoll asked the logical question: "Why didn't you ask them, if you were hungry, for a few nickels or something to enable you to get something to eat?" Miller responded, "I never thought of it." Stoll pursued the point: "Didn't you have any idea that after you had divided your lunch with them they would have helped you get something to eat if you were hungry?" The boy could say only no, the idea had not occurred to him. When Charley stated again that he "did not know" why he had killed the two clerks, Stoll asked: "If you don't know why you killed why did you take the money and watch and knives and pistol?" Once more, Charley responded that he didn't know, so Stoll persisted: "Did you kill them because you were hungry?" When the witness said yes, the deft attorney hit him again with the same damning question: "Why didn't you wake them up, or when you got into the [box]car why didn't you ask them for money to get something to eat." Charley's response was again brief and unsatisfying: "Never thought about it."

Taggart must have known that his client's nonanswers—"I don't know" and "Never thought of it"—were digging a grave for the defense, but there was not much he could do to stop Stoll's line of inquiry or change the nature of his client's responses. Unlike coaching on the athletic field, commentary from the sideline was impossible in court. After yet another painful review of how Miller had rifled the bloody corpses and ignored Fishbaugh's terrible moans, Stoll put it to the witness sarcastically: "So you thought the proper way in order to get something to eat was to kill two human beings. Is that it?" Charley replied no, but Stoll pressed on: "What was it? Can you answer the question? If you killed them for the purpose of getting their money to procure something to eat, why was it necessary to take Emerson's watch and chain and the pistol and the knife?" By this time, Charley's "I don't know" was pitiful and incriminating, but Stoll hung on to his witness like a pit bull: "If it was hunger that caused you to take the life of two human beings you must have been very hungry." In response, Charley spouted, "I was thinking I was ragged and far away from my brother." This answer generated a response from the prosecutor that verged on ridicule: "You didn't attempt to take their clothes did you? Overcoat or anything? I would like you to explain if by shooting them you could mend your clothes or improve your appearance in any way?" No explanation followed. Charley Miller was unable to think his way through Stoll's dizzying, late-in-the-day attack.

When the defendant finally left the stand it was close to the hour of five. The gaslights in the courtroom had been lit, and some people were beginning to leave for their supper now that the star witness was done. A boy of limited words, Charley nevertheless left a firm impression, and the newspapers the next day made it clear that he had won few hearts with his unperturbed, unrepentant demeanor. Most people found him callous, even cunning. According to the *Leader*, Charley was a flop in terms of aiding the defense: "His story scarcely created as much sympathy as might have been expected from his friendless position." The *Sun* observed that everyone was offended by his undisturbed air: "His calmness in admitting the killing was something simply amazing. He admitted commission of this awful crime with the nonchalance of one telling of carrying a package to the depot." Denver's *Rocky Mountain News* repeated the idea that the boy "betray[ed] no emotion" at hearing the testimony of others or even when he offered his own; in Missouri, the *St. Joseph Daily News* thought that Miller talked of the double murder "as though it were a petty offense."

Unfortunately for Charley, the only people who ever saw him cry over what he had done were back in Leonardville, and the defense never called any of them. One reason may well have been the cost of the trip; another the possibility that their testimony would open the door for the prosecution to question others about Charley's prior bad behavior. In the courtroom, people surely wanted to see the boy murderer show some visible remorse, or hear him say explicitly that he was terribly sorry for the evil he had done, but he did neither. Although his body language revealed his nervousness—a reporter observed "he moved his fingers a great deal and shifts his position frequently"—no one gave voice to the idea that Charley's steely, unflinching demeanor might be just a façade, an expression of a long-standing need to be like a man in a world that provided him few of the pleasures or protections of childhood. As a result of his terse language, his lack of affect, and his failure to shed even a single tear, Charley Miller was proclaimed "indifferent" by the press, and that label stuck, undercutting any claims to the contrary, that he was sad and guilt-stricken as a result of a horrible, impulsive mistake.

Some of the responsibility for the bad-apple image lay with Frank Taggart, who flubbed an important opportunity to show that his unrefined client had some sense of morality and duty—hence, the confession—despite a lack of adult guidance. In the courtroom, Taggart never developed the idea that when Miller turned himself in to the authorities it was a brave act of moral conscience, a marker of responsibility, and not a desire for notoriety, as some people proposed. The boxcar murderer might have gone undetected if Charley had not volunteered himself because of the emotional torment he experienced as a consequence of his behavior. In order to win the sympathy of the jury, Charley needed to have someone argue persuasively that he was a morally developed boy despite his gruesome crime. Instead, his energetic but outclassed defense attorney took the opposite tack, exposing his client to more intimate, embarrassing scrutiny, which made Charley even more unlikable.

————— ❖ —————

Frank Taggart literally changed his strategy overnight. At 9 A.M. on the third day, he called Charley to the stand to begin the process of proving that his client was insane, that he did not know right from wrong. This definition of insanity had been established in 1843, when Daniel McNaughton shot and killed the private secretary of British Prime Minister Robert Peel. McNaughton suffered from paranoid delusions, believing that Peel's Conservative Party was trying to kill him. Instead of the death penalty, he was sent to Bethlem Hospital and then the Broadmoor Criminal Lunatic Asylum on the grounds that he suffered such a "deficit of reason" that he did not comprehend his own act. Although the McNaughton Rules had no statutory basis, they were afforded the same status as actual law in both England and the United States. By the time Charles Guiteau stood trial for plotting and assassinating President James Garfield in 1881, most Americans were acquainted with the McNaughton defense, but it failed to save Guiteau, even though he was unbalanced and claimed to be on a mission from God. Taggart would now make an earnest attempt to use McNaughton, but he did so in a controversial way.

Taggart began with a shocking directive to his client: "State whether or not you have ever been guilty of an unclean practice on yourself, and, if so, to what extent?" Although the prosecution objected to the question on the grounds that it was immaterial, since "nothing of that kind" led to insanity and homicide, Judge Scott allowed the defense to continue, because the idea that insanity could be caused by excessive masturbation was not seen as entirely ridiculous given medical ideas of the day.

Taggart must have spent the night with his law books preparing for this last-ditch effort to get Charley off. He had probably also had some conversation with Charley the evening before to warn him about the new, unusual line of questioning he would face. As a legal matter, Taggart needed to draw the boy out about his sexual behavior and also provide convincing medical testimony to the destructive effects of "self-abuse" on the human mind. This would be a hard row to hoe, because there was little certainty in the field of medical jurisprudence about what constituted masturbatory-induced insanity, and Cheyenne had few medical experts qualified to discuss the matter. Most American physicians in the 1890s agreed that masturbation had deleterious physical and emotional consequences for men and boys, but few would substantiate a direct link between masturbation and homicide. Despite these problems, Frank Taggart set out to prove that his young client's perverse personal habit made him incapable of making moral decisions. To be sure, it would be a difficult and delicate interrogation, but Taggart reckoned that the jury might buy the argument that the boy had become morally indifferent and less culpable as a result of his private depravity.

With Judge Scott's approval, Taggart rephrased his initial question—"You may state whether or not at any time you practiced masturbation"—but Charley answered blankly, almost as if he had never heard the word before. "I don't know what you mean," he responded. Taggart tried again with more colloquial language: "Don't you know what I mean by saying an unclean act? Have you been guilty of practicing upon yourself this unclean act?" To this, Charley admitted "yes." Asked when he began his habit, he answered, "Before I was twelve years old." Pushed to be more specific about how long before, he muttered: "Two or three years." Taggart continued: "How often have you been guilty of this practice—this unclean act?" And Charley replied unabashedly, "Sometimes three or four times a day," an answer that cast him as habituated—not casual—about his solitary vice.

To this indecent admission, Taggart responded with more questions, some designed to show that his client's foul habit was not entirely his fault, because he had received no moral training as a child: "Did anyone at the time you were at the asylum and before you were twelve years old, tell you that [masturbation] was wrong?

Did anyone since tell you it was wrong?" According to Charley's response, he had had no guidance on this point at all—that is, until Frank Taggart told him that it was a bad, nasty thing to do. When Walter Stoll declined to cross-examine him, Charley left the stand, probably with great relief. Taggart's strategy required that he admit to something embarrassing, more humiliating than bedwetting, in order to improve his position. This was clearly painful, and Charley's minimal responses indicated that he was unable even to say the "m" word, or any slang equivalent, out loud.

Over the next few hours, the defense tried to establish, and the prosecution to debunk, the notion that Charley was insane at the time of the crime because of the effects of so much self-abuse. The experts called by both sides were all local doctors from Cheyenne. The first, for the defense, was Dr. William W. Crook, a well-known local physician and surgeon, educated in medicine at the University of Iowa before coming to Cheyenne to practice his profession and run a drugstore. When Taggart brought Crook to the stand, Stoll immediately objected on the grounds that he was not an expert on insanity, but the court still allowed the local doctor to have his say. This decision opened the door for other nonexperts to testify for both sides, a pragmatic solution in a frontier town where there were few specialists in diseases of the mind.

Crook admitted immediately that he had never given "more than an average attention to the subject of the soundness of the human mind," and that he had never really seen chronic insanity because it was usually treated in special institutions, not in a general practice like his own. Taggart would not allow Crook to pass himself off as totally ignorant, however. He used his witness to establish that the "standard authority" on these issues, the Englishman Henry Maudsley, had proposed a relationship between masturbation and diminished moral responsibility. Taggart asked Crook if he knew the work of this eminent expert, and Crook affirmed that he had read "some" Maudsley.

When Dr. Crook stated that he could not testify to the stability of the defendant's mind because he had never seen the boy before that morning in court, Judge Scott called a twenty-minute recess so Crook could examine Charley and report his clinical findings. When he returned, Taggart tried to get Crook to corroborate Maudsley's idea that the boy's pernicious habit had lowered his capacity for moral thinking, and thereby his criminal responsibility for the murders. Despite Stoll's objections to this line of argument, Taggart was allowed to ask if, on the basis of his brief examination, Crook thought that Charley was "guilty" of masturbation. When the physician responded in the affirmative, Taggart asked him to state his opinion on the effects of self-abuse if practiced daily from childhood until the age of fifteen, the age at which Charley committed his crime. Although Crook thought some "natural depredation" was inevitable, he equivocated on just how much: "I cannot exactly tell what effect and the extent of injury done to his nervous system and the brain." On cross-examination, when Stoll asked him if there was any impairment of Miller's mental faculties sufficient to make him "irresponsible for killing two individuals," Crook said, "No, I cannot say so," an answer that essentially ruined the defense case.

The second physician, also called by Taggart, turned out to be even less effective in forging the link between masturbation and homicidal mania. Dr. J. J. Marston received his medical education at McGill University and then practiced in New York City before heading west with the United States Army. By the time of the Miller trial, Marston, a member of the elegant Cheyenne Club, had been a physician and surgeon for over twenty-five years, and he spoke with a tone of scientific rigor and authority. When asked by Taggart what he had found in his examination of Charley, Marston stated that he found only slight evidence of self-abuse and nervous prostration, explaining that he determined the latter by having the boy hold up his hand to see if, or how much, he trembled. Unhappy with Marston's moderation, Taggart suggested that, if Miller was the habitual masturbator he claimed to be, there should be more than a slight effect on his mind and health. He asked Marston again: "If what he told you be true [about the duration and intensity of his masturbation] what would you say as to the effect on the boy's mind?" Marston again replied with an answer based on what he had observed in the present, not on speculation about the past: "The only effect it shows now is his manner of indifference." Stoll, on cross-examination, queried Marston as to whether or not there was anything to indicate that Miller was "not responsible for his acts" at the time of the killing, but Marston dodged the question: "I don't know what the condition of the boy was at the time of the killing." The only judgment that the steely Dr. Marston would offer was that Charley Miller was responsible and sane at present.

When a third physician was called, this time by the prosecution, the argument shifted to whether or not Charley Miller actually masturbated as much as he said he did. According to Dr. William A. Wyman, the physician who presided over Ross Fishbaugh's death and also tended to Charley in the Laramie County Jail, Miller was in "inordinarily [sic] good health," prima-facie evidence that "the practice had not extended far enough to produce very serious results." Although Wyman did not think the boy was particularly bright, he was certain that his mind was unaffected, because his memory was very good. Memory was widely held to be an indication of sanity, so Wyman's clinical observations were important for the jury to hear: "He seems to be able to remember events that happened, and speak consecutively in regard to them, and those are points which would be injured or impaired in him by the practice of the habit to any great extent." Stoll queried his witness again to make sure that the jury heard it from the mouth of the doctor who knew the boy best: "You found no impairment of his faculties?" "I did not," Wyman answered.

Obviously, the local physicians were not at all certain about the effects of masturbation on the mind of Charley Miller. Although witnesses for both sides affirmed Henry Maudsley's principle that masturbation weakened willpower, they did not agree on whether the practice contributed to the kind of impulsive action that often led to homicide. Taggart consistently tried to establish that masturbation was both enervating, in the sense of weakening and lowering moral reasoning, and also exhilarating, in the sense of stimulating "animation" and impulsivity, two characteristics of homicidal mania, the diagnosis he hoped to pin on his client.

Skeptical of how these two opposite effects could coexist, Stoll called yet a fourth physician, Dr. J. C. McGillvary, a native of Canada, who claimed that his medical education included weekly visits to an insane asylum over a number of years. Stoll directed his expert to tell the court, "as a matter of medical science, whether or not the practice of masturbation indulged in its excess, can present homicidal mania?" McGillvary replied, "I don't think it can," and went on to offer an opinion that further deflated the idea that Miller was a bona-fide homicidal maniac. When asked about the general effects of masturbating three or four times a day, McGill-vary implied that the boy was just lying: "My opinion is that it would have a serious effect upon his mind. More serious effect than the defendant appears to show." Like all of the doctors who testified before and after him, McGillvary could not find in Charley the kind of physical or mental deterioration that masturba-tion was supposed to cause. As a way of explaining the absence of this deterioration, McGillvary told the court what he had learned in his professional training about the veracity of chronic masturba-tors: "We are taught that persons who are in the habit are among the most incredible of all people. As a rule, you will not find one in a hundred that will confess to the truth of the matter."

Frank Taggart countered with a fifth and final physician, Dr. Major C. Barkwell, a Civil War veteran who had fought with the Union Army and then served as a surgeon at Fort Russell before starting his medical practice in nearby Cheyenne. Barkwell had been educated at the Miami Medical College in Ohio before at-tending a postgraduate course at Bellevue Hospital in New York City. Convinced that masturbation first showed its effects on the physical body, Barkwell examined Charley and then enumerated his vital statistics—namely, his height and weight as well as his chest, waist, and hat measurements. All of these numbers were low

On the day after his execution, images of Charley Miller appeared in newspapers on both coasts and points in between. In the *San Francisco Chronicle* (*top*), Charley appeared almost prepubescent; in the *New York World*, he seemed more manly. These "pen portraits" were probably done from life; no photograph seems to have survived.

These youngsters, from an immigrant neighborhood close to where Charley was born in New York City, were left unsupervised while their parents worked to feed them. Like Charley and his siblings, they fended for themselves, making space to play wherever they could.
Collection of the author.

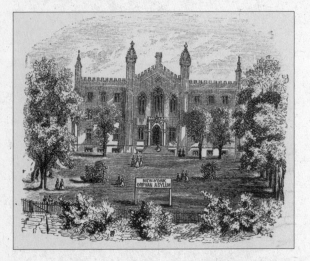

Charley Miller spent five years at The New York Orphan Asylum, located on West 73rd Street. Like many custodial institutions in the late nineteenth century, its managers attempted to instill middle-class values in its charges, in preparation for being "placed out" with good families, usually at the age of twelve.
Collection of the New-York Historical Society.

Charley Miller and his two brothers each left New York City on "orphan trains" bound for points in the West. This column from a Kansas newspaper includes a reminder to local farm families that a shipment of orphan boys will arrive the next week at the Leonardsville Depot, pictured here. Fred Miller, Charley's beloved older brother, arrived with this particular "ship-ment" in July 1886. He remained with his adoptive family for the rest of his life.
Collection of Riley County Historical Society.

Charley's placement in a farm home near Chatfield, Minnesota, was unhappy. His adoptive family required him to spend most of his time in the fields and in this barn, the only surviving remnant of the farm where he spent more than a year. The village was miles away, and it offered few attractions to an urban youngster.
Top: Collection of Minnesota Historical Society.
Bottom: Collection of the author.

At the age of thirteen, Charley was returned to this railroad station in St. Charles, Minnesota, where he was abandoned by William Booth, the farmer who had selected him at the orphan train distribution. Left without food or money, he set out looking for work. In letters to his brother Fred in Kansas, he described his plight and asked for help.

Collection of the Winona County Historical Society.

Preston Loofbourrow, Fred Miller's surrogate father, was willing to take Charley into his home after the traumatic experience in Minnesota. Although Charley did not stay very long, Loofbourrow taught him the basics of the printing trade and arranged for him to live with another respectable Kansas family. After the murder, when Charley decided to confess, Loofbourrow accompanied him to the police.
Collection of the Kansas State Historical Society.

Charley celebrated his fourteenth birthday along with Fred in the Loofbourrow's Leonardville home (*top*). The brothers worked together in Preston's shop, and they socialized with their peers as well as travelers from the railroad in the commercial district (*bottom*), directly across from their house.
Collection of the Riley County Historical Society.

Charley Miller was a fan of cheap, easy-to-read fiction for working-class men and boys, known as "dime novels." Books like these, with protagonists whose names linked them to geographical areas, probably inspired him to adopt the moniker "Kansas Charley." *Hess Collection, University of Minnesota.*

Many young men in Miller's generation liked to pretend that they were manly and tough. This staged photograph, taken in a photography studio in the 1890s, used whiskey glasses and a gun to create the personal style that Charley admired and tried to imitate. *Collection of the author.*

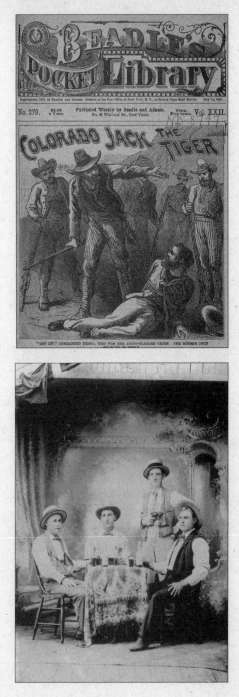

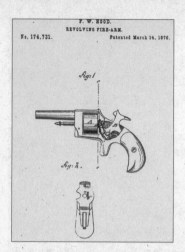

The murder weapon used by Charley Miller was a .32-caliber revolver, widely available in stores and catalogues and relatively inexpensive by the 1890s. Charley purchased his used, in a Kansas City pawnshop, for only $1.50.
United States Patent Office; Patent US0174731A.

Just a few hours before they were murdered, the two youths who were Charley's victims, Waldo Emerson and Ross Fishbaugh, ate an ample, early morning breakfast in a small hotel in Pine Bluffs, a raw Wyoming town where the Union Pacific stopped to take on coal. Afterward, they hopped back on the train and went to sleep in the same boxcar as Charley Miller.
Collection of Polly B. Burkett and Larry Brown.

Less than two weeks after the "box-car murders," Charley surrendered himself to the sheriff at the small Riley County Jail in Manhattan, Kansas. In a special front parlor, a local newspaper editor took his confession and then transmitted it to newspapers across the nation. The editor was Albert Stewart, shown here in his youth, when he was superintendent of printing at Kansas State Agricultural College and a stalwart of the local Sons of Temperance chapter.
Above: Collection of Kansas State Historical Society.
Right: Collection of Kansas State University.

Charley's victims first boarded the Union Pacific railroad at the depot in Grand Island, Nebraska (*top*). When Emerson was found dead, and Fishbaugh barely breathing, in a boxcar in Hillsdale, Wyoming, both boys were conveyed by rail, as swiftly as possible, into the Cheyenne station (*center*). Only a week after they left home, their parents received their corpses for burial at the railroad depot in St. Joseph, Missouri (*bottom*), where their unhappy adventure had started.
Top: Collection of the author. Center: Collection of the Wyoming State Archives. Bottom: Collection of the author.

Charley Miller's crime and punishment were discussed at The Cheyenne Club (*above*), an all-male, by-invitation-only social association that was nationally renowned for its fine cuisine and vintage wines. The elegant clubhouse, located in the heart of Wyoming's state capital, provided its powerful, elite members with opportunities for camaraderie and deal making.
Collection of The American Heritage Center, University of Wyoming.

Richard H. Scott (*left*) was the presiding judge at Charley's three-day trial and the person who sentenced him to death. State Supreme Court Justice Herman Groesbeck (*right*) extended an important stay so that the defense could prepare an appeal for a new trial, but the appeal failed. When it became clear that Charley would actually be hanged, Groesbeck, who had concurred in the Supreme Court decision to turn down the appeal, told a newspaper reporter that if he were the governor, he would grant clemency to Charley Miller on the grounds of his youth and early life experiences.
Collection of The American Heritage Center, University of Wyoming.

FRANK LESLIE'S ILLUSTRATED NEWSPAPER

In 1888, the date of this popular middle-class magazine, the idea that women voted in Wyoming was clearly a novelty worthy of attention. Many Americans believed that when women won the suffrage, politics would change, and that a female sensibility would prevail, particularly around humanitarian issues such as clemency for Charley Miller.

Therese Jenkins *(left)* and Amalia Post *(right)* blended suffrage and temperance work with an interest in saving and rehabilitating Charley.
Frances E. Willard, Woman of the Century.

John Wesley Hoyt (*above left*), the third territorial governor and the first president of the University of Wyoming, was in favor of clemency for Miller as was Ethelburt Talbot (*above right*), an Episcopal bishop, and Sidney Dillon (*right*), the aged railroad magnate who was the former president of the Union Pacific Railroad.

Above left and right: Collection of The American Heritage Center, University of Wyoming; right: Harper's Weekly (1882).

After graduating from the University of Pennsylvania Medical College, Amos Barber was lured west by the prospect of becoming the resident physician at the "Cowboy Hospital" in east-central Wyoming. Barber's rough appearance in this photo, *(above)* probably taken in the late 1880s, contrasts dramatically with his sophisticated appearance as the Acting Governor and a member of the Cheyenne Club *(right)*. In 1892, he was the only person with legal authority to grant Miller clemency and save his life.

Above: Collection of The American Heritage Center, University of Wyoming.

Right: Collection of the Wyoming State Archives.

Miller spent over a year and a half in the Laramie County Jail where he forged a complex relationship with Sheriff A. D. Kelley, a local grocer and father of five. Kelley was fond of Charley, but it still was his responsibility to make the arrangements for the boy's execution.
Collection of the Wyoming State Archives.

> Cheyenne, Wyo.,
> April 1st 1892
>
> Mr. Harter,
> As you have followed out my instructions, in order to recieve an invatation to my execution, which comes on April 22nd 1892, I hereby invite you to be present
> Chas. E. Miller
>
> OK
> A D Kelley Sheriff

Charley sent out invitations to his own execution but they had to be approved by the sheriff. This one, written in his own hand, was dated early in April when there was still a slim hope that he might not be hanged. The recipient was probably one of the "celebrity hounds" who liked to visit "the boy murderer" in jail, bringing cigarettes, doughnuts, or messages.
Collection of Johnson County, Jim Gatchell Memorial Museum.

Charley Miller was executed on April 22, 1892, within an interior courtyard attached to the back of the Court House in Cheyenne. There were only sixty people in the official gallery, but the streets around the site were thronged that day with people hoping to see the hanging. Some climbed up trees and telephone poles hoping to peek down at the gallows.
Collection of Wyoming State Archives.

he said, a convincing indication of the habit of self-abuse. Barkwell then revealed an intimate detail about the defendant's puny
body that no other doctor had mentioned: Charley was circumcised, unusual among boys, but understandable given his bedwetting and his residence at the New York Orphan Asylum. For
Barkwell, all the data about Charley confirmed that masturbation
in youth made boys sallow, sickly, and small.

When Taggart asked him questions about the strength and
condition of Miller's mind, Barkwell reported, just as the other
physicians had, that Charley passed the memory test: "From what
I saw of the boy his memory is good." He also theorized, without
reference to Charley specifically, that masturbation produced a
"desire to slink away from people and lead a life of solitude." Although Barkwell mentioned melancholia and suicide as possible
outcomes of this antisocial frame of mind, he would not be pushed
too far on the issue of the defendant's mental state at the time of the
crime because he had not been there, the crime, after all, had happened some months ago. Because his examination of Charley was
so rushed, Barkwell felt the need to offer some disclaimer about his
clinical judgment: "No man can tell in five minutes what there is in
any man, so it requires a series of observations upon a subject before a man can give his opinion." He also felt compelled to add that
he had "never been a specialist."

Despite this admission and his warnings about the complexi-
ties of diagnosing mental disease, Taggart used Barkwell to provide the jury with a short course in nineteenth-century medical
theory about the organic origins of insanity. Barkwell, like many
other Victorian physicians, believed that mental disturbance was
caused by actual problems in the physical structure and composi-
tion of the brain. (Mind was matter, in this case.) Taggart asked his
last medical witness a series of questions about the sanity of Frederick Muller, in the hopes of connecting the father's suicide to the
crime of his son. "What is the condition of the mind at the time
when it determines to commit suicide?" Taggart queried. Barkwell
responded: "If the brain is healthy, the mind must be also. The

brain is simply the substance of the mind, and without a healthy brain there is no mind, memory or will." When asked if a suicidal person could be of sound mind, Barkwell replied: "I don't believe anyone ever committed suicide who was sane." This was an important answer, because it empowered Taggart to argue that his client was the product of an insane father, giving Charley a lineage that implied the possibility of hereditary insanity.

In the end, the parade of physicians in the courtroom created little certainty for those who observed and listened. After hours of testimony, there was no consensus on the impact that years of constant masturbation would have had on Charley's mind that fateful day in the Union Pacific boxcar. None of the experts offered any proof that there was anything wrong with his brain or that he had ever experienced an episode of homicidal mania. Moreover, it was abundantly clear that Charley was not a lunatic—he saw no visions and heard no voices—and that made it hard to buy the defense argument that he should be freed of criminal responsibility for the murders because of his mental state. Taggart tried to introduce a new medical vocabulary that justified application of the insanity defense, but it was a language, and a way of thinking, that most of the tough-minded people of Wyoming were not willing to embrace.

Whether he masturbated once a week, once a day, or once an hour, Charley's masturbatory history never aroused much sympathy. Instead, the fact that he admitted to these unclean acts without contrition reinforced the notion that he was morally indifferent and perverted as well. There was no mention of masturbation in the press, however, because the subject was unsuitable for family reading. But the word must have leaked out of the county courthouse, giving the entire case a lurid tone that it had not had before.

Taggart's last move on his client's behalf brought another unclean act in Charley's past to the attention of the now exhausted courtroom. Earlier in the trial, the prosecution had introduced the murder weapon, a cheap .32-caliber revolver, which the defendant said he bought in order to "protect himself from bums." Now Taggart recalled the defendant and told him, "You may state to the jury why it was that you bought that revolver at Kansas City." The prosecution objected on the grounds that the question had already been answered, but Taggart retorted that it had not been answered fully. When Judge Scott directed the boy to reply, Charley repeated what he had said earlier, but Taggart insisted that he say more: "You may state how and why you needed it to protect yourself from bums." Stoll objected again, this time on the grounds that Miller's motivation was immaterial, but he was unable to stop the impending revelation of sexual abuse.

In his characteristic deadpan, Charley then uttered a half-dozen words that suggested Taggart was treading on painful ground—"I don't like to answer it"—but Taggart would not allow him to be silent. "Answer it. Tell the truth," he said firmly. Charley then spoke his last words on the witness stand, words that the defense hoped would help the jury see the full extent of his youthful victimization. As soon as he said it—"Bums in the boxcar take my pants down and do something to me"—the defense rested.

The revelation that Miller had been sodomized at the age of fifteen was never challenged by the prosecution. The subject was too terrible, and the emotion it stimulated potentially detrimental to the prosecution's case. From a modern perspective, the revelation suggested the dark, unspoken possibility that Emerson and Fishbaugh might have been sexual predators whose behavior toward Charley, or in relation to one another, reminded him of the awful incident near Omaha. But no one in Cheyenne ever raised that possibility, because the murder victims seemed to be reputable, middle-class youths whose morality and sexuality were beyond question. Stoll dropped the sodomy issue like a hot potato, and quickly recalled Albert Stewart, his star witness, and then John Martin, the Laramie County sheriff who had brought Charley back from Kansas. There were a half-dozen final questions and challenges—all about what was said when Miller left Manhattan—but absolutely no new information.

The change in tenor orchestrated by Stoll brought everyone

back to the immediate reality: the boy who stood before them had already confessed to a double murder. Regardless of what awful things may have happened to him in a railroad car a month or so before the crime, he had admitted, seemingly without remorse, that he shot Waldo Emerson and Ross Fishbaugh at close range in their heads, as they slept. He had also admitted, again without visible embarrassment or apology, that he masturbated frequently. In hushed tones, many a Cheyenne moralist probably concurred that what had happened in the boxcar was a natural consequence of the boy's perverted practice rather than any disease in his brain.

<hr />

Over the next four hours, Stoll and Taggart made their summaries to the twelve-man jury empowered to decide Charley's fate. Each side now had the chance to rehash its best arguments, in its most persuasive language. Although the actual texts of these final arguments do not survive, the trial transcript provides a good guide for determining what each attorney thought was most important. Stoll wanted the jury to believe that the immoral and malicious Miller had stalked the two boys and killed them deliberately for their money; Taggart hoped that the jury could see the defendant as a victim of sorry circumstances and imperfect upbringing, all of which came together in an instant, causing him to act impulsively, if not insanely, in a manner he never had before. Charley's fate depended on which narrative the jury considered most convincing, along with the directions they would receive from the judge as soon as Mr. Stoll stopped talking.

As he summed up, the shrewd Cheyenne prosecutor used a cattle metaphor to make the argument that the jury really had only two choices. There are "two horns to the dilemma," he advised: either acquit the boy, or find him guilty of murder in the first degree. As the hours wore on, even the stalwart Walter Stoll weakened from the heat of so many bodies in the stuffy room, which could not be ventilated because of the fierce winds outside. Feeling some discomfort, Stoll cut his summary short, "completely exhausted."

The following morning, he returned with vigor to say more about the "two horned dilemma," and also to provide, as backup, an explanation of the distinction between murder in the first and second degrees. Because premeditation was the defining characteristic of a first-degree offense, Stoll belabored the point that Miller had hatched a plan to murder when he saw that his companions carried ample cash. "Conceived" and "conception" were words he used again and again.

In the end, Stoll probably did not have to work as hard as he did to make the case for first-degree murder, because the final instructions imparted to the jury by the presiding judge made it virtually impossible for them to find anything else. Judge Richard Scott told the jury that any murder performed in the act of robbery constituted murder in the first degree, and he proposed a definition of malice and premeditation that further supported that level of offense. If Miller was sane and there was no provocation, he said, then the defendant had displayed malice simply by the act of shooting Emerson and Fishbaugh. On the question of premeditation, the judge told the jury that it did not matter how much time it took for Miller to murder his companions, because premeditation could happen "in a flash," a clear dismissal of Frank Taggart's argument that his defendant had had no time to think before he acted. For the jury to find the boy insane, Scott said the defense must demonstrate that he was both "incapable of telling right from wrong" and also driven by an "uncontrollable impulse" to kill. In effect, he set the insanity bar so high that even the most sympathetic juror could not jump over it. Charley had to be demonstrably out of his mind to be judged insane in Scott's court.

Frank Taggart saw the handwriting on the wall as Scott ended his remarks about eleven-forty-five that morning. The tired defense attorney duly registered his objections, arguing that the judge should give the jury many more ways to find Charley Miller insane or mentally incompetent. According to Taggart, the burden of proof should be on the state to show beyond a reasonable doubt that Charley's mind was *not* weakened by masturbation, and that the boy's moral conscience was *unaffected* by his brutal life. Although these objections formed the basis of a later appeal, they were put aside now, and the jury left the box to begin its sequestered deliberations. Within fifteen minutes—just a little after noon—the word was conveyed to the sheriff that a verdict was ready to be rendered. The court reconvened. All the major players took their seats, and the jury foreman passed the verdict to the county clerk, who read it aloud: "We do find the defendant Charles Miller guilty of murder in the first degree in manner and form as indicted."

Although his future depended on these words, Charley remained impassive. He did not flinch, cry, or even drop his head. In his stiff, unexpressive body language, most observers thought they saw the same indifference that he had displayed throughout the four-day trial. He exhibited his "usual lack of feeling" and "never turned a hair," the *Leader* reported. Despite the awful news, he managed to smile at someone he knew, saying that he felt "all right about the verdict." Others in the courtroom—especially some of the women—were visibly distressed, because they suspected that the verdict was the first step on the way to hanging a minor in Wyoming. As the sixteen-year-old passed out of the hot and noisy courtroom, following behind the deputy sheriff, a sympathetic woman in the gallery leaned over and told him in a "hysterical" tone: "Now, Charley, when you are led out on the scaffold, be sure to bear yourself like a man."

<hr>

Although privacy would have helped at this moment, it was not in the cards for Charley that day. After the short walk back to jail, he found himself in Sheriff Martin's office, sitting face to face across a table from the parents of Waldo Emerson. This awkward, unanticipated encounter was a plum for the irrepressible local press, who were invited to cover it. Surprisingly, they did so without quoting the exact words of any of the players. The meeting was intended to give John Emerson the opportunity to meet with his son's killer— to have his say—but also to give Charley another chance to admit he was sorry, if he really was. For both parties, the meeting must have been excruciating, albeit for different reasons.

The Emersons had been in Cheyenne for the entire trial, watching their son's killer as he took the stand and admitted to the gruesome murders as well as his revolting personal habits. Now that it was over and the boy faced the possibility of a death sentence, they must have felt some satisfaction. But John Emerson, a decent, churchgoing man, was still struggling for the reason his beloved older son had met such a violent, undeserved death. Emerson had come to Cheyenne on a personal mission, and now he wanted the opportunity to talk to the boy murderer on his own, in person. Apparently, the aggrieved father wanted to confirm his pet theory that Miller was "morally irresponsible" and filled with "grotesque ideas" as a result of reading trashy novels. Like many Americans at this time, Emerson disliked certain forms of popular culture, especially cheap fiction, because it allegedly stimulated immorality, sexual license, and criminal behavior in the younger generation. John Emerson was convinced that Charley Miller, an admitted dime-novel reader, had confessed to his brother only because he wanted to induce Fred to join him in a bandit gang—in imitation of Jesse and Frank—and not because he felt any honest guilt about the terrible thing he had done. (As he left the interview, John Emerson told the press that he had "satisfied himself" that his theory about Miller's motivation was correct.)

At this agonizing moment, when he had to face the people who understandably hated him, Charley managed to behave courteously, like an adult man. As the interview drew to a close, he extended his hand to John Emerson, and the father actually shook it. Mrs. Emerson, who was hostile and mute, had greater difficulty when it was her turn to do the same. The *Leader* drew out all the emotional nuance in the interaction between the murderer and the victim's mother: "The lady hesitated for the moment with the natural antipathy of a mother to the murderer of her son but finally touched his hand with the tips of her fingers."

By all reports, Charley told the Emersons that he was sorry he had killed their son, but the way he said it was not convincing enough to make them feel any better or convince the journalists who listened in. "His tone and manners did not indicate any depth of feeling on the subject," a reporter explained, confirming, as almost all firsthand observers did, that the boy they had watched in the courtroom was callous and morally indifferent. Little attention was paid when he provided any shred of evidence to the contrary. As soon as the Emersons were gone, he telegrammed Fred in Leonardville about his desperate situation: "Verdict of murder in the first degree. Please come."

CHAPTER SEVEN

The Politics of Clemency

O VER THE NEXT sixteenth months, the question of whether Charley Miller would live or die absorbed the attention of the people of Wyoming as well as many other Americans. Those who followed the case knew that the boy's future rested first in the hands of the state courts and then in those of Wyoming's Acting Governor Amos Barber, who had the power to grant both a reprieve and clemency. In the effort to save his sixteen-year-old client, indefatigable Frank Taggart began another round of defense activity even before Charley Miller was sentenced. Only three days after the boy was found guilty of murder in the first degree, Taggart filed a motion for a new trial, but that motion was quickly denied. Then, on January 27, 1891, Judge Richard Scott sentenced Miller to death, claiming that he had no discretion in the case, and that he was compelled to follow the requirements of the law. As the young defendant stood in the dock, Scott told him that he would be "hung by the neck until he was dead" sometime between 10 A.M. and 4 P.M. on March 20, less than two months away.

Although there was a solemn hush in the courtroom right after Scott's awful pronouncement, Charley Miller appeared "unconcerned, unabashed, and entirely self-possessed" during the sentencing. Only one reporter thought he saw a slight flush on the boy's face when he heard the word "hung." Wires were sent immediately to the Emersons and Maria Fishbaugh announcing the outcome they had clearly hoped for, and reporters scurried over to the Laramie County Jail to see how Miller was handling the frightening news once he was out of the courtroom and the public eye.

Apparently, the first thing Charley did was ask Sheriff Kelley to help him send a wire to his brothers in Kansas, but he stumbled over the date of his death as he wrote out the dreadful message. "What day is this thing to come off?" he asked matter-of-factly. "What thing?" inquired the sheriff, unclear what the boy meant. "I mean what day am I to be hung. Did the judge say the 28th or the 27th?" the boy responded. Kelley had to tell the youngster that the execution date was actually a week earlier, but Charley took it all with his characteristic impassivity, showing neither disappointment nor anger.

With the headlines announcing that his client was "Booked for Hanging," Frank Taggart began the process of drafting the documents necessary to appeal to the governor for a stay of execution and to the Wyoming Supreme Court for a new trial. Time was short, especially for an attorney acting on his own with so little criminal experience. Throughout the winter of 1891, Taggart worked resolutely to develop a list of errors made in the Miller trial (known as a bill of exceptions), and also an appeal to the higher court (known as a writ of error) that would eventually elaborate twenty-three reasons why the judgment against his client should be overturned in favor of a new trial. All the while the clock kept ticking, as people on Charley's side hoped for intervention from Amos Barber, the former Wyoming secretary of state, who had replaced Republican Governor Francis E. Warren when he went off to Washington as one of the first two United States senators from Wyoming. All eyes were on the new state to see what it would do with the sixteen-year-old New York City orphan who was sentenced to hang. If Charley Miller died on March 20, he would be the youngest person to be executed in the history of Wyoming, and also one of the youngest in the history of the nation.

⟫━◆━⟪

Charley used his time in jail to do some of the things he had never been able to do, either in the regimented environment of the New York Orphan Asylum or as a boy tramp. Having access to paper and pencils, newspapers, books, and regular meals was an experience he seemed to appreciate despite the price he might have to pay for this unusual form of R&R. In jail, he read the "blood-and-thunder stories" he had always favored; played checkers on an improvised, handmade board; and worked on decorations for his walls. Even though he occasionally shared his cell with a short-termer, by early February his tiny space was transformed into a room of his own. After Charley provided a tour of the pictures and mottoes he had on display in his cell, a local reporter wrote: "He enjoys himself as keenly as a child in cutting out pictures that attract his attention, and arranging and rearranging them as his restless fancy may dictate. He also spends much time in printing signs with a pen. These he arranges fancifully, laboriously drawing the various letters and surrounding them with ornamentation." Sheriff Kelley, a magnanimous father of five who also ran a successful wholesale and retail grocery business, actually liked the boy, and was quick to tell reporters that, at this point, Charley Miller was "not a source of trouble." His fellow prisoners considered him "the life of the prison" because of his harmonica playing, poems, and youthful buffoonery.

Ironically, Charley probably felt better physically at this point in his life than he had in years, largely as a result of regular meals and the hygienic conditions provided by Laramie County. The newspapers noted that he was not "losing flesh" and that he remained a "good feeder" despite the terrible shadow that hung over him. As with many adolescent males, food was a major preoccupation, and he was unabashed in talking about finding ways to satisfy his appetite. Allegedly, he told a deputy sheriff right after sentencing: "Now if I am going to be strung up sure enough, I want a good restaurant breakfast on that morning. Common grub won't be good enough for me that day." Two days later, he asked if he could really have anything he wanted to eat now that he was sentenced to die. Sheriff Kelley asked the boy where he got that idea, and Charley told him that when he was sentenced to death someone said that he could now "feed as he liked at state expense." Kelley actually agreed to supply the youngster with whatever he wanted, but the story of this exchange—published in the local papers—fueled the notion that Miller was an unfortunate drain on the community purse, a leech on the body politic, deliberately taking advantage of everyone, including Sheriff Kelley, right up until the end.

Whenever Charley Miller was asked what life was like in jail under sentence, he invariably responded in terms of food. "How are you being treated?" a reporter asked, and Miller answered: "Oh, we still get the same old soup." This was his formulaic response throughout the winter of 1891, the period when Frank Taggart was working so doggedly to save him from hanging. Instead of complaints or anger about his situation, Taggart's client filled the ears of anyone who would listen with genial commentary about the big meals he liked to eat. "Miller's appetite is his chief consideration," observed the *Sun*, an observation that had different meanings, depending on your point of view about the boy. For those who were sympathetic, his unrelenting hunger was a sign of long-time deprivation; for those who wanted to see him die, the preoccupation with food made him seem like an animal, motivated only by the need to fulfill basic urges.

As the temperature dropped well below freezing and the winds howled outside, Charley Miller was glad to be inside and comfortable in his involuntary hotel. His cordial, almost cheery demeanor was regarded by many, however, as proof that he was immoral and not interested in meeting his maker in an appropriately remorseful or reverent way. "[Miller] doesn't seem to give a thought to the future," was the way the *Leader* described his frame of mind: "With his creature comforts supplied, in the midst of snug and cleanly surroundings, with nothing to do, he is perfectly content to let the future take care of itself. He doesn't appear to have any hope of a reprieve, or perhaps it would be better to say that he isn't troubled one way or the other."

Only time would tell if Charley really was as accepting of confinement as most observers thought. In all likelihood, he was "in denial," a modern way of saying that he was unable to accept the idea that his life would be foreshortened, or that the same men who provided him with good company and tasty food were really going to lead him to his death. In a manner typical of adolescents, he pushed the dreaded event out of his mind, thinking that there was plenty of time for Mr. Taggart to win him a reprieve or a new trial. During the many hours when he lay alone on the cot in his cell, he probably also harbored secret fantasies of escape and heroic acts of survival while he was on the lam. But he said nothing to that effect and never groused about life as a prisoner. From all reports, he lived life day by day, willing to be satiated and soothed by ample food, decent clothes, and a clean bed, all things he had been unable to have with any regularity since he left the orphan asylum.

While Charley lived in the moment, Frank Taggart hustled to head off the impending execution. During the first week of March, Amos Barber granted a reprieve of sixty days in order to give the defense attorney time to bring the matter to the Wyoming Supreme Court. The conditional reprieve was regarded as the fair thing to do, because it meant Miller would have every legal opportunity to avoid the ultimate sentence. Two weeks later, Chief Justice Herman Groesbeck of the Wyoming Supreme Court allowed a suspension of sentence that gave Taggart and Charley even more time. Groesbeck, a Laramie resident who hailed from Syracuse, New York, was known for his interest in children, although he had none of his own. On March 19, he heard Taggart's bill of exceptions and ordered the defense to submit its appeal for a new trial, an appeal that would not be heard until the October term of the state Supreme Court. Groesbeck ordered suspension of the death penalty until decision on that appeal, a pronouncement that meant Charley Miller would now live for at least six more months.

For Miller, six months seemed like an eternity. Life would continue now, along with the glad prospect of more good food and the hope that Fred and Willie might be able to come see him once the weather was better. Charley's confidence in Mr. Taggart's ability to protect him from Judge Scott's awful decree grew rather than diminished as a result of the governor's reprieve and the latest court action. Although he seemed a little "bleached out" from the anxiety of waiting, the reporters who arrived to capture the boy's reaction to Groesbeck's decision found him "cheerful over the status of his case" and looking forward to his seventeenth birthday.

———◦∗◦———

Charley Miller got a new lease on life as a result of the actions of Chief Justice Groesbeck, but his fate could ultimately be determined in the governor's office. If the Wyoming Supreme Court failed to grant him a new trial, Charley Miller's life could still be saved by Acting Governor Amos Barber, if he decided to commute the death penalty. Soon after Miller was sentenced to death in January 1891, letters making different arguments about how he should be handled began to cross the desk of the man who would be the likely arbiter of the boy's fate.

Amos Barber was born in Doylestown, Pennsylvania, in 1861 to a family that had enough resources to send him, the fifth of six children, to a local academy. Later, he attended the University of Pennsylvania Medical College, graduating in 1883. For the next two years, he served as a resident physician at the Hospital of the University of Pennsylvania and staff physician at Children's Hospital, Pennsylvania Hospital, and Episcopal Hospital, three of Philadelphia's most highly respected medical institutions. Barber seemed to be making a niche for himself in a sophisticated medical community, but in May 1885, when he was offered a position in the Wild West, the adventurous, unmarried twenty-four-year-old seized the opportunity and left a profitable urban practice behind.

The organization that lured Dr. Barber from his Eastern roots was the Fetterman Hospital Association, a newly formed cooperative of cattlemen and cowboys who came together to bring decent "doctoring" to a region that lacked good health care. Most of the physicians in Wyoming at this time were clustered in the railroad towns—such as Cheyenne, Laramie, and Evanston—a pattern that meant there was little accessible treatment for isolated ranch managers, their families, and cowboys, whose lives were filled with almost constant physical danger. As a result of the urgent need for medical care, in the spring of 1885, at the height of the cattle boom, some of the biggest livestock men in the territory joined forces with small operators and individual cowboys to form a medical association that would hire a trained doctor and give him a place to work.

The "cowboy hospital" that resulted was located in east-central Wyoming, near the site of the abandoned Fort Fetterman, once a center for military activity against the Sioux, Cheyenne, and Arapaho Indians. It was housed in a former army barracks, purchased from the U.S. Army by a successful cattle baron. The association offered Dr. Barber one hundred dollars per month to entice him to practice medicine in this isolated, incommodious setting. During the first six months of operation, the association attracted as subscribers more than two hundred individual cowboys as well as twenty of the largest cattle ranchers, who paid a dollar per month for the medical care of each cowboy they employed. These group memberships added up, making the support of prominent cattlemen, most of whom were members of the WSGA, critical to the operating budget of the cowboy hospital.

Dr. Barber arrived to do the demanding work that the Fetterman Association needed in June 1885, at a time of year when the prairie was flowering, and the weather and winds were relatively mild. Even as the weather became less hospitable, the young Easterner handled the rigors of life in the West with great skill. In addition to his general proficiency in setting broken arms and legs, a common problem in the cattle industry, Barber earned renown for his adept handling of gunshot wounds and rattlesnake bites, conditions that he saw infrequently in Philadelphia. (Allegedly, Silas Weir Mitchell, the reigning dean of neurology and nervous disorders back east, taught him how to use injections of permanganate of potassium as an antidote to rattlesnake poison.) According to local lore, the youthful and energetic Dr. Barber once rode fifty miles on horseback to attend the daughter of a frontier rancher after she was bitten by a poisonous snake. When he realized that the young woman could not be treated in her home, he carried her back to the cowboy hospital himself, where he subsequently saved her life.

In only a few years, Dr. Barber made an enviable professional reputation, which grew even stronger as he helped cattlemen, cowboys, and families cope with the harsh effects of the drought, overgrazing, and severe blizzards that deflated the cattle bubble in the late 1880s. In 1889, he moved to the new town of Douglas to begin a private practice, but he continued to serve association members and to stay in touch with the territory's most powerful cattlemen. When Wyoming became a state in 1890, Dr. Barber was so well known and so well liked that he received the Republican nomination for secretary of state, the second-highest elected office in the state. (Wyoming's constitution provided no lieutenant governor and the attorney general was appointed by the governor.) As a result, when Republican Governor Francis E. Warren left for senatorial service in Washington, the thirty-year-old Philadelphia doctor stepped in as the new chief executive.

Amos Barber was clearly an enterprising, ambitious man. Eager to affirm his professional connections and credentials, he became a member of the American Academy of Railway Surgeons, the Rocky Mountain Interstate Medical Society, and the Wyoming Medical Society, serving eventually as president of the state group. Barber also found time for the fraternal orders that dominated male culture in most of the settled areas of the region. He was a 32nd Degree Mason, a Shriner, and, most important, a member of the Cheyenne Club. At the time he became involved in the case of Charley Miller, the unmarried acting governor was actually living full-time at the Club, sleeping in one of the ornate walnut-paneled bedrooms, and taking his evening meals with Wyoming's richest cattle barons. As the state's chief executive, the bachelor governor also had a prominent place in receiving lines at the capitol's most glittering receptions, the kind where his stylish handlebar mustache and polished Eastern manners attracted attention, especially among the eligible daughters of Cheyenne's first families.

Dr. Barber's transition from cowboy hospital to governor's office took less than five years, and it was owed, in large part, to

WSGA members with Republican Party connections who saw him as smart, genial, and one of their own. He was loyal to the interests of the cattle growers who had brought him to Wyoming, and he was comfortable in their company, eager to listen to their boisterous stories about early successes as well as current problems with weather, markets, and unpunished rustlers. Amos Barber so enjoyed life at the Cheyenne Club that he urged his friend from medical school in Philadelphia, Charles Bingham Penrose, to join him there late in 1891. Penrose, who was both a doctor and a physicist trained at Harvard University, was recovering from pulmonary tuberculosis when Barber wrote him recommending recuperation in Cheyenne's dry, clear, and sunny environment.

Penrose took Barber's advice, arriving at a moment when his friend, the governor, was feeling pressure from both sides on the Miller case. Some people wanted him to intervene on behalf of the boy and commute his sentence to life; others urged him to hold firm for hanging or stay out of the affair altogether. Aware that he was in the middle of something controversial, Barber appeared at first to be interested in hearing out both sides. For that purpose, he kept a scrapbook of articles about the case that he clipped from the newspapers he read while chatting with Charles Penrose in the plush surroundings of the reading room at the Club. Over a cognac or a cigar, he probably also told Penrose that the Miller case had captured the attention of the "ladies," some of whom he knew personally and some who were interlopers from back east.

━━◆◈◆━━

For many reasons above and beyond the issue of his youth, women of different social classes and regions were troubled by the prospect that Charley Miller might die on the gallows of the new state. Women, more than men, embraced the idea that Charley's crime was a result of the impoverished, emotionally barren environments in which he had spent his early years. Moved by the story of his life without parents, shelter, or regular meals, they cast the boy as a "waif" rather than an "incorrigible" or a hardened criminal. Waifs, like stray animals, were unthreatening, requiring care and nurture. A waif needed to be taken in and absorbed into someone's home or maternal heart. In the letters that crossed his desk in Cheyenne, Barber learned that the female perspective on Miller's future was laced with religious values epitomizing the spirit of the New Testament and its emphasis on forgiveness.

Shortly after news of Charley's sentence reached New York City, the trustees of the New York Orphan Asylum met to discuss what action they should take on behalf of their now infamous alumnus. Ever since the NYOA began sending children westward on orphan trains they had bragged about their results. But in 1891, after Charley's story hit the national press, the annual report took a much more somber tone: "Although we are disappointed in some of the children who leave us for other homes, still by far the larger number turn out satisfactorily."

With Miller awaiting death, the apprehensive and embarrassed trustees concluded that the best way to help the errant boy was to approach Wyoming's chief executive through a petition signed by the trustees but introduced by a letter from Edwin Mitchell, a prominent attorney who lived on Gramercy Park with his wife, an asylum trustee. Among the eighteen signatories only two were men: Cornelius Demarest, the asylum's superintendent at the time, and John L. Campbell, the doctor who had treated Charley Miller. The others were all women born to privilege who gave their time and money to the cause of the city's impoverished orphaned children. All of them had ample money and a vast web of connections, but the conventional wisdom in 1891 was that they needed a man to present their cause, because to take charge themselves could be construed as unladylike political activity.

In a letter bearing the imprimatur of the Office of the U.S. Attorney for the Southern District of New York, Edwin Mitchell put forth the women's case for imprisonment rather than death. An introductory statement about the organization's stellar record with orphans was obligatory: "Since the foundation of the Society some ninety years ago, not one of the children who have been under its care has met so sad a fate as threatens this poor boy." After reiterating Charley Miller's personal history, Mitchell gave voice to the trustees' argument that the boy was not all bad. This was a sentiment that he had heard many times from his wife and her friends, women who believed implicitly in the work of the asylum and its ability to create moral youngsters and decent citizens. "[Miller] must have some conscience and good parts or he would not have been moved to confess his act," the attorney asserted. And then he made a legal analogy likely to have been his own: "Had there been an accomplice of his who had confessed and whose testimony had been used to convict [him], would not the accomplice have been equitably entitled, if not to pardon, to some executive clemency?" The same principle should be applied in the Miller case: the boy should get clemency because he provided testimony against himself.

The New York attorney did not let his argument rest there, however. He wanted Amos Barber to understand the nature of the New York women he represented, as well as their unique relationship to the friendless and unfortunate boy facing death on the gallows in the Wyoming capital. "The excellent estimable women who are Trustees of the Orphan Asylum feel in a certain sense that they are <u>in the place of his parents</u> who are dead." Mitchell's deliberate underlining was meant to emphasize the trustees' sentiments about this boy: they were his surrogate parents, and if Barber allowed it, execution would be an unnatural act against the maternal bond, an event likely to break the hearts of some of the finest, most well-bred women in the city of New York.

Closer to Cheyenne, women of more moderate means, without social pedigrees or distinguished husbands, were also animated by Charley Miller's plight, and they too sought ways to influence Wyoming's chief executive. In Kansas, a state that for all practical purposes had outlawed the death penalty in 1870, Miller's cause was embraced enthusiastically by the stouthearted middle-class women of the Women's Christian Temperance Union, who were

eager to energize their "White Ribbon Army" in the clemency effort. The name came from the sashes worn by the membership in
their official campaigns against alcohol, saloons, and tobacco.
There were over two hundred local unions in the state by 1890. In
Kansas and elsewhere, the WCTU could be fierce, capable of taking aggressive extralegal action on behalf of women and girls in
local communities. They were known, for example, for forcing pu-
tative fathers to marry girls they had impregnated, and rumored to
be responsible for tar-and-feathering abusive husbands.

In the 1890s, the WCTU was the largest organization of
women in the United States, and it embraced many social reforms
beyond prohibition. Under the leadership of Frances Willard, a
powerful stump speaker and inveterate organizer, the WCTU
turned its attention to broader philanthropic work, including the
need to provide custodial care and moral instruction for impoverished criminal youth. Frances Willard used the term "incapables"
to convey her sense of this class of people. Whenever she could,
she visited the most up-to-date prisons and reformatories and encouraged her "white ribbon sisters" to expose the links between alcohol, crime, and violence. When the Kansas WCTU got wind of
the Miller case, it began to deploy its network of local chapters and
publications to stimulate impassioned letters to the Wyoming governor on Charley's behalf.

At the outset, the likelihood of success in the Miller case
seemed good, because Wyoming was a state where women already
had some record of real political participation. Women in the
Wyoming Territory had been granted the vote (as well as the right
to serve on juries) as early as 1869. This revolutionary measure was
approved largely in anticipation of its economic value, not because
of any broad commitment to justice or gender equality. Giving
women the vote was seen as a way to attract attention and bring
more people to the sparsely populated region. Elizabeth Cady
Stanton, one of the most influential leaders of the American
women's rights movement, was so excited by this development in
Wyoming that she called the territory "the first genuine Republic

the world has ever seen." Susan B. Anthony, Stanton's longtime compatriot, urged women to immigrate to Wyoming and make it a model state. Among the nation's pro-suffrage community, the theory was that, when women finally got the vote, politicians who failed to do the right thing would be voted out of office.

Wyoming had the potential, then, for being a demonstration project, a place where women's interests might prevail in shaping public policy. In the summer of 1890, at the festive moment when ten thousand people gathered to celebrate Wyoming's new status as the forty-fourth state, the political potential of women was captured in the ceremonies. A flag handmade by the state's women was presented to the governor on behalf of their gender, and in honor of the unique equality provided in the state constitution; in turn, a copy of that constitution was presented to and accepted by the women of the state. The flag bearer was Therese A. Jenkins; the receiver of the hallowed document, Amalia Post. Both were residents of Cheyenne, and both symbolized the heady optimism felt by the state's women at that point. Jenkins and Post also embodied the ways in which suffrage, temperance, and clemency for Charley Miller would all be fused in Wyoming over the next year.

Therese A. Jenkins was among the first women to join Cheyenne's fledgling WCTU local in 1883, the year when the beloved national leader, Miss Willard, made her first trip to Wyoming. Jenkins was also a pro-suffrage activist, who lectured in thirteen states; and she became the first woman delegate to a national party convention (Republican) in 1892. Jenkins was neither reticent nor demure. She had been trained in oratory side by side with Robert La Follette, the Progressive Wisconsin senator, who was a former classmate and friend. As teenagers, Therese and "Bobbie" attended the same academy in Fayette, Wisconsin, where they participated in weekly public-speaking exercises— known as "Rhetoricals"—which required writing and delivering original speeches as well as performing Shakespearean soliloquies from memory. Jenkins, like many women in her generation, was a "bride of the open range": she left her native region soon after she was educated and headed west in the company of a young husband, James, who eventually became one of Cheyenne's leading shoe merchants. She managed to raise three children, all girls, while she wrote and lectured about temperance and women's rights.

Amalia Post, also a Cheyenne resident, shared Jenkins's political agenda—temperance, suffrage, and eventually clemency for Charley Miller—although she tended to be more of a behind-the-scenes organizer than a stump speaker, using personal connections and a persuasive, genteel manner to obtain access to powerful men. Amalia Post personally begged Wyoming's territorial governor to sign the woman-suffrage bill in 1869; then, in 1871, when the legislature repealed it, Post went directly to Governor Campbell to get him to veto the regressive act. Although Campbell did as she requested, there was an effort afoot to pass over his veto with a two-thirds majority vote. Post quickly sized up the situation and recognized that the override would hinge on one vote. As a result, "with political sagacity equal to that of any man," she courted and cajoled the relevant legislator until he agreed to vote no on behalf of the women of Wyoming. In 1871, she reported on her success before a thrilled audience of five thousand at the National Woman Suffrage Association convention in Washington, D.C. And while her husband, Morton, a successful Cheyenne grocer, served in the U.S. Congress from 1880 to 1884 as a Democrat, Mrs. Post—a Republican—spoke publicly on behalf of her favorite cause, soon becoming vice-president of the National Woman Suffrage Association, Stanton and Anthony's organizational home.

With women like this as their allies, the alert and assertive women of the Kansas WCTU felt there was a decent chance they could save the poor waif who was in jail in Cheyenne. The Kansas woman who activated the 1891 campaign to save him was less well known than Jenkins and Post, and she played no particular role in the history of women in her state. Ohio-born E. Louisa Smith was a fifty-three-year-old mother of three whose husband, Charles, fourteen years her senior, was a retired dry-goods merchant in Garnett, Kansas, a small farming town in Anderson County that experienced an orphan-train distribution in 1885. There was nothing extraordinary about Louisa (as she was known) or, for that matter, the Smith household. At the time she first got wind of the Miller story, her two younger children—Celeste, age eight, and Fred, age four—were attending grammar school, and she was assisted with housework by a hired girl and a hired boy, both local teenagers. Domestic help made it possible for Louisa to attend monthly meetings of the WCTU and also have time to spend a quiet hour with the *Union Signal* and *Our Messenger*, the national and state journals of the temperance cause. When she took pen in hand to express her feelings about the Miller case in the winter of 1891, it was the first time Louisa Smith had ever been involved in politics, so she spoke principally as a mother, empowered by her Christian convictions.

Smith wrote first to Therese Jenkins, someone she did not know but trusted implicitly on the basis of their common WCTU connection. "Dear Sister," she said, "I find your name as [Wyoming] State Reporter for the *Union Signal* and in reading your communications I believe you to be a sister W.C.T.U. willing and ready for every good work for God, Home and Humanity." Louisa Smith went on to explain that, just like Miss Willard, she had a "great interest in poor unfortunate boys, one of whom is in jail in Cheyenne awaiting the time he must die."

Louisa Smith told Therese Jenkins how she felt when she first read reports of Charley Miller's confession in the Kansas papers: "We who have never suffered with cold or hunger can have little idea what an experience like that must be, to be cold, hungry and Homeless. Would it not drive you to the verge of despair? Wouldn't it have a tendency to make the strongest and bravest insane?" The Kansas matron thought the physicians who had testified at the trial were wrong about Charley's mental state: "Why not give this poor unfortunate the benefit of the doubt, as to his sanity at the time the deed was committed? Who can say under oath [that] he was in his right mind when he did the deed?"

Smith's displeasure with the doctors and the trial was unmistakable, as was her sympathy for Charley, who was orphaned so young, about the same age as her own little Fred. "Poor boy," she said of him, "he has never in his life known what it was to be comfortable," but she carefully defined comfort in emotional as well as material terms: "No mother to go to and tell his boyish sorrows, and be comforted as only a mother can comfort her darling boy." And then she broke into the fervent language of evangelical piety, lamenting how this "waif of humanity" was "thrown out into the blustering sea of life with no one to pour oil on the troubled waters. No one to make the places smooth for his feet to tread. No one to build him up and lead him into the Highway of Holiness."

Louisa Smith was sentimental and conventional in her thinking about the power of Christian motherhood, but she was biting in her questions about what good would be gained from carrying out an "inhuman" punishment that was a violation of Christ's teaching. Jesus would "do away with capital punishment," she stated confidently. She asked Therese Jenkins in an astringent tone: "On the morning of the 21st of March would it be an honor to the new state of Wyoming in making history to have it wired around the world that a boy was hanged on the 20th till he was dead, dead, dead?"

Smith and others like her wanted the death sentence commuted to life imprisonment, so that Charley Miller would have an opportunity "to grow spiritually" in an appropriate setting, such as a reformatory. Yet she offered no actual brick-and-mortar alternatives to the gallows. When she spoke about redemption, it was in broad generalities rooted in her familiarity with Scripture. Louisa Smith was quick to remind Therese Jenkins: "In Bible times there was a City of Refuge. We ought to have one here. It is a part of our mission as members of the W.C.T.U. to be merciful and care for the unfortunate." Smith's purpose, however, was not to engage in a discussion of rehabilitation options. Ultimately, she wanted Sister Jenkins to help her organize the good women of Wyoming in a specific way: "I very much desire that Mothers in the W.C.T.U.

who have sons present a petition to your worthy Governor asking him to commute the death sentence of this boy Miller to imprisonment."

Besides her own household and family, Mrs. Smith had never really organized others before, so she awaited a reply from the more experienced Jenkins with great anticipation. Yet, only a few days later, certainly before she had any answer from Cheyenne, the Kansas homemaker took up her pen again, this time in a letter that provided a more organized twelve-point enumeration of the reasons why Charley Miller should be saved. Her points were pithier and less sentimental, because this letter was intended for the desk of Wyoming's governor, and she sensed that she needed to adapt her voice to the larger world of men and politics.

In more confident, succinct language, intended for the ear of a powerful man, Louisa Smith argued first that Charley Miller's death sentence should be commuted because he was a boy, "one of God's most irresponsible creatures." Then she asserted that he was made irresponsible, possibly even insane, by hunger, cold, and homelessness. The situation called for mercy, not retribution, a recommendation that set her up to enumerate all the familiar arguments against capital punishment that were circulating in the 1890s. Capital punishment, she assured the governor, never prevents crime or restores life to the victims; it "hardens the hearts" of those who witness it; and it contradicts the teachings of Jesus Christ.

Louisa Smith also told the governor that there was a woman's point of view on the Miller case that he needed to consider. The points she numbered seven and eight were an observation about the history of her sex in Wyoming coupled with a subtle political threat. Seven read: "Wyoming is a State where Mothers and Sisters of Boys have a voice in the Government." In eight she stated: "I don't think there is a Mother or Sister in Wyoming what would advocate taking a life." Although she had no polling data to support this claim, Louisa Smith was banking on the fact that Wyoming's governor did not want to incur the wrath of pro-clemency women, who had the power to vote against him in Wyoming. In her twelfth point, the fervent author used strategic underlinings for emphasis, displaying her self-righteous side, and also some confusion about the identity of the person to whom she wrote: "If you commute this sentence, you will <u>never regret it</u>. Whereas if you refuse, <u>repentance</u> will profit you <u>nothing</u>. Yourself and your wife (of whom I have read in the *Union Signal*) will be happier, and your sleep will be sweeter on the night of March 20, and as long as you both do live, if you refuse to have the boy executed."

The problem with Mrs. Smith's impassioned letter was that it was addressed to the wrong person. Instead of Amos Barber, the current acting governor of the state, who was a bachelor, Louisa Smith's letter was addressed and sent to John Wesley Hoyt, the third territorial governor of Wyoming, a married man, who was long gone from office, having completed his term in 1882. In the winter of 1891, when Smith wrote her letter, Hoyt had just retired from the presidency of the University of Wyoming, and he and his wife, Elizabeth Orpha Sampson, were probably the state's foremost intellectual pro-suffrage couple. (Elizabeth was also a soldier in the "White Ribbon Army.")

The Hoyts did not need Louisa Smith's disquisition to see the merit in saving the orphan from New York. Hoyt wrote back to her in Kansas to say that he was already on board. Hoyt then forwarded her original letter to Amos Barber, with a note explaining that he thought the appeal for executive clemency was not intended for him, yet he took a moment to add his own plea that the acting governor give the request "careful consideration in view of the extreme youth and apparent moral irresponsibility of the criminal."

A few weeks later, Hoyt conveyed to Barber yet another letter sent to him by the same Mrs. Smith from Garnett, Kansas, who seemed to think that he still maintained considerable influence in Cheyenne. This one was knowingly addressed to "Hon. J. W. Hoyt, Ex-Governor of Wyoming," and it reiterated many of the points made earlier, with one notable exception. This time Louisa

Smith actually suggested that Charley Miller be remitted to the care of the WCTU, although she did not specify a chapter or name an institution willing to supervise the undertaking: "I would say let the boy live, and see what the W.C.T.U. with their plan for building of fallen humanity can do with him." Hoyt once again sent the letter on to Amos Barber, explaining that it would "better fulfill its mission" on the current governor's desk than on his own. And, once again, Hoyt added words in support of the petition: "The author is evidently very earnestly philanthropic and a worthy representative of a host of noble American women." Hoyt, who liked to think that he and his wife were highly evolved thinkers, encouraged Barber to show his intelligence by acknowledging that the human sentiment against the death penalty expressed by so many women was emblematic of "the present advanced age." He did not, however, recommend turning Charley Miller over to the WCTU in Cheyenne, or anywhere else. Hoyt was enough of a realist to know that Miller was a matter for law enforcement, not a bunch of pious women.

By this time, Louisa Smith was not alone in the push to bring Amos Barber around to what many perceived as the women's position on Charley Miller. Although no records exist for the WCTU in Wyoming in this time period, the newspapers provide some evidence that Therese Jenkins may have tried to follow up on Smith's suggestion that the Wyoming organization begin an organized petition drive among the mothers of boys. Soon after the Smith-Jenkins exchange, a small note in the *Cheyenne Daily Sun* suggested that there were some differences among WCTU members in Wyoming about how to respond to the situation of the boy murderer awaiting his fate in the Laramie County Jail. According to L. Annette Northrup, state president, and Mary E. Spoor, president of the Cheyenne chapter, "the members of the Women's Christian Temperance Union are not trying to get Charles Miller released. It is not the object of the society to interfere with justice." Despite this abrupt denial, with its suggestion that women should not meddle in the Miller business, the *Sun* acknowledged that it had already been informed of a WCTU effort to have the boy's sentence commuted to life, an indication that there was some difference of opinion in Cheyenne about how involved women should get in influencing the political decision-making that surrounded issues of crime and punishment.

In Kansas, Charley's adopted state, WCTU activity on his behalf was out in the open. The *Union Signal* reported that, at the Topeka meeting of the State Executive Committee in April 1891, a vote was taken to "petition the Governor of Wyoming to commute the sentence of the boy murderer to imprisonment." The next day, Fanny H. Rastall, Kansas state president, and Sarah H. Thurston, corresponding secretary, sent a letter on Miller's behalf directly to Acting Governor Barber, requesting that "an opportunity be given this child for *reformation*, making it possible for him to grow to manhood capable of doing some good, even though confined by prison bars." The State Executive Committee also appointed Olive Bray, Thurston's fifty-three-year-old, unmarried sister, and a graduate of the Salem (Massachusetts) State Normal School, to follow up on the Miller boy's situation. Although she was given no clear-cut agenda of things to do on his behalf, Olive Bray was a good choice, because she was already knowledgeable about efforts in Kansas and nationwide to cope with the problem of troublesome boys. Bray was a founder of the Waif's Aid Society of Kansas, a collaborative group in Topeka that joined the WCTU, the Young Men's Christian Association, the Ministerial Union, and the Salvation Army in work devoted to the interest of boys in prison as well as wayward and neglected boys on the outside. In 1892, the group finally opened a progressive custodial institution of its own, but it was too late for Charley Miller. The benevolent ideals that motivated this effort were emblazoned prominently on the front page of the Waif's Society's journal, in large print, in a prominent box on the left: "It is not the will of your heavenly father that one of these little ones should perish." On the right: "Under every human skin God has placed a human heart. Go find it."

Most of the letters that crossed Amos Barber's desk came from women like Louisa Smith and Olive Bray, whose deep faith in the ideal of rehabilitation was sustained by their religious faith as well as the ideals of the single-sex benevolent groups to which they belonged. Occasionally, however, there was a passionate voice from an individual who simply felt compelled to say how pained she was at the thought of executing a young boy. An appeal sent by Adelia Conduitte, a matron from Clarke County, Missouri, probably struck the educated governor as incredibly naïve, if not simpleminded. "I feel like if I had all the wealth on earth," Conduitte wrote, "I would gladly give it to be allowed to go and see the poor child and ask him, 'Charley if you could have your freedom once more, wouldn't you be a good boy and never do another wicked thing and have him tell me yes.'" Then she added wistfully: "[When] I tell him that the Governor has reprieved him and see the look of life once more on that poor pale face. No words could express the joy. God alone should know." In the *Cheyenne Daily Sun*, this letter was ridiculed and run under the headline "Oh, My! Oh My! A Tender-Hearted Missourian Wants Miller Turned Loose."

Arguments made in effusive, sentimental language were intended to stimulate sympathy for Miller and evoke religious ideas of mercy, but they often backfired. Many men in Wyoming had little tolerance for the avalanche of gushy empathy generated by women trying to make Charley Miller's case into a moral crusade. In Cheyenne, the advocates of execution made fun of the behavior of local women whose "jail work"—reported proudly in the *Union Signal*—had them distributing temperance pamphlets and singing and praying with prisoners every Sunday. Those who hung around supplying young Miller with special attention and favors were the worst, and they drew scorn in a March 1891 editorial: "A man may be the vilest, lowest wretch alive and all he need to do to become a hero and be presented with choice edibles and fragrant flowers by fair women, is to murder some good citizens, prolong the trial and enlist the sympathies of the ladies."

What these hardliners disliked even more than the sympathy of

Cheyenne wives and daughters, however, was the interference of brazen women from outside Wyoming: "Fortunately, there are not as many female fanatics here as in the effete east—the ones for example sending the letters to Governor Barber and otherwise, dipping into an affair that is none of their business." As they began to understand the intensity and breadth of female interest in Charley Miller, the editors of at least one prominent Wyoming paper drew their guns against the opposition: "The sickly sentimentality of the American women in relation to murders makes us tired." The clear message to women was to bug off and let men handle this one. Although Wyoming seemed progressive on the issue of female participation in politics, there was plenty of opposition when women meddled in arenas such as crime and punishment, still considered a male prerogative.

⋯⋯⋯◆⋯⋯⋯

The cry for clemency actually came from a mixed chorus, although the men arguing for mercy were generally less deferential and sentimental in tone than the women. One of the most powerful pro-clemency arguments to cross Amos Barber's desk came from a distinguished cleric who rejected the idea that the Bible provided support for capital punishment. (In the 1890s, those opposed to capital punishment were usually called "abolitionists"; those in favor "retentionists." The latter found Biblical evidence for their belief in the famous dicta, "An eye for an eye, a tooth for a tooth," and "Who so sheddeth man's blood, by man shall his blood be shed" [Genesis 9:6].)

Within two weeks of Miller's sentencing, Ethelburt Talbot, the Episcopal bishop of Wyoming and Idaho, wrote Barber arguing for life imprisonment rather than death. Writing from Bible House in New York City, the well-known Astor Place establishment that housed a conglomerate of evangelical religious organizations and publishing groups, the visiting bishop took time out of a busy schedule to pressure the young governor, who just happened to be an Episcopalian, one of his own flock.

Talbot probably knew Amos Barber personally, because he had been almost everywhere in Wyoming, traveling by rail, stage-coach, wagon, horse, and foot to stimulate religious organizations and institutions even among the most remote and "uncivilized" people of the territory. Before he was consecrated bishop in Christ Church Cathedral in St. Louis in May 1887, he was for fourteen years rector of St. James Church in Macon, Missouri, and also headmaster of St. James's Military Academy, a school for boys which he founded. By his own admission, Talbot so "cherished" the work of Christian education among boys that he initially de-clined the call to become a bishop when it was offered. Four years later, after he had established his center of operations in Laramie, the plight of Charley Miller in nearby Cheyenne awakened his long interest in issues of rehabilitation in youth, prompting him to offer young Barber advice from an informed spiritual point of view.

The bishop's argument was simple and direct: clemency was the only Christian position in the Miller case. Talbot's hard-hitting letter insinuated that the death penalty was inhuman: "This boy of sixteen—left an orphan—probably mentally imbalanced [sic]—it seems one ought not, in the interests of humanity, to be hung." Al-though the awfulness of Miller's crime was apparent, the bishop was deeply impressed by the mitigating circumstances: "He is a mere child—confessed his crime—has had no such opportunities as would educate his social sense." For this reason, the religious leader urged Barber to be governed in his difficult decision-making by his "highest and best judgement," meaning God's law rather than the legal code of Wyoming. It was the governor's duty, he said, to commute the boy's sentence based on his age, his life circumstances, and Christ's commitment to rehabilitation and re-demption. After offering his opinion as a man of the cloth, Talbot showed that he had a worldlier, strategic side by suggesting that clemency was the smart political position for the governor to take: "I believe the enlightened conscience of the entire state would vin-dicate and sustain you in giving [Miller] a chance to atone for his crime by imprisonment for life."

Barber also heard from men whose power was based in commerce rather than the church. Charley Miller found a surprising champion, for example, in Sidney Dillon, the former president of the Union Pacific Railroad, the line that had been the unwitting host to the boy murderer and his victims. Dillon was nationally known for having taken part in the laying of the ceremonial spikes that marked completion of the transcontinental railroad. At the time he became a supporter of Charley Miller, Dillon was an eighty-year-old widower who had recently resigned from leadership of the Union Pacific after a long career. His enormous fortune, made from investments in partnership with financier Jay Gould as well as railroads, made it possible for him to live comfortably between two lavish homes, one in New York City, the other in Connecticut, where he enjoyed the company of his children and grandchildren. His eldest daughter, Cora (Dillon) Wyckoff, married to a New York City physician, was one of the asylum trustees who petitioned the Wyoming governor for clemency. When Cora told her famous father about the case, the elderly Dillon took it to heart and wrote Amos Barber on his own. (Sidney Dillon never forgot his humble origins, earning wages, at age seven, by carrying water to railroad workers on the lines outside of Albany, New York.)

The railroad magnate argued for clemency on the grounds that deprivation in childhood was an important mitigating circumstance in the Miller boy's case. He asked Barber to acknowledge that Miller showed real "remorse of conscience" when he voluntarily confessed to authorities in Kansas. Dillon urged Barber to give Charley a chance to turn his life around: "In the face of his youth and the pitiful circumstances of his life, I beg to add my petition to those already sent imploring your mercy for this poor boy, and praying you to change the death sentence to imprisonment for life." Except for the letterhead from his Wall Street office, the railroad magnate's letter was remarkably similar to those written by ordinary women, many of whom had no bank accounts at all.

Other male petitioners made a point of distancing themselves from what they called the "sentimental" case for Charley Miller. Instead of arguing for clemency on the basis of life circumstances or religious ideals of mercy, these petitioners sought to impress Amos Barber with the legal and political reasons for overturning the death penalty with a life sentence. The most noteworthy of these appeals came from George Weaver, the Rochester entreprenuer who had "adopted" Carrie Miller. As a result of his involvement with the Lawyers Cooperative Publishing Company, Weaver was familiar with a number of well-known legal writers (whom he published), lawyers (who bought these books), and legislators (who made laws). When he heard about Charley's possible fate, Weaver turned to this professional network, looking for assistance.

One of the men Weaver worked with most closely in Rochester was Robert Desty, an attorney who had already written and edited ten books of law before he came to join the LCPC in 1887. Desty began his career as an expert on California law; later, he expanded his perspective, writing and editing texts on tax and criminal law, laws of commerce and navigation, and even the Constitution. His *Federal Citations: An Alphabetical Table of English and American Cases Cited in the Opinions of the Courts of the United States*, first published in 1875 and then revised in 1878, indexed and annotated over twenty-seven thousand cases. (It also developed a useful legend of thirteen letters that referred users to other cases where the decision was cited.) Desty's *Citations* was regarded as a classic handbook for every lawyer who practiced in the federal courts, and it was rumored to be used "exclusively" by the judges of the United States Supreme Court. Desty's *Compendium of American Criminal Law*, published in 1882, was another famous and highly regarded text used by both defense and prosecuting attorneys. For George Weaver, Desty was an on-the-spot legal expert—he lived close by, and the two shared an office—available to guide him through the arguments that he needed to make in a letter and petition that eventually reached Amos Barber's desk in April 1891.

When Weaver's clemency petition arrived in Wyoming, it was

significant because it had originated with someone respectable who knew the Miller family. But it was even more noteworthy because it was signed by a number of prominent, no-nonsense professional men. The Rochester petition was different from all the others, departing from the usual sympathy arguments. "Nearly every other communication on this subject has been of the sentimental order," the newspapers explained. In contrast: "Mr. Weaver argues the question and cites authorities."

Most people who saw or read the petition understood George Weaver to be an attorney, a mistake that meant that Desty was effective in helping his colleague create an authoritative professional voice. (The embossed letterhead also helped: Weaver was listed officially as treasurer of the Lawyers Cooperative Publishing Company.) The Rochester petition made an appeal for clemency on the grounds of American criminal law—namely, legal arguments drawn from Desty's volume on that subject: "The extreme youth of the boy—being barely past the legally recognized age of criminal responsibility—when he committed the crime together with the circumstances of his life are matters worthy of careful consideration." And: "Some states prohibit capital punishment under seventeen years of age." Although Desty and Weaver knew that boys fourteen and older were often treated like adults in the eyes of the law and therefore subject to the same possible punishments as adults, they wanted to provide the Wyoming governor with a legal pathway around the death sentence. This made good sense, because Wyoming, only a year into statehood, probably hadn't had much experience with minors who committed murder.

Charley Miller was already an adult according to the American criminal code, which was similar to the British. Children under the age of seven were considered incapable of criminal intent, and therefore they could not be convicted of crimes. Children over seven but under fourteen had a presumption in their favor that they did not have criminal intent, although the presumption could be overcome by strong evidence. (The level of evidence varied from state to state, as did the age range: in some states, the age range was ten to fourteen, in others nine to thirteen.) Fourteen, plus or minus one, remained a landmark age that was tied to all kinds of historical and cultural traditions, as well as the physical changes in the body associated with puberty. In England it was the age at which boys could contract for marriage, and in nineteenth-century America it was a popular age for undergoing religious conversion, leaving school, and starting an apprenticeship. At the moment when Charley Miller put his gun to the heads of Emerson and Fishbaugh, he was, inconveniently, fifteen. That made him an adult in matters of criminal responsibility—at least according to prevailing American laws, a decade before the invention of the juvenile court system.

The Rochester petition implied that American law was more humane than it actually was on the issue of the death penalty for minors. In his criminal-law text, Desty noted an 1879 case, *Axe v. Texas*, in which that state prohibited the death penalty for individuals under the age of seventeen, but he provided no other citations to states with similar prohibitions, precisely because they did not exist. He wanted to fight Miller's death sentence on the basis of age, but the summary he provided Barber of the state of affairs in 1890 was not altogether accurate. In fact, according to a historical roster of executions constructed by Victor Streib, a contemporary legal scholar, in the twenty-year period from 1880 to 1900, all of the following states executed youngsters between the ages of fourteen and seventeen: Alabama, Arizona, Arkansas, Delaware, Georgia, Indiana, Kentucky, Louisiana, Maryland, Massachusetts, Minnesota, Mississippi, Missouri, New Jersey, New York, Ohio, South Carolina, Tennessee, and Virginia. Although Weaver and Desty wanted to make it seem that Wyoming was going against the American grain by sentencing a boy this young to death, such an execution was actually in step with much of the nation. In New York State alone, the state Weaver knew best, three boys had been executed within recent memory: a seventeen-year-old was hanged in 1882 for the murder of a domestic servant girl who rejected his sexual advances; and, in 1886 and 1888, two boys, one sixteen and another seventeen, were executed for murders performed in the act of robbery. Both were homeless youngsters, billed as vagrants and tramps, much like Charley Miller, and it was likely that Weaver knew about them, but he and Desty finessed these precedents in the interest of their particular cause.

Still, there were plenty of American men who thought clemency was the right and just thing to do in the case of someone so young, and they lent their names and titles to Weaver's efforts, in the hopes that these would make the petition even more persuasive when it reached Amos Barber. Of the twenty-five cosigners beyond Weaver and Desty, eighteen were "powerbrokers" within the state of New York, men who were heads of major legislative committees. Thomas Raines was a Republican state senator from Rochester who served as a manager of the State Industrial School there, an assignment that probably made him more familiar than most with errant, troubled boys. John Francis Ahearn, born to Irish immigrant parents in New York City, was a Democratic state senator with Tammany connections who chaired the State Banking Committee. Signatories from around the Empire State represented cities other than Rochester, such as New York, Brooklyn, and Syracuse, as well as rural areas, including a number of upstate counties; and they included many lawyers, both Republicans and Democrats, as well as a few temperance men. Weaver apparently did some soliciting in Washington, D.C., where he secured the names of three U.S. senators, all Republicans—Lyman Carey (North Dakota), John B. Allen (Washington), and Nathan Dixon (Rhode Island). And there were two U.S. congressmen from New York, John Raines and Charles Baker; a former chief justice of the Indiana Supreme Court, Charles A. Ray; and a retired U.S. Army general, I. A. Reynolds. Weaver told Amos Barber that it was "only the demands of business on my time that prevented my securing ten fold the names—and as good ones as I have—upon the petition."

Beyond all the eminent names, Weaver made some important points in his cover letter to Amos Barber. At the very start, he told him that he had obtained personal assurance from U.S. Senators Carey and Warren that their governor would take this petition seriously even though neither of them was able to sign it. The reason they gave was that senators should not interfere in this kind of internal decision-making within the state. Weaver also made it clear to Barber that his cosigners were all men whom he knew to be in favor of punishment "as prescribed by law," that none were the kind who regarded the death penalty as a form of "legal murder." Weaver evidently wanted to put some distance between himself and the abolitionists, considered by many in Cheyenne to be a sorry coalition of impractical, wild-eyed social reformers supported by naïve, pious do-gooders, most of whom were women.

Having assured Amos Barber that he and his group were realists and true men of the world, George Weaver put a final, pointed query to the governor that may not have been as welcome as some of his earlier rhetorical attempts to persuade about points of law. "It is urged and perhaps not unreasonably," Weaver explained, "that the young and poorly settled State of Wyoming demands different criminal jurisdiction than Eastern states; still, if this boy ought not to hang in New York State—and I cannot find a single eminent criminal authority who says he ought to or would—would it not be a crime to hang him in Wyoming?" (This was not entirely honest, given that New York State had executed those two young boys within the past five years.)

The suggestion that Wyoming would be backward and barbaric if it hanged Charley Miller was never taken well, regardless of the gender of the person bearing that opinion. The Rochester petition got special attentioin in the Wyoming press because it came from "prominent men" who had more claim to the ear of the public than sentimental women. Yet it was still considered meddling by pro-execution forces, who wanted all the advice and intervention to cease and desist, especially when this came from east of the Mississippi. An editorial in Evanston, Wyoming, implied that Weaver and his ilk were arrogant in the way they made "a strong point of what the people of the East may possibly think about hanging a boy in his seventeenth year." And the parents of Waldo Emerson weighed in again, indicating that they too disliked the Easterners' air of moral superiority. What they wanted from Governor Barber was a guarantee that he would not grant clemency to their son's murderer. To that end, they assured him and the people of Wyoming that the plea of the Honorable G. W. Weaver had "no grounds whatsoever," and they posited that the signers must have been misinformed about the true facts and circumstances surrounding Miller's dastardly deed. If these men had been informed, the Emersons reasoned, they "would not have affixed their signatures to such a petition."

In the spring of 1891, as Frank Taggart prepared to argue the case for a new trial at the Supreme Court level, many in Wyoming saw self-interest in the arguments of outsiders who urged leniency: "The orphan asylum authorities are particularly interested for the reputation of the institution since no boy ever yet sent out from it has been hanged. They seem more concerned about the good name of their kid caravansary than they are about the atrocity of the crime." In Cheyenne, but also in other towns around the state, a segment of the population was irked by the attention the boy was getting, as well as by the idea that the outcome of the case would be a litmus test of Wyoming's stature as a civilized place. They wanted the case to be determined by local people and local sentiments. As the summer passed, the busy governor chose to put the Miller case on the back burner. The sympathy types could send him all the letters and petitions they liked; those in favor of seeing the boy "stretch hemp" could accost him in the street; but until the justices of the Supreme Court decided if the original trial and sentence would hold, there was no reason for Amos Barber to take any action at all.

CHAPTER EIGHT

Acting Out

As Amos Barber waited, so did Charley Miller. With the heat of summer giving way to the crispness of fall, the sixteen-year-old who was the source of all the trouble spent one long day after another eating and entertaining himself at the expense of the taxpayers of Wyoming. By all appearances, Sheriff Kelley and his staff had him under their control, but appearances turned out to be deceptive, and Miller's compliance only a façade. As he lay on his cot, contemplating his drawings and cutouts, Charley must have harbored fantasies of escape.

In late September 1891, without warning—at least from the perspective of his jailers—Charley abandoned his usual pattern of obedience and escaped from the Laramie County Jail. According to reports of the event, William Troy, aka "Curly Cleveland," a vagrant known for petty offenses such as stealing beer, entered the jail early on a Sunday morning with the intention of freeing Frank B. Parkinson, a convicted murderer awaiting transfer to the state penitentiary, where he was supposed to serve twelve years. Parkinson, a corporal in the U.S. 17th Infantry, had killed Roy Barker, a private in his own company, after a disagreement in a brothel the year before. When Curly Cleveland showed up to rescue his friend, the two older men must have felt some sympathy for the convicted boy murderer, because they thought to include him in their breakout. Curly Cleveland apparently called for Charley to leave with him when the moment was right, and Charley did.

The flight into freedom was short-lived. By noon the same day, Charley was found without his companions, ten miles east of

Cheyenne, walking the rails, as if he were heading back to Kansas. The local authorities caught him easily, because he made no effort to conceal his identity and bragged to tramps along the way that he was the famous boy murderer. The escapade seemed to be spontaneous, involving no prior planning or duplicity on his part, but many regarded it as proof that Charley really was incorrigible. The fact that his partners in crime were unseemly, violent men only added to the perception that he was reverting to type.

———◆◆◆———

While the bad taste of this misadventure lingered, the Supreme Court finally, in early October, began to hear Frank Taggart's elaborate multilayered argument on his client's behalf. The appeal laid out twenty-three reasons why the Supreme Court ought to grant Miller a new trial. Many of the points were complaints about the instructions Judge Richard Scott had or had not given to the jury, as well as the lack of evidence presented by the state to sustain murder in the first degree. Other points reiterated familiar ideas about age and life circumstances that were at the heart of the national debate about Charley's fate. Taggart predictably asserted that his client had barely reached the age of criminal responsibility, which meant, he said, that "malice should have been made clear from the evidence and not left for implication." He also developed his own pithy formulation of the environmental argument about Miller's mental state at the time of the double murders: "A mind disordered by hunger is as much insane as if disordered by disease."

As the justices listened and deliberated, they must have realized that the Miller case embodied thorny economic, social, and philosophical questions about the relationship between poverty, crime, and punishment that were at issue throughout the country whenever and wherever a young person turned to violence. Their immediate charge was not to resolve social problems, however; it was to judge the merits of Taggart's claim that Miller had not gotten a fair shake in the courtroom of Judge Richard Scott, and that the jury in the Miller case had been irregular in a number of ways.

In addition to procedural problems in impaneling them, Taggart decried the fact that the jurors were all male. No women sat on either the grand jury or the petit jury, he argued, and that lapse meant that the verdict against his client was rendered in violation of the state constitution. He cited chapter and verse: from section I, article I: "The laws of this state affecting the political rights and privileges of its citizens shall be without distinction of race, color, sex or any circumstances or conditions whatsoever"; from section I, article 6: "Both male and female citizens of this state shall equally enjoy all civil, political, and religious rights and privileges." By suggesting that women, who were electors, must also be jurors, Taggart was calling the Wyoming Supreme Court on the state's unique commitment to sexual equality. If there was another trial, having women on the jury would certainly help, or at least it seemed that way to the defense, given the disproportionate number of female voices raised on the boy's behalf.

As the autumn went on, Chief Justice Herman Groesbeck and Associate Justices Asbury Conaway and Homer Merrell heard and evaluated these and other arguments offered by both the defense and the state. Throughout the proceedings, two of the justices, Groesbeck and Merrell—as well as Charles Potter, the attorney general representing the state—socialized with Amos Barber at the Cheyenne Club, where they all were members. No one in this inner group seemed to be in a hurry to make the decision to carry out the difficult, unpleasant sentence. At first, delay appeared to be in Charley's best interest, because it extended his life, but dragging out the decision-making process also served the state of Wyoming. The older the boy got, the easier it would be to justify his execution, in terms of both existing law and public opinion. In November 1891, Charley turned seventeen, a birthday that received no special attention even though it had threatening legal implications: in most states, a boy of seventeen was subject to the same penalties and punishments as a grown man. Charley also gave the impression of being more manly as time passed, perhaps because of an adolescent growth spurt, and also because reporters talked casually about seeing him smoke or shave in his cell.

Then, on the afternoon of December 31, 1891, almost as if he needed a flamboyant way to ring in the new year, Charley Miller made banner headlines again, this time by busting out of the county jail for a rigorous two-day taste of freedom. The story of the second jail break and Miller's bizarre near-death experience while on the lam dominated the news in Cheyenne for a number of days. Many who were sympathetic about Charley's first flight into freedom lost their patience over the second, because it confirmed that the boy was neither contrite nor honest.

The defense's public-relations disaster began at the start of a festive holiday weekend, at a moment when Sheriff Kelley was out of town on a trip to Omaha. Cheyenne was alive with the prospect of good times on New Year's Eve and New Year's Day. Over the span of twenty-four hours, there were countless private parties where people played whist and charades; an elaborate cotillion organized by the National Guard; and a private leap-year ball sponsored by five of the city's leading ladies, including the wife of Senator Carey. Amos Barber was a guest at that event along with Amelia Kent, the daughter of a wealthy merchant family and a likely prospect to become his wife.

Miller and his companions made their break as the cakes were being decorated and gowns and jewelry selected. Charley left the Laramie County Jail in the company of two older prisoners, William Kingen, a convicted cattle rustler from Nebraska who had already served fourteen months, and Richard Johnson, an African American U.S. Calvary trooper convicted of selling alcohol to Indians. As the deputy sheriff cleared away supper dishes through the unlocked, grated door of the jail, the three prisoners rushed him, pushed him to the floor, and stole his keys, binding his arms and legs with ropes they had stolen and concealed beforehand. Then they returned to their cells, donned as much warm clothing as they could, and headed out into the icy Wyoming winter with a sack of food prepared for the escape.

Everyone agreed that Kingen was "the big game," the brains behind the operation, and that Charley Miller was unlikely to have planned or carried out such an audacious escape on his own. Since Kingen was presumed to have a large number of pals on the outside waiting to assist him, sheriffs throughout the eastern part of the state, near the Nebraska border, were alerted and put on guard. "It is predicted by all who pretend to know anything about the facts in the case that Miller, the semi-idiotic boy murderer, will be picked up and returned," the *Leader* advised within the first twenty-four hours after the jailbreak.

The local paper was prescient, but the story of what actually happened as the threesome made their way north and east toward Hillsdale showed that Charley Miller was far from idiotic. As they fled on foot toward the Nebraska line, the temperature dropped to zero. The fugitives found no allies; their food reserves were gone by the second day. Kingen, once a large and brawny man, was surprisingly weak from his stint in jail and unable to keep up the pace; Johnson, sturdier and determined, drove the three onward. At Archer, a settlement eleven miles from Cheyenne, they stole a horse, but the animal was so old, and so sedate and methodical in his movements, that riding proved no faster than walking. Kingen then devised a plan based on his memory of the area near the Nebraska border. In order to avoid the cold, he proposed that they take cover in a small structure that sat, he recalled, beneath a windmill marking a good well on the Van Tansell ranch. (R. S. Van Tansell was a transplanted New Yorker who just happened to be a close personal friend of Senators Carey and Warren, as well as Governor Barber.) It was an easy landmark, not far from where they were, but in order to reach it, they needed to cross land unmarked by roads or footpaths and avoid walking on the rails, where they might encounter other people. The journey ended abruptly, however, only a mile short of their goal. Kingen collapsed, saying that he could not continue, that he would prefer to be recaptured than to keep up the frantic pace. Johnson urged him on, even threatened him, but then took off on his own, leaving Miller to spend the night on the open prairie with Kingen, who was sinking rapidly.

The convict and the boy murderer slept huddled together, on the ground, using each other's body warmth as protection from the frigid temperature and winds. Both went to sleep easily, because they were exhausted, but Kingen never woke. As the sun rose, Charley Miller realized that the body he was using as a windbreak was stark and stiff. The newspapers later provided all the graphic details: as the result of hypothermia, Kingen's tongue swelled to twice its normal size; his lips, bloodied and rigid, froze in place; and the skin on his face turned purple, almost black, in places. Miller lay side by side with the distasteful corpse, trying to conserve his own energy. A few hours later, employees from the Van Tansell ranch found him, delirious and frostbitten, with a flour sack over his head, nestled in Kingen's rigid armpit. Unable to move independently or sit up, he was loaded into a cart. "You're pretty nearly a goner," his rescuer said, and Charley managed to mutter plaintively: "I wish I was a goner."

At first, the boy's recovery was in doubt. The initial telegram from the Van Tansell ranch said: "Don't think he can live. Gave him stimulants but can't rally him. He don't appear to be frozen, but fatigued." From Leonardville, a telegram from brother Fred indicated that news of the jailbreak had spread, that Fred was worried: "Is my brother Charley dying? Let me know the truth." Despite dehydration and circulation problems in his feet that ultimately resulted in the amputation of some of his toes, Charley was nursed back to health by William Collum, the cook at the Van Tansell ranch, and, later, at the county hospital, where he was cared for by a series of local doctors, some of whom had testified at his trial. In the initial stage of recovery, he slept and drank water incessantly, refusing to say much about his thwarted escape. When he did talk, he told Collum that William Kingen had three hundred dollars in cash, provided by his lawyer, and that Kingen gave five dollars to him for remaining at his side the night he died, and fifty dollars to Johnson for helping with the breakout.

Charley's glib story was transparent from the start. Everyone saw it as a fabrication intended to explain the five dollars the authorities found in the pocket of his stiff, icy pants. Charley had evidently mustered the energy to rifle Kingen's corpse even as he fought to maintain his own life. The authorities also found evidence on Charley that he had planned to disguise himself if he got away. A small bottle of purplish powder capable of turning wet hair black suggested that he hoped to achieve a new identity and a new life. He also carried with him the lyrics to a number of popular songs that he favored, neatly copied out in long hand: "Come all you Texas Rangers, Wherever you may be, I'll tell you of some trouble that's happened unto me." When the newspapers got a crack at these, they said they were all "metrical laudations of criminals, robbers and thugs"—in other words, the musical version of the bold, swashbuckling Western tales and dime novels that Kansas Charley had always adored.

The New Year's Eve breakout had implications for the outcome of Charley's case. Even as he lay recovering from a serious case of hypothermia, he managed to offend with his sickbed requests for high-priced oranges as well as ordinary doughnuts. The escape, and his reaction to being caught, made it apparent that he was not idiotic or simple-minded. Instead, the truth became clear: beneath the veneer of his jailhouse camaraderie there lurked a hostile individual, capable of deception and calculation, anxious to flee, and willing to engage in criminal activity to further his own ends. The second jailbreak suggested that he would continue to be a costly danger to society if he was allowed to live. "Miller is by no means such an idiot as he has been credited with being," advised the *Leader* the day Charley was brought in, "He is criminal in every instinct and possesses a good deal of low-grade cunning." Another editorial the same day proposed that he was "irredeemably bad."

The audacious escapade added to the arsenal of arguments mustered by those who believed that Charley Miller was a bona-fide threat to law and order. Miller would be a "dangerous character in an ordinary jail," advised the *Sun* whenever anyone proposed sending him to the state penitentiary in Laramie with a life sentence. But some people doubted that Miller could be contained even there: he would require a "first class penitentiary surrounded with high stone walls and guards." No one on either side of the controversy wanted to put up with another jailbreak, but it was something that could happen if Miller was given a life sentence. As a result of the New Year's Eve escape, Charley lost some toes, and also the sympathy of many who had once thought he was a law-abiding, decent kid, sorry for what he had done.

The timing of this affair could not have been worse. In mid-February 1892, only six weeks after the highly publicized jailbreak, the Supreme Court of Wyoming refused to grant Taggart's client a new trial and affirmed the action of the lower court and jury. Charley, still fragile from the amputation of his toes, was hauled into court again by Sheriff Kelley, this time to stand before Chief Justice Groesbeck, who told him that "the sentence would be carried out." He then asked the convicted boy murderer if there was anything he had to say, but Charley responded only with a "faint negative," followed by "the same supreme indifference," which was now regarded as his trademark.

After Charley was told to sit down, Associate Justice Conaway proceeded with the judgment, including the critical information about when he could expect to die: "The court now appoints Friday, the 22nd of April, A.D. 1892 for the execution of the sentence." With the date only two months away, Charley and Taggart both had a lot to think about. The legal summaries that followed were boring for Charley and disheartening for his attorney, who had worked so hard, for more than a year, to find a way around the death penalty. From the bench, Taggart heard Conaway (for the entire court) and Groesbeck (concurring) approve all the actions of the lower court and dismiss his hard-fought claim to insanity and jury irregularities. The justices also found the evidence presented by the state compelling—"no jury with any regard for their oaths could have acted otherwise." Chief Justice Groesbeck closed the concurring opinion with these words: "It is a sad case and has been well considered by the court owing to the youth of the plaintiff in error. He was at the age of accountability at the time of his great crime and he must suffer the extreme penalty of the law. The court can not burden the public with the expense of another trial of this case from mere sentiment. There has been no prejudicial error in the case." In the end, the decision in *Miller v. Wyoming* demonstrated that even the highest legal authorities in the state regarded the orphan from New York City as a flawed boy, a belief that made their decision to uphold the trial and sentence much easier. Out of court, a disappointed Taggart finally vented and told a reporter that if Charley Miller was hanged it would be "the most monumental crime that this community ever perpetrated."

≫—◦—≪

The Miller case was now a hot potato in Amos Barber's lap as a result of the Supreme Court decision. On March 22, exactly a month before the scheduled execution date, the *Sun* noted: "Miller, the condemned wretch, is in his cell awaiting the action of the governor or the hangman." On the same day, Barber was seen at the Club, where he was asked if he had reached any conclusion about the case. Like a good politician, he answered with a statement about how busy he was: "No, sir. I have been horse back riding and attending to my several duties. I have come to no conclusion yet." Further questioning revealed that he was under considerable pressure to consider an act of gubernatorial clemency: "I have been waiting for all to have a fair show in their petitioning and after all have been considered carefully by me then I shall when it seems proper, make my decision in the case public."

Barber's indecision only a month before the scheduled hanging made the drama of Charley's situation all the more intriguing and intense. Barber was one focus of journalistic attention; Charley, of course, was another. Since everyone wanted to know how the boy was coping with the prospect of being hanged, newspapers sold briskly whenever there was a tidbit of information about his behavior or emotional state. Only hours after the Supreme Court decision, the *Leader* had a man on the spot, right in the county jail, reporting on Miller's demeanor. As always, Charley was "inclined

to be jocose," appearing to be relatively unperturbed by the idea
that he was going to die: "I am ready to go when the time comes
and I am pretty sure that it will come all right."

Charley's stalwart refusal to admit to any disappointment about
the Supreme Court judgment was betrayed that afternoon, however, by an uncharacteristic rush of words indicating a sense of resentment, a feeling that he was misunderstood. "I never expected
to get a new trial," he told the reporter dismissively. "Ever since I
attempted to escape last September with Parkinson the people
have had it in for me. When I attempted to get away with Kingen
that was the straw that broke their patience. That is what I am told
and that is what I believe. I do not understand how they can blame
me so much for trying to escape. I think the majority of people, if
they had been placed in my stead, would have done the same
thing."

Charley Miller made no effort to appear contrite. To his mind,
escape was a rational choice for someone who faced the prospect of
death by hanging. Given the nature of his reading about the James
boys, escapes were also familiar imaginative terrain, a form of high
drama that he relished. He apparently told one reporter that he
would never cease in his endeavors to gain his liberty. And, a few
weeks later, as the execution came closer, Sheriff Kelley discovered
that Miller was using a razor stolen from the County Hospital to
attempt to carve wooden keys for use in yet another jailbreak. In
the wake of the Supreme Court decision, Charley never attempted
to present himself as a penitent fellow, but he did make a poignant
public admission about his inner terror: "I tell you I do wish that I
had died at the same time Billy Kingen did. If I had then it would
have been over. I would rather have frozen to death than to be
hanged."

Uncertainty about whether Miller would live or die stimulated
newspapers from around the state and region to weigh in with their
opinions. There were pointed editorials from other cities, such as
Denver, Salt Lake City, and even Philadelphia, all reiterating the
familiar arguments for and against clemency, some in passionate

language. From the *Tribune* in Utah's capital: "Most certain it is that the world will lose nothing by the death of young Miller, but the question is, what right has a jury to convict a man of willful murder when every jot of testimony goes to show that the man was just as entirely irresponsible morally as a wild animal? The place for young Miller is in a cell where he would see no one but his keeper, and where he would remain until the law that gave him life intervened to take it away." Commentators at the *Press* in distant Philadelphia countered with an editorial expressing distaste for the growing number of legal cases that made insanity, and its corollary moral irresponsibility, an excuse for crime: "Whether Miller's moral irresponsibility was hereditary or acquired may interest students of criminal problems, but that it should not relieve him from punishment is a canon of good law and common sense that ought to rule in all capital offenses against society. Moral irresponsibility or moral insanity as a successful plea means a practical annulment of all our laws."

In Wyoming, newspapers from around the state tended to be less theoretical and more direct, regardless of their point of view. Miller "should have stretched hemp long ere this," was the word from the *Derrick* in Casper, a town where many believed that the state courts were already too lenient with criminals. On the other hand, the *Evanston Register* railed against the prospect of judicial murder in Cheyenne, arguing that the spectacle of hanging a boy by the neck until he was dead would dishonor the state. The newspaper in Evanston used man-on-the-street polling to demonstrate that public sentiment in their community favored commutation of the death sentence to life imprisonment, largely on the basis of the boy's age. The Evanston respondents, all men, came from different walks of life, and they all repeated the same reason, even though it was incredibly naïve: "I have no knowledge of a person being hung at such an early age"; "I know of no state in which a person has been hung at such an unmature [sic] age"; "I never heard of a person so young as Miller being hung"; "I do not know of a single case where a boy was hung for murder."

With all the controversy and speculation about what was the right thing to do with the boy murderer, Cheyenne's Debating Club decided to hold a formal discussion of the issue on the evening of March 12, about six weeks before the scheduled execution. This meeting lasted well beyond midnight because of the intense interest and emotion provoked by the case. There were two speakers who spoke for the affirmative (the clemency position), two for the negative (the death-penalty position), and three judges. When the formal debate ended, the judges found for the affirmative, and then opened the floor to general discussion. Men (no women attended) spoke for and against the question, and at the end of the evening, a vote was taken of the entire house. The argument was heated, and much of it familiar and predictable, since the community had been preoccupied with the case for over fourteen months.

No one said very much that was new that evening, except for the introduction of the economic argument that was in the minds of many although infrequently stated out loud: Miller's probable life term would be forty years, costing the state over six thousand dollars to maintain him, a sum that made it cost-effective to execute him. Execution was a better option, they said, than vacillating and listening to the "sentimentalists of the east who want [Wyoming] to perpetuate the existence of another Jessie Pomeroy." Despite this frightening reference to the nation's most notorious boy murderer, a sexual psychopath who had terrorized Boston in the 1870s, the team in favor of hanging still lost: the final result was nine in favor of commutation and only five for the death penalty.

As Amos Barber sifted through the different points of view about the Miller case, he must have wondered about the boy in question. To satisfy his own curiosity, he apparently made a visit one Sunday to see Charley in jail, but the conversation there was not recorded by any reporter. Barber's problem was that most of the written appeals for clemency never spoke directly to the practical concerns he faced as a governor. A letter from Esther Weaver, the guardian of Charley's sister, was a notable example. Like those of so many of her supplicating, religious sisters, Esther Weaver's letter asked Barber to think of the boy in the Laramie County Jail as a "poor, hopeless little object," a "child" who was never able to find even "one bright spot." Barber had considerable difficulty thinking of the impudent young man in that way, just as he had difficulty relating to Esther Weaver's appeal to him as a father, which he was not: "Have you dear sir a child of your own? If so could not your love of him speak to your heart asking, pleading that you do what lay in your power to save this poor boy from the horrible fate hanging over him?" This kind of simpering talk made a hardheaded realist feel uncomfortable. Moreover, if he did commute the boy's sentence, his reward, according to Mrs. Weaver, would be in heaven, not on earth, a pious platitude that did little to sway his scientific mind or capture his secular heart. To men like Barber, Mrs. Weaver's point of view seemed like mistaken philanthropy, brushed with naïveté about human nature.

In contrast, a letter from Frank Bond, chief clerk for the Wyoming District of the General Land Office, U.S. Department of the Interior, conveyed the kind of realistic arguments that Barber was inclined to hear, because of its shrewd recommendations and manly tone. Frank Bond had already made his name in Cheyenne as an energetic member of the city's Fire Committee, a designer of municipal improvements for Lake Minnehaha, an important water source; and an inveterate birdwatcher who identified a wide range of native birds. He was also a member of the state's House of Representatives. His boss, whose name adorned the letterhead on the handwritten six-page letter, was William Alford Richards, surveyor general of Wyoming and a prosperous rancher from Red Bank. Both Bond and Richards were good Republicans with an allegiance to the faction of their party headed by Senator Warren. Both were also on their way up: Richards, a Cheyenne Club member, would become governor of Wyoming in 1895; Bond later went to Washington as chair of the United States Geographic Board, an organization responsible for place-naming throughout the nation.

Frank Bond presented Amos Barber with an articulate, hard-hitting statement of the law-and-order position in the Miller case. His argument never relied on the conventional, Old Testament notion that retribution—"an eye for an eye"—was the best punishment for murder. Instead, Bond's starting points were the twin facts that Miller had admitted his guilt and that his trial had been judged fair by the Wyoming Supreme Court. On that basis, Bond offered his opinion about what Amos Barber should do: "I may be wrong in my views of the circumstances under which Executive clemency can properly be extended," he wrote, "but it appears to me that the pardoning power ought not to be considered a privilege granted to an Executive to undo the work of a just tribunal, but if exercised at all, it should be only in those rare cases where, after all the searching inquiry concerning the innocence or guilt of the defendant prior to, during, and even after a fair and impartial trial under the laws of an enlightened nation, grave doubt shall have crept in as to the guilt of the accused." Unless the acting governor thought that Charley Miller was innocent, there was no reason to intervene on his behalf. Miller sealed his own fate with his Manhattan confession, Bond asserted, and though he displayed some "eccentricity of character," he had never been insane, because he had always been able to distinguish right from wrong.

There was a critical local concern, however, that Bond and his boss wanted Amos Barber to remember as he deliberated about granting or denying clemency. If the state of Wyoming failed to deliver retribution in the Miller case, private groups—vigilantes—would do it instead. Bond unhappily evoked a bit of recent history: "In the past the citizens of Wyoming have repeatedly had cause to blush for the good name of their Territory on account of the regularity with which appeals were made to mob law to settle the debt due to loss of a human life. Mob law seemed to have become part of the unwritten law of the Territory." The universal excuse for this behavior, Bond explained, was "either that the courts were unable to visit the proper penalties for capital crimes or were careless in the discharge of their duties." Bond wanted Barber to use the Miller case as an opportunity to demonstrate that Wyoming would no longer be ruled by vigilantism. "Mob violence belongs to past history," he asserted, urging Barber to show that the state had the power necessary to carry out the sentence of its juries, judges, and courts. The "general welfare and good name of Wyoming," he assured Barber, depended upon people understanding and accepting the "majesty and efficacy of the law."

In his travels around the state and in conversations at the Club, Amos Barber had heard this argument before, but Bond's letter laid it all out in a concise, effective manner. Since there was talk that an act of gubernatorial clemency might provoke ruffians to seize the boy and string him up on their own, Barber felt that Bond was offering him wise, preventive counsel—namely, that an execution would serve as a deterrent to the rough justice that had characterized the early settlement of the territory. Barber also knew that the management of the Union Pacific Railroad, a critical player in Wyoming's economy, was anxious to prosecute illegal riders like Charley Miller in order to scare off tramps and assure the public that their cars would be safe.

As a result, Barber made his decision, and the letter he subsequently sent to Charles Miller and Frank Taggart on March 23 was published in the newspapers the following day. The acting governor denied the petition for commutation on the grounds Bond outlined: the boy was a self-confessed killer found guilty of premeditated murder by a fair trial; he was not insane; and he was "much beyond the legal age of accountability." "In view of all the circumstances of this case," Barber explained, "I cannot, without yielding to mere sentimentalism, interfere with the sentence of the court." At this point, some of Charley's supporters still held out hope that Dr. Barber would be responsive to their passionate arguments for saving a young life. In late March, there was no way to foresee that in just a few short weeks the politics of the state would explode, causing their governor's position to solidify rather than soften.

It took Frank Taggart two days to work up the courage to tell Charley Miller that his cause was probably lost and that he had no plans to take the case to a higher court. The boy was told of the governor's decision in the presence of Sheriff Kelley and his deputy, along with a *Sun* reporter who felt no embarrassment intruding on the painful moment. A trembling Taggart gave the boy the actual letter from Barber and then led him through its most salient parts, but Charley never swooned, paled, or even acted upset as he got the drift. "He didn't quail in the shadow of the gallows," a reporter observed; he just "chewed his tobacco at the same speed and held to the bars with the same grip." To Taggart's surprise, when Charley was asked if he was satisfied with the decision, he responded in a surprisingly upbeat way: "Yes. I guess it's all right. I'm not afraid of hanging and if I went to the pen there wouldn't be any chance to get out."

Since the boy's spiritual state was a concern at a time like this, Sheriff Kelley asked him if he believed in the hereafter. Charley responded: "Well, these preachers have told me there was [a hereafter]. I have been taught lately that there was punishment and a heaven." (The "lately" was a reference to the local clerics and WCTU ladies who had been visiting him every few days since the Supreme Court decision.) The boy also said that he thought he "might" go to heaven if he did what was right—namely, "reading the Bible and believing in it, and some praying and [getting] others to pray for you." When one of the men suggested caustically that Charley had started his "training for heaven rather late in the day," the boy countered by saying that being hanged would be punishment enough to get him into heaven. "Then I'll be alright in the hereafter, if there is a hereafter," he quipped. In the tension of the moment, Charley also made a sly, mischievous suggestion to the group that he still had a "great mystery" left to tell, words that shook Taggart to his boots, causing him to ask anxiously if Charley was taking back his confession or suggesting an accomplice, either of which would have major legal implications at this point. But when Charley was pressed to explain himself, he backed off, saying he would tell it all on the scaffold. And then he turned his attention to his fellow inmates, whom he wanted to impress with his astounding news and the official, signed letter from the governor.

Taggart did agree to participate in a second clemency appeal to Governor Barber; local citizens began to canvas for signatures on

Miller's behalf. By late March, a sense of urgency had developed about the gruesome event that had been only hypothetical until now. In order to devise an effective way to hang the boy, the authorities engaged J. P. Julian, a Cheyenne architect, who was well known for his design of the First Methodist Church, commercial buildings in Omaha, and also the Wyoming state capitol. The instrument of death, a unique new "self-killing" system, would be built by local carpenters according to Julian's design, and housed within the interior yard of the Laramie County Courthouse. This strategy was intended to keep the execution from turning into a large public spectacle, something considered distasteful to an increasing number of Americans as the nineteenth century ebbed. By the 1890s, even retentionists thought that a modern execution ought to be swift, painless, and "aesthetic," meaning without observable blood and gore.

Amos Barber let other people worry about the mechanical details of how Miller would be hanged, although it was a surefire subject of conversation whenever Cheyennites got together. By late March, everyone knew that planks of wood for the scaffold were being delivered to the courthouse, and people could hear the noise of energetic hammering inside. Sheriff Kelley made the event all the more real when he told a local reporter that he already had in hand a "regular hangman's twine, tested and with the knot made," borrowed from a sheriff in Illinois. In case of an accident—usually a failed attempt at the drop, something that was not uncommon in hangings—he had another half-inch-wide piece of hemp as a backup. But Kelley would not actually do the deed himself. According to Julian's masterful killing scheme, after Sheriff Kelley put the noose around the boy's neck, Charley would step onto one panel of a divided trapdoor and thereby set in motion a shifting balance of water and weights that would jerk away the support beneath his feet. Death was supposed to come instantly, in a refined manner, and the gallery looking on would be small. It would be the first legal hanging in Cheyenne in fifteen years, a historic event, marking both the inception of innovative gallows technology and also the newly-flexed muscle of a fledgling state.

CHAPTER NINE

A Stormy April

J ACK LONDON noted that Cheyenne had never been a hospitable town for tramps, but in April 1892 concerns about vagrancy and violence escalated as winter ebbed and the prairie took on more color. On the hills surrounding the town, wild purple crocuses and gray-green sagebrush waited to bloom, and the air was scented with the aroma of vivid green pines aroused by the new warmth of the earth. It was a particularly early spring, but the signs of the new season were not completely reassuring. As the cold subsided and opportunities for outdoor work expanded, the Wyoming capital was vexed by a "tramp nuisance," a perception that did little to help Charley Miller as Amos Barber deliberated his fate.

Tramps had been arriving in large numbers for the past few weeks, and the language used by the local press to describe the seasonal phenomenon was anything but welcoming: "The city has been infested with a horde of loafers who have no visible means of support, and whose very presence is a menace to respectability in any community." Allegedly, these vagrants and hoboes were unwilling to work and earn their daily bread—a narrative that evoked the image of Charley Miller, working the back doors, making his way ominously into Wyoming: "Instead of going to someone and asking to shovel coal or do some sort of chores, these gentry flock in crowds and impudently enter the court house, the capitol, the stores, offices, anywhere in fact, that they wish and ask for money on the plea of starvation." These men were a "nuisance of the worst sort" and the local police were encouraged to "remedy the evil" by arresting them and putting them to work.

Charley Miller was an unmistakable reminder that vagrancy was laced with danger. The familiar story of the "double blood letting" in the boxcar was still vivid enough to shape the way many people in Cheyenne reacted to the dozens of homeless men who arrived in town that April, looking for handouts but also for legitimate work. Some actually thought that hanging Miller would be a sensible deterrent to the crime wave alleged to follow from the influx of tramps. E. J. Pasmore, a "Professor of Music" who conducted a local percussion band, tried to counter that notion in a letter to the local press: "There is no epidemic of homicide in our midst that calls for, as an example, the terrible exhibition of the gibbet." The migration of homeless, unemployed men that April did nothing to improve the lot of the orphan boy who had once been a member of the tramping fraternity. On the contrary, it helped make him an easy target for all the anger and resentment that anxiety about crime inevitably breeds.

⟫══──══⟪

As Cheyenne prepared itself for the landmark hanging of the boy murderer on April 22, the town's attention was diverted northward by a different kind of violence, in the Powder River region, the north-central section of the state, due east of Yellowstone and west of Sundance. The Powder River was the "river of roundups," 486 miles of stream and tributaries running eastward down out of the Big Horns and extending into a huge section of grazing land rich with sagebrush. It was land where cattle was king, and where large and small stockgrowers had been engaged for a long time in what one Laramie editor called an "irrepressible conflict." An outbreak of armed violence there (known as the Johnson County War), combined with local anxiety about vagrancy and tensions over the fate of Charley Miller, made April 1892 a tumultuous moment in the history of the new state.

On April 5, a special train composed of six cars left the Cheyenne depot for Casper, the best point of access into the Powder River region. The train carried an array of bellicose passengers: nineteen Wyoming cattlemen (including the owners and managers of some of the largest ranches in the Powder River region); five stockyard detectives; and twenty-two hired gunfighters from Texas who arrived in Cheyenne earlier in the day aboard a Pullman car with its shades pulled down. Although the train and its purpose were supposed to be secret, there were two newspapermen on board who expected to cover the coming action, as well as a physician who went along to treat those who might be wounded. The doctor was Charles Bingham Penrose, Amos Barber's old friend from medical school and the Cheyenne Club. According to Penrose: "Governor Barber knew all about the expedition and he advised me to go on it."

Although Amos Barber gave lip service to the ideal of law and order, he did nothing to stop this illegal initiative, which involved marching a private army through a peaceful area of the state to shoot, hang, and burn all those who stood in opposition to the cattle coterie and its economic interests. The cattle barons who were behind the rash plan believed that their armed invasion was an appropriate response to the problem of the small ranchers, too many of whom, they believed, stole their cows and got away with it. According to Dr. Penrose, the "regulators" knew exactly who among the "rustlers" they wanted to kill, and they intended to target these men unmercifully, along with their property and their families. The focus of their aggression was Johnson County and its small cattlemen, many of whom were former cowboys who had homesteaded successfully and acquired small herds.

Barber was not the only state official who looked the other way as the regulators planned their hit list for the unauthorized foray into Johnson County. Railroad managers surely knew about the train bound for Casper, which was carrying horses, wagons, and a cadre of armed men along with an unusually large supply of munitions, but no one had the courage to call a halt to the well-funded operation. Union Pacific officials supplied six cars with full understanding of the travelers' intentions. The National Guard also co-operated. Usually in cases of civil disturbance, Wyoming law provided that local sheriffs could call out the National Guard if the legislature or the governor did not. But in late March, just weeks before the invasion began, Adjutant General Frank Stitzer of the Wyoming National Guard issued an edict that changed the rules. Now, he told his company commanders, the guard could only be deployed if there were orders directly from his headquarters. Since Stitzer reported to Amos Barber, this meant that the National Guard was virtually immobilized, paving the way for the invasion forces. Nearly two weeks later, after it was clear that the situation in Johnson County was tantamount to war, the sheriff there tried to call out the local guard in order to stop the invaders, but the effort failed because of Stitzer's new order.

A vast number of Wyoming's first citizens, especially wealthy cattlemen, were enmeshed in planning this flagrant act of vigilantism. According to Dr. Penrose, even Willis Van Devanter, a former chief justice of the Wyoming Supreme Court and later associate justice of the United States Supreme Court, gave the expedition tacit support: Van Devanter gave Penrose a telegraphic code so that he could communicate with him personally as the adventure developed. John Clay, president of the Wyoming Stockgrowers Association at the time, did not approve the invasion, but he knew exactly who was involved. He confirmed later that men at the highest level in the state and federal government knew about the undertaking beforehand, and sanctioned it, either by lending concrete support or by remaining silent. The invaders, he said candidly, "were backed by every large cattleman in the state," and they also had behind them "the moral influence of two senators, Warren and Carey." This revelation meant that the two most powerful men in the state, both United States senators, were in cahoots with the regulators, as was their younger friend and supporter, Acting Governor Amos Barber.

As a result of their long-standing loyalties to the cattle barons, the triumvirate of Barber, Carey, and Warren was chagrined to learn that the invasion army was surrounded, outnumbered, and in jeopardy within a week of its departure. After brutally killing two suspected rustlers and burning down a cabin at a ranch near Kaycee, the vigilantes headed north, toward Buffalo, stopping along the way to care for their horses at friendly ranches. As they neared Buffalo, they were advised that a large counterforce was advancing their way, news that drove them back to another sympathetic ranch, where they expected to hunker down temporarily. (This was the TA Ranch, owned by Dr. William Harris, a supporter of the invasion.) By the morning of April 11, however, the invaders at the TA were threatened by almost two hundred well-armed men, and a bloodbath loomed. When Amos Barber learned about this state of affairs a day later, he immediately wired the President of the United States, fellow Republican Benjamin Harrison, telling him that an "insurrection" existed in Johnson County against the government of the state, an interpretation that was deceptive, if not a lie. "Open hostilities exist and large bodies of armed men are engaged in battle," he reported, before asking the nation's chief executive to call out United States Army troops at nearby Fort McKinney to suppress the insurrection. Senators Carey and Warren allegedly rushed to the White House and roused the President from his bed in order to add their fervent support to Barber's recommendation for a rescue with federal troops. Without this kind of help, both senators knew it was likely that many of their friends would be wiped out.

By April 13, nine days before Charley Miller was scheduled to die on Cheyenne's adept new gallows, U.S. Army troops intervened in Wyoming so that no one else was killed. The invaders were led off to Fort McKinney to be protected from angry citizens who thought they should answer for the murders of the two men at the TA Ranch. Everywhere in the state and across the nation, the Johnson County War made headlines, stimulating discussion about who was in the right—the cattle barons who sought to establish some law and order in a region where cow theft tended to go unpunished, or the smaller ranchers who stood up to the invaders and demanded that the cattle coterie pay for their arrogant violation of law. Powerful interests in the state made sure that the invaders were handled with kid gloves. Their trial, for example, was moved from Laramie to Cheyenne, because sympathy for the regulators was strongest in the state capital; and two trappers who saw the ugly events at the TA Ranch were conveniently escorted out of the state, to the east, so they would not supply damaging information for the prosecution when the trial began that summer. Judge Richard Scott, the same person who sentenced Charley Miller to death, eventually dismissed charges against all the invaders, on the grounds that Johnson County had failed to pay the bill for their keep while in jail and for the wages of the men who guarded them. The dismissal meant that the hired guns from Texas went home, but only after a celebration with plenty of champagne.

As the people of Wyoming dealt with the news of this belligerent assertion of cattle power, their governor had to decide the fate of Charley Miller, scheduled to hang in less than ten days. Although most people probably did not see the two events as related, the Johnson County War made Amos Barber all the more committed to denying clemency, so that he would appear to be a stalwart law-and-order supporter. "Appear" is the key word, since Barber was deeply enmeshed in the whole unseemly affair, and his personal allegiance was to the regulators, vigilantes who took the law into their own hands. In April 1892, he needed some cover for his involvement with the invasion, so it seemed only logical to take a stand in the Miller case that would convince people that he was a solid supporter of the state's formal justice system, someone detached and capable of standing above the passions that drove Wyoming's irrepressible conflict. Executing Charley Miller was a convenient way to make this point. There was little likelihood Barber would change course now, because his reputation depended on how he acted in the wake of the paramilitary blunder along the Powder River.

⟨⟨⟩⟩

As talk of the gibbet and "the drop" intensified, Frank Taggart made one last-ditch effort to forestall his client's imminent walk to the scaffold. On April 12, he took pen in hand to write to John

Emerson, Waldo's father, to ask him to embrace Miller's cause now that hanging was near. It was a fruitless, naïve appeal, surprising for someone who had observed the Emersons in court and read their earlier angry attack on his client. "I feel assured that you will not favor the execution of Miller," Taggart said, and then he urged the victim's father to join him in the movement for commutation: "Will you not express yourself in a brief letter to me, or to the *Sun*, or some other paper here?" Taggart posited that the parents had undergone some softening, a change of heart, but John Emerson's response, written four days later, was a hard, insulting rebuke: "Mr. Taggart, I do favor the execution of such a cold blooded murderer and thief, who not only murdered his sleeping victims but robs his dead. I have no use for sympathetic cranks who uphold criminals." Taggart's effort to enlist the victim's parents was inept, and he was probably not pleased when both letters ended up in the newspaper (at John Emerson's request, not his). All Taggart could do now was make a personal face-to-face appeal to the acting governor. And he could continue to visit Charley, along with his wife, Lula, someone the boy always seemed to enjoy.

A week later, on April 19, George Weaver made his final attempt to influence the situation in Cheyenne. In a letter written for publication in the local newspapers, Charley's advocate in Rochester offered his rationale for commutation based on ideas about community and how it should function. These ideas were drawn, in part, from the work of Washington Gladden, a proponent of what came to be called the "Social Gospel." "Our whole body politic—our entire entirety as a community," Weaver explained, "is made up of individuals, each one of whom is obligated to the whole. Likewise the whole body owes a certain, and in these days a reasonably defined debt to each individual." In the case of Charley Miller, Weaver felt that American society was a passive party to the heinous crime: "The community ha[s] never fulfilled its obligations [to Charley Miller] in any degree."

Weaver's message was hard for the people of Cheyenne to accept, particularly at a moment when their fears were raised by the presence of so many drifters and outsiders for whom they felt no particular responsibility. Weaver suggested that, in addition to the well-known inadequacies of Miller's early life, all Americans bore some responsibility for the boy murderer's distorted view of himself, what we call today "self-image." As if he were a modern clinician, Weaver explained that Miller was trying to be a "frontier hero," a fantasy stimulated by his "morbid" taste for dime novels and other forms of readily available, lurid literature such as the crime papers. In the mind of Carrie Miller's guardian, American society, and its lawmakers in particular, bore responsibility for allowing racy, sensational material to get into the hands of the young. "Is not this class of reading authorized simply by its sufferance?" he asked. Weaver's final recommendation was congruent with his political theory: confine Charley Miller in an insane asylum, a reformatory, or a penitentiary as punishment, but also as "a protection to the community, which actively he has outraged and passively at least [he] has been wronged by."

Anxious to avoid any sentimentality, Weaver made no mention in his letter of the absent Miller family. There was no information on how Charley's sister, Carrie, felt about the impending execution of her younger brother; and he gave no suggestion that he or anyone else would make the trip westward to be at the boy's side when he approached the gallows. Nor was there any further plea from the Loofbourrows in Kansas. Although Fred Miller was certainly mature enough to travel to Cheyenne on his own, he stayed at home in Leonardville, avoiding any public role. All he did was send a studio picture of himself, as a way of saying that he cared but that he would not come.

≈◆≈

Frenetic petitioning became the order of the day in the final week of Charley's life. Many citizens still believed that it was possible to get enough signatures to convince Governor Barber that he would insult the will of the people if he allowed the execution to proceed. As a result, the clemency constituency eagerly passed petitions in the streets and parlors of the city, sometimes to the annoyance of those who wanted no part of any effort to save the boy. "The only petition I will sign concerning Miller would be one to have him hanged, if possible, a little earlier than has been designated," T. Joe Fisher, deputy treasurer for Laramie County, told a solicitor who asked for his signature. The circulating petition homed in on three pithy arguments: Charley Miller's life should be spared because of the "demoralizing and unfavorable surroundings" of his childhood and youth, his age at the time of the crime, and the fact that he had been his "own accuser."

There was no easy way to categorize the pro-clemency community. It included such well-known local figures as ex-Governor George W. Baxter, a planner and backer of the recent Johnson County War; Roman Catholic Bishop Maurice Burke, leader of the see of Cheyenne; Dr. W. W. Crook, the longtime Cheyenne medical man who had been a witness at the boy's trial; and E. A. Slack, the editor of the *Sun*, the local newspaper most sympathetic to his situation. There were also ordinary folks among the signatories, prompting Slack to editorialize that "nearly every working-man in the city who has had an opportunity gladly signed the petition." In the interest of making it seem that commutation was the will of the masses, the *Sun* posited that the drive to commute came from people "who can appreciate the struggles of those who are thrown in early life upon their own resources." Charley was one of their own, Slack implied, and they did not want to see him punished so cruelly.

In reality, there were signatories from all walks of life—skilled laborers as well as professionals and wealthy businessmen—but a notable absence of Protestant clergymen. Only the Reverend A. G. Lane and Reverend George S. Rocker, from the Presbyterian and Congregationalist churches, lent their moral authority to the drive for commutation. Cheyenne had at least seven other Protestant denominations, some with multiple churches in town, but no clergy from the Baptist, Episcopal, Lutheran, Methodist, or Methodist Episcopal denominations signed the pro-clemency petitions that April. Ten days before the execution, a clemency advocate by the name of D. C. Bridges called on all the ministers of the city, asking for their support, but his success was "not flattering," by his own admission. With the exception of Bishop Burke and Father Carmody, a parish priest who regularly visited Charley in jail, Bridges felt that the local clergy had not yet moved beyond "the old doctrine of an eye for an eye." It is "singular," he told the newspapers, that "all the Protestant preachers of this city should favor hanging the boy, or at least are not opposed to it."

One reason for their passivity may have been that, as Charley Miller anticipated death, it seemed likely that he would approach the scaffold and the Lord with a Catholic priest, not a Protestant pastor, ministering to his soul. Despite his Lutheran roots, Charley's turn to the spiritual would take the form of a last-minute conversion to Catholicism, something that many Protestants found abhorrent. It was also possible that certain congregations were so deeply split over the issue of life or death for Miller that their pastors saw no reason to exacerbate tensions by taking sides in the heated controversy. A more cynical explanation suggests that Protestant clerics were silent because they realized that the state's wealthiest and most powerful men, some of them members of their congregations, agreed that Charley Miller should be hanged, especially after the debacle in Johnson County.

Cheyenne women stood alongside men in the final effort to sway the governor. Although there were still some hidebound traditionalists who found this kind of political activity "unwomanly," approximately one-third of the published names were those of women, drawn from a variety of Protestant denominations, and linked to husbands and fathers engaged in a wide range of trades, businesses, and professions. Some of the female signers were predictable and already associated with social causes that led them to take on public roles, but even these women—such as suffragist Amalia Post and WCTU President Ellen Lee Bristol—identified themselves as "Mrs. M. E. Post" and "Mrs. S. A. Bristol" in a nod to middle-class convention and propriety. Careful scrutiny of the female signers reveals, however, some surprising fault lines within Cheyenne families. Bessie Potter, the talented organist at the Congregational church (rumored to have had the only pipe organ in the Wyoming Territory), was willing to offer her name on Charley Miller's behalf even though her husband, Attorney General C. N. Potter, presented the case for the state in Miller's unsuccessful attempt to win a new trial. Likewise, Harriet Richards, a Baptist who sang in her church choir, differed from her husband, W. A. Richards, the state surveyor general, who supported Frank Bond in winning over the governor with their strategic arguments against clemency.

By April 21, the list of names on the clemency petition had grown to six hundred, stimulating a countereffort by those who wanted to see Charley hang. Although the names of those in favor of execution were never published because time was so short, the six men who carried the counter petition claimed that within two hours they had one hundred signatures in hand, causing them to stop to make more copies for people to sign. The counter petition said: "We the following taxpayers and residents of the City of Cheyenne, do earnestly petition your excellency to let the law take its course, and thereby permit Charles Miller to hang tomorrow at 11 o'clock."

The chief spokesmen for hanging were Charles M. Smith and G. R. Palmer, both employees of the Warren Mercantile Company, a large and lucrative firm dealing in furniture, carpets, pianos, and coffins, founded and owned by Senator Warren. Smith and Palmer appear to have been the senator's mouthpiece on the Miller issue, and they were quick to tell the newspapers that they had little use for the sentimentalists who wanted to save the vicious boy tramp. As the clock ticked, those who wanted to see Miller hang boasted that they had acquired five hundred signatures, but there was also talk from their quarter of less peaceful means of expression, some rough justice, if events did not unfold the way they wanted. One man told editor Slack that any citizen who dared to petition for clemency should be "tarred and feathered", another allegedly threatened to lead a mob to lynch Charley if the hanging did not take place.

Declarations of this kind confirmed Barber's decision to be firm and let the sentence stand, even as pleas for commutation kept coming at him. Alice Downs Clark, wife of U.S. Congressman Clarence Don Clark, wrote Barber hurriedly on her husband's letterhead from the nation's capital begging him to see that the situation required "mercy rather than justice," the rhetorical formula espoused by so many women and pious men. And Chief Justice Herman Groesbeck, who had denied Miller a new trial, admitted to the newspapers two days before the execution: "If I were governor I would commute the sentence of Charles Miller. My grounds would be his youth and handicap through life. He is a waif and a vagabond. If he was a wealthy boy who had been educated my position would be different. It would be merciful and just to spare his life." A man of humble background who campaigned for the Socialists in later years, Groesbeck understood that Miller's story made a valuable point about the handicaps and privileges of social class in America. But hypothetical messages about mercy and social class were unconvincing to a chief executive besieged by more practical issues of state governance. For the women of Wyoming, there was a terrible irony in what was about to happen to Charley Miller: although they had the vote and should have been able to bring their influence to bear, the politics of men and violence clearly prevailed.

—————◆—————

Two days before the execution, Amos Barber still had the power to commute, although there were no indications that he would change course. On April 20, Sheriff Kelley sent out gilt-edged invitations to the unpleasant event that he was likely to supervise. (Deputy Wilkes would be in charge of the actual "strangulation"—that is, holding the rope.) The invitation asked people by name "to be present at the execution of Charles Miller" and stated the date, place, and hour: April 22, A.D. 1892, 11 A.M., at the court-house. Charley had actually begun to extend his own invitations somewhat earlier; he was entitled to six. The first, a handwritten note, went out to Ed Towse, a sympathetic *Sun* reporter: "As you have treated me fairly during my various troubles, I invite you to witness my execution April 22, 1892. It will be by hanging and at the courthouse in this city. Yours truly, Charles E. Miller." Another went to a local fellow named Harter, who hung around the jail and gave him a dozen doughnuts in exchange for a gallows-side seat. Whether Charley sent invitations to family in Kansas and Rochester remains a mystery.

On April 21, a day after the sheriff dispersed the gruesome invi-tations, Amos Barber agreed to a noon meeting with representa-tives of the commutation movement—Bishop Burke, ex-Governor Baxter, Frank Taggart, and others—who brought their impressive petitions. However, Barber also received the counter petition, "not so numerously signed," he admitted, but compelling all the same. Later in the afternoon, he may have considered an alternative plan laid out in a letter from an unidentified citizen and published in the local press. It proposed that Taggart and Attorney General Potter sign an agreement ensuring that if the sentence was commuted Charles Miller would "never request a pardon" at the hands of any other governor. It was a compromise that might have satisfied those who preferred the death penalty to jail because they feared Miller could be released to threaten the community and kill again. Barber seemed to be deliberating seriously, but the suggested com-promise, if it was ever entertained, must have been discarded, be-cause it was never mentioned again. Still later that day, the acting governor announced to the press that he would make a final pro-nouncement the next morning, a development that left everyone on edge, including Charley Miller.

Sheriff Kelley dealt with the uncertainty of the situation by test-ing the new gallows one more time. His staff gave Charley a fitting for the straps that would pinion his arms and legs; the thick hemp rope used for strangulation was treated carefully with melted can-dle wax so that it would work efficiently. Simulations of the anticipated event were also performed by placing on the deathtrap blocks of wood equal to Charley's weight. After calculating the time and the height of the drop, Kelley gave the newspapers his projection that it would take Charley Miller between forty and sixty seconds to die, if they really had to do it the next day.

The following morning, at eight o'clock, Cheyenne learned that the hanging would go forward. In a month already marked by unprecedented violence, the execution seemed almost fitting. In the letter written to explain his second and final denial of clemency, Amos Barber virtually repeated what he had said in March: Charles Miller had had a fair trial before an "impartial jury and a learned judge," and their combined judgment was affirmed by the highest court in the state. As acting governor, he felt no compulsion to do anything to disturb the present situation, especially when a hanging seemed to be a deterrent to even more violence. A local using only the name "Justica" applauded Barber's decision: "I think we should sustain our judges and jurymen in their hard duty, unless we wish to lapse into more violence again."

Timing is everything, they say, and Charley's experience reinforced that old adage. If he had committed his crime just minutes earlier, in Nebraska rather than Wyoming, the outcome might have been quite different. And if, in the eleventh hour, when he most needed mercy and understanding, the Johnson County War had not intruded, the Wyoming governor might have been able to see his way through the morass of sentiment and anger in the state to effect a compromise that would preserve the boy's life but also impose severe, consistent punishment. But at that moment in 1892, with the state in agitation and uproar, it seemed to Barber and a number of other men at the highest echelons of the state and federal government that Miller was more valuable dead, as a symbol of order and restraint, than as a lifer in the penitentiary at Laramie. It was time, they thought, to carry out the execution of the human maverick who had wandered into the state and caused so much trouble. For reasons peculiar to Wyoming that April, Charley's fate was sealed.

CHAPTER TEN

"I Can Die Game"

SAMUEL JOHNSON once wrote: "When a man knows he is to be hanged it concentrates his mind wonderfully." In the last weeks and days of his life, Charley Miller did exactly that. As regulators and invaders faced off with their guns, Charley underwent a life review driven by the local reporters who hounded him for interviews, and by an inner need to tell his own story. As the awful day approached, he was more talkative then ever before. "He talks not a little of the approaching event," was how the *Leader* described the way in which his tongue was loosened by anxiety.

In addition to chummy conversations and smokes with local newspapermen, Charley authored a final narrative account of his life, penned a number of sentimental poems and songs, and developed an inventory of his possessions with clear directions about how these meager goods should be distributed after his death. This "estate," along with his spoken and written words, captured the essence of a lonely young man caught between his ideal of bravery and the wash of fear and sentiment that overcame him as he contemplated his own mortality.

Because his time was so short, Charley's keepers indulged him: "He is fed upon restaurant fare now, is provided with a plentiful supply of cigarettes and every reasonable request is granted." Reportedly, he spent most of his time playing his harmonica, although he was interrupted nearly every day by curious people who wanted to talk to him. Before doing so, he usually asked for cigarettes, doughnuts, or two bits in return for conversation. But, as cagey as he was about obtaining payment first, he was also generous about giving it away. When he realized that "it was getting pretty close now" and he would have no use for money, he gave more than two dollars to an inmate who was being discharged, and provided another handful of coins for Richard Johnson, his surviving accomplice from the New Year's Eve breakout, who had also been recaptured. On April 20, two days before the execution, Sheriff Kelley announced that there would be no more visitors and sightseers, but he never restricted the access of the town's two leading dailies, whose reporters were at Miller's side right up until the end.

Stories of Charley Miller's behavior on death row showed that his bravery in the face of death sometimes slid into foolish bravado, and that his anger at the people who had wronged him was still keenly felt. When all was said and done, he remained remarkably consistent about one thing: he did not understand, and could not find the words to explain, the sudden, brutal acts of violence that had brought him to national attention. Yet in his final days he showed that he was not amoral. In fact, he had a coherent value system and a set of loyalties that he tried to honor, as best he could, given his circumstances and the time he had left to live. In the last hour, he acted conventionally, doing what he thought he should do in order to get himself ready to die. In effect, he "got religion," and though his understanding of Christian faith was never more than rudimentary, it was clear that he wanted to die properly. He said this, in a raw, inelegant way, the day before he was hanged: "I feel [now] that my sins are forgiven in heaven, and that I can die game."

——◆——

Charley always said that he wanted to die bravely. That was a goal he had set for himself based on the stories he had heard and read about cowboy heroes, outlaws, and Civil War soldiers. Although he was frightened by the thought of strangulation and wanted assurances from Sheriff Kelley that it would not hurt, he maintained the appearance of being calm and collected most of the time. The reporters noted that he continued to keep himself nicely—"Miller looked as fresh yesterday as a newly blown daisy"—and that he received visitors with a handshake and a smile. At the end of March, he told the press that he was quite certain that he could maintain a "stiff upper lip until the end." According to Kansas Charley's code of ethics, appearing manly was an important part of acting "game" in the business of dying.

Facing death without fear or tears is a hard assignment for anyone, but for a seventeen-year-old, alone in the world, the situation was an extraordinary emotional challenge, leading to displays of bravado that were tragic and comic at the same time. Within the society of the jailhouse, Charley was unusual. He was literate, whereas many others weren't; he could read for enjoyment and also sing and compose songs. The music he played on his harmonica helped pass the time for bored inmates, and the sheriff and the deputies found his poetry, however awkward and contrived, a better form of entertainment than most of the crude stuff they heard from the more run-of-the mill criminals in their care. As a result of the receptive audience he had in jail, and those farewell soliloquies he had seen on the stage in Rochester or read in books, Charley got the grandiose idea that he should perform his own work on the scaffold.

He told the reporters who made him their beat that he was writing something special for the occasion, and on the night before he died, he allowed the press to see his versification, noting proudly that he had composed it entirely by himself. His final lament was a poem in four stanzas, probably intended to be sung. Though the rhymes were forced and sometimes redundant, it was structured, sequenced, and punctuated in much the same way as thousands of other undistinguished poems written by amateur poets in late-nineteenth-century America. Miller's life since the murder was his muse, his voice that of someone who had been wronged:

> *1.*
> The jury found me guilty
> Judge Scott to me did say,
> I sentence you to hang, Miller,

March 20th the day.
I took my case to a higher court,
There I met the same fate,
Refuse me a new trial
And fixed the execution date.

2.
It's fixed for the 22nd of April,
In the year 1892,
And expect it to take place
'Less the governor carried me through.
But that he will not hardly do
Because I am a boy
And not very hard to manage
But hard to destroy.

3.
Remember this life, e're so young,
Is soon to fade away,
Fade where at last it has been hung,
April the 22nd day.
My life in the world is not long,
It hangs only by a thread,
Soon forever I'll be gone
When to the gallows I'll be led.

4.
My blood in life will soon cease.
When Kelley leads me to my doom
Then forever they will release
Me, when I meet my doom.
I had a four days' trial,
Which seemed to me so long,
But time now is precious,
I'll end my dear old song.

Charley's plaintive swan song managed to convey the solemnity of the situation as well as the author's sense of foreboding. Its language revealed, not surprisingly, that he was preoccupied with dates—the death date he had escaped as well as the one he was about to face in just a few days. More than once he mentioned April 22; and more than once he used the term "fixed" and the expression "my doom." Yet there was a glimmer of youthful defiance in his sad lament. Although he realized that Governor Barber would probably never pardon him because of his age, he took pride in the fact that the state of Wyoming had had to delay his execution for more than a year. "Not very hard to manage / But hard to destroy" was Charley's elegy to his own tenacity.

As the execution approached, Cheyenne wondered if Charley Miller would actually have the audacity to sing and play his mouth organ on the scaffold. He was the kind of kid who liked to tell a big story and make flamboyant claims. And in his final days, he bragged about the escapes he attempted, his special legacy, he thought, to those who succeeded him in the Laramie County Jail. In a poem written especially for Sheriff Kelley, Charley warned:

> Do not think when I am gone,
> Jail breaking will stop its all;
> As soon as I have this world left
> It will commence again in the fall.

Charley's poetic swagger was a relatively mild provocation compared with the way he defamed the Bible by scribbling bawdy rhymes within the inside cover. He was at home with cussing and lewd street jargon, and he was not averse to using them both when the mood struck him. (In public statements to the press, however, he could be deliberately decorous, even pompous.) By scribbling indecent ditties in the Scriptures, Charley knew that he would shock and offend the pious women and clergy who came to call on him in order to pray with him and save his soul. It was a perverse, defiant act, unfriendly to many who supported him, but it was followed by something even more outrageous.

Charley Miller wanted a woman before he died. Using his

hand was no longer enough. Given his age, the length of his confinement, and the amount of time he had spent in jail with adult men who talked about sexual exploits with women, his assertion of manhood should have been no surprise. A boy with Miller's credentials was unlikely to be chaste; and everyone knew that Cheyenne had flourishing brothels, with women and girls available for a price. But Sheriff Kelley would have no part in making a match between this particular prisoner and a whore. A single line in the newspaper on April 17 signaled that Charley's adolescent libido had not been extinguished by his impending doom: "Miller made one request to the Sheriff yesterday which cannot be printed in a newspaper, but under the circumstances [it] is very ludicrous." Providing the boy with doughnuts and restaurant food was one thing; procuring a prostitute was another. On death row, even a sympathetic sheriff could not satisfy a randy boy.

<hr/>

Despite these willful displays of bravado, Charley Miller realized that he needed to do some quick moral accounting before April 22. As a result, he issued a final statement to the *Sun*, the paper he favored, on April 19. He told his personal story in a lengthy chronological narrative that was familiar to anyone who had read accounts of the crime and trial, but this time the story was entirely in his own words, with his emphasis. Authored in part to garner public sympathy, this final autobiography also fulfilled Charley's desire to speak "the truth." He wanted to set the record straight on a number of issues, including his motivation for the crime, and the kind of person he really was. To do this, he reviewed his life and generated a list of what he thought he had done wrong, as if the act of "settling up" would improve his lot with God and the people of Wyoming.

But it was hard for Charley to hold a clear mirror to his life, because there were so many old hurts. In his final accounting, his resentments were packaged tightly, and he still made enuresis—not sexual abuse—the primary misfortune of his early life. Although it was an embarrassing subject, Charley did not let it drop: "During the seven years, I was in the home I had a complaint," he explained, "[and] medicine did me no good." This complaint, as we know, followed him to the Babcocks', the Booths', and the Robinsons', causing upsetting hygienic problems, social ostracism, and, in the Booths' case, violence. "I got a slashing [there] every morning," he reiterated, "I thought sometimes that would kill me." As he pieced this sad quilt together, hardship, duress, and misunderstanding were the dominant patterns.

In the interest of appearing contrite, Miller conceded that he had done a few things wrong. He lied, for example, under oath about his birthday. (In court he said that he was born in September 1875, although he was actually born in November 1874—a fabrication intended to make him appear younger so that he could avoid adult responsibility for his crime.) Two other dishonest acts were aired now as well. The first was stealing the valise from the Colts in Kansas, a story he told with lingering bitterness. The Kansas couple failed to provide him with the clothes he needed, even though they worked him very hard. And when he left their home, with a suitcase worth "a dollar at most," they made an awfully big fuss. Even now, he assured everyone, Mrs. Loofbourrow would substantiate his side of the story: "I can prove [by her] that I never got as much as a pair of stockings while there." In short, Miller felt that the Colts deserved what they got: ".'I do not feel sorry about the valise, because they did not treat me right." Charley claimed that stealing the valise was the only robbery he had ever committed outside of taking pennies from Minnie Robinson, but his behavior in this instance was rationalized as well: "It was a case of necessity. I could have taken three good sized cups full of money when I was leaving." (Charley never mentioned the pocket watches that he stole from the Pohls.)

When he finally mentioned the murders, Charley admitted for the first time that his own behavior had driven him to despair, at least momentarily. "When we got to Hillsdale, I began to think what I had done and was going to throw myself under the train." But with that quick admission, he rewired the anger he still felt for

Albert Stewart, who, he continued to say, betrayed him by saying that robbery was the motive for the crime: "He sent me a copy of his paper giving what I said, and it came out that I said that I killed them for their money. I would say that I never told anybody that I killed those men for their money." Still searching for a motive, Charley blamed alcohol, claiming that he was inebriated at the moment he murdered the boys from St. Joe. There was a bottle in that boxcar filled with at least an inch and a half of "licker," and he now claimed that he drank it all: "I commenced feeling pretty good and [then I] felt dizzy. It made me pretty drunk." But he told the entire story without a dollop of contrition for the lives he had snuffed out in his intoxicated state.

Charley Miller then made a showy pronouncement about the kind of person he believed himself to be: "It is a known fact that where people have treated me good they have <u>received in return the same</u> [underlining added]." This restatement of the Golden Rule was an attempt to articulate his theory of reciprocity based on his life in the asylum, as a foster child, and on the tramp. Miller had had very little control over his own life, and he was buffeted about by all kinds of forces—the death of his parents, the needs of the strangers to whom he was assigned, the desires of men he met on the road, even the weather. In order to survive, he reacted rather than initiated, waiting to see what others' intentions might be. If they were decent, he tried to respond in kind—at least that is what he wanted people to remember about the philosophy of Kansas Charley.

Sadly, when Miller reviewed his life there were very few people he could cite who treated him "good," and most of these were women. He said of his mother: "She was pale and sickly and I don't remember much about her, only she was good to me." There was the unnamed schoolteacher in Chatfield who took pity and saved him from early-morning beatings at the Booths'; and there was Minnie Robinson, who, he claimed, told him before he robbed her: "Remember, Charley, if you ever need a home again this one is always open to you." Charley's connections to other human beings were minimal and shallow. People like Preston

Loofbourrow were memorable because they helped him out, not because he knew them well or cared for them in any deep sense.

Fred, Carrie, and Willie were the only people Charley Miller was attached to. The reporters noted that he "prize[d] very highly," and was quick to display, the up-to-date studio photograph he had of his older brother, Fred. He also had a picture of Carrie, probably carried with him since his Rochester days. In his final accounting, Charley's emotional need for his siblings was unmistakable: "If my brothers were here in my lonely cell tonight and sister Carrie, I would tell them that if it had not been for that whiskey, I never would have done such a wild thing. I would ask [them] to pray that God would forgive me, and that we could see mother in heaven." These were, of course, conventional sentimental pieties picked up from the religious folks who wanted to convert him, but the longing he felt for Carrie, his surrogate mother, was authentic and deeply troubling to him.

As execution day approached, Charley Miller could neither accept nor understand his siblings' nonappearance, and he struggled to explain it to himself. "I would like to see Carrie before I die," he said plaintively, "but I am afraid she could never stand it." The idea that his sister was too sensitive to see him hanged was a convenient explanation rooted in traditional Victorian notions about gender and femininity. (Women were too weak, it was alleged, to stomach the sight of an execution.) Charley also came up with a rationale that was a tragic form of self-deception, given that his sister still lived in the home of George Weaver, who had been following the case closely. "If Carrie knew I was to be hung she would come," he posited. What Charley did not say aloud was the most hurtful of all: in the search for middle-class respectability, Carrie, Fred, and Willie all seemed to be abandoning their stray brother to his fate, since there was nothing much that any of them could do to change things. For Charley, this probably felt remarkably familiar, something like the time when his mother had left them, so many years ago in New York. On the evening of April 21, as he played cards with Deputy Sharpless, the *Sun* reporter noticed that Charley looked listless and pale, while the fellow from the *Leader* said he had a haggard, hunted stare. All plans seemed to be off to versify and entertain on the scaffold.

———⊱•⊰———

On April 22, Charley woke early, about 6:20 A.M., without knowing for sure if this would be his execution day. By seven, a reporter from the *Leader* appeared to see him, so he quickly changed out of his nightclothes in order to meet with the fellow and answer his query: "How did you sleep last night?" His response to this kind of journalistic prod was a model of composure and also understatement. "First rate. Thank you," Charley replied. Then he spoke of his wager with Deputy Sharpless the night before, and added the kind of details the press wanted to hear: "Not a dream nor a beastly nightmare appeared to me in my slumbers, and my rest was natural and refreshing. I needed it all too, for I have now, and have had all the time, a presentiment that today will be a trying one for me."

The next hour confirmed Charley's "presentiment." He tried to eat from a special basket of breakfast sent over from the nearby Capital restaurant, but after poking at his eggs, he gave up: his usual appetite was gone. The reporter who observed his distress offered him an early-morning cigar, which he accepted with thanks, and the two smoked and talked about what might happen next. At nine o'clock, Father McCormack arrived, one of the two priests who had been visiting him since his sentencing in the hopes of tending to his spiritual needs. (McCormack was a visiting priest, probably one of a number of Capuchins from Ireland who were active in the area.) When the deputy admitted him to Miller's cell, he asked explicitly if the priest wanted to be alone with the boy, but Father McCormack said no, it was fine for the reporter to remain. Then, in "kindly but unmistakable words," he told Charley Miller that Governor Barber had refused him clemency again and that he was destined to die in just two hours.

Charley Miller never sobbed, cried out in anger, or even struggled to keep back his tears, according to the journalist in attendance. In this terrifying moment of certainty, he resorted to what he did best: acting the part of the tough guy, unmoved and invincible.

"Is that so," he responded impassively without a tremor or twitch of any kind. The priest then let it be known why he was there, and why he wanted a reporter in attendance: "Now, Charley, your fate is sealed, what do you want me to advise you in regard to the new life you will soon enter? I want you, without any compulsion or suggestions, to state that. Do you desire to die a Catholic or not?" Miller replied calmly and deliberately, as if he had prepared ahead of time: "For the last two days I have given up all hope of living, and of course I have studied about the great hereafter and religion. I desire to embrace the Catholic faith, and to be baptized and meet my doom as a Catholic."

Back in March, the people of Cheyenne had learned from the press that Miller had been "taking some interest in religion." At that point, Father McCormack began to visit him more regularly. Charley's situation understandably prompted thoughts about death and its meaning, and he seemed to want answers that would work for him quickly. His choice of faith bemused the Cheyenne community, however, even though Bishop Burke, Father McCormack, and Father Carmody were prominent leaders in the effort to help him, both in this world and the next. Miller was especially fond of the two priests, and in the last week of his life he wrote a poem for Father Carmody in which he conceived of himself as a "troublesome rolling stone," prepared to exit this life for a better one:

> God in His image made this world alone
> In which children always fret and moan
> Where happiness throughout is never known
> Nothing but the troublesome rolling stone.
> God made the other world beyond to adorn,
> Where children will not fret nor moan;
> Where nothing but happiness throughout will reign
> No trifling sorrows or no pain.

On the surface, Charley Miller's new piety was admirable, although most of the people in Cheyenne would have preferred to see him die a Protestant instead of a Catholic. In an era when

Catholics were still feared and demonized for their ritual practices, Charley's last-minute conversion to "Popery" and the Church of Rome was a slap in the face to the many evangelical Protestants who had been working for commutation of his sentence. If Charley was naïve about the social costs of becoming a convert to Catholicism, his priest was not. The savvy Father McCormack expected to be accused of forcing his faith on a vulnerable boy, so he made sure that the *Leader* reporter made the conversion discussion very public. Before ten o'clock, Father McCormack had prepared Charley for death by propounding the catechism and administering baptismal rites.

Slightly after 10 A.M., the Taggarts arrived, a development that seemed to buoy Charley up and also heighten his emotion. There were now seven people in his "support group," including Sheriff Kelley and a reporter from the *Sun*. The boy who was the center of attention took a moment to express his gratitude to his attorney, but when he tried to do the same with Taggart's wife, it finally drove him to tears. As he sobbed, he told Lula Taggart that he "did not know there were such good women" as she, an utterance that embodied all of his sadness about the mother he had lost as well as the sister who was not at his side. Lula Taggart was sufficiently moved to offer to walk to the scaffold with Charley, but the men in the room dissuaded her in favor of Father McCormack.

As the clock ticked unrelentingly to the fateful hour, Father McCormack and Lula Taggart adopted various tactics to divert the boy's attention from the impending event. One matter still left to resolve was his clothing, something Charley always cared about a great deal. For the occasion he was provided with a pair of new shoes, a dark-blue woolen shirt, a black tie, and a cutaway suit jacket, creating a "somber costume" which he seemed to like. Sometime before Sheriff Kelley left to supervise the apparatus, Charley announced to everyone in the room that he would neither sing nor speak on the scaffold, as if he needed to assure them that he intended to die decorously, by the rules, causing them no further embarrassment. Taggart, perplexed to the end by his client's inability to provide a convincing explanation of his crime, asked if there was anything he wanted to say or add to his confession, and at first Miller said no. But then he added that he was "sorry," a reaction that prompted a final interrogation from his attorney: "So why did you kill those boys?" Miller replied now with discernible anguish, but the answer was the same: "I don't know. When I saw what I had done it all seemed like a dream to me. I have tried to give reasons to myself and to [you] and to other friends, but I can't tell." To the end, Charley Miller did not understand why he had exploded so violently in the Union Pacific boxcar.

A few minutes after eleven, Sheriff Kelley gave the word to get ready, prompting a hard set of goodbyes to the Taggarts and his newspaper friends. The boy listened now to every word that Father McCormack said, and he repeated what the priest told him as best he could. As the two waited in the cell for the call to proceed into the hanging theater, guests for the event passed through a corridor that Charley could see quite plainly. For a moment, he thought that someone might appear with a pardon; but that hope faded when the heavy iron door swung shut, announcing that everyone was in place, except for him.

There were approximately sixty people in the gallery, most of them sheriffs from other Wyoming or Utah jurisdictions who had come to see the state's first legal execution, but also some business and "sporting" types who had inveigled an invitation. In the gallery was T. Jeff Carr, the infamous buster of tramps, now a deputy U.S. marshall; Dr. W. N. Hunt, from the County Hospital, who would inspect the corpse afterward; and the few local people whom Charley had invited. Outside, more than a thousand people milled around the courthouse; a group sat high up on top of Castle Dare, a turreted stone mansion, in order to get a view of the special platform within the courthouse next door; and a number of daredevils shimmied up telephone poles for a peek into the protected courtyard that Miller now entered.

When Sheriff Kelley arrived to take him to the scaffold, Charley figured he might be able to get a stiff drink to dull his senses. Kelley responded with a firm "no," but allowed the boy a few extra minutes with Father McCormack before leading them both outside, followed by the two deputies, who were trailed by Frank Taggart. Charley Miller walked arm in arm with Father Mc-Cormack to the platform, repeating "God have mercy on me" and "Jesus save me," in an audible, unquivering voice. He had a cruci-fix firmly clasped in his hands, and he concentrated fiercely, evi-dently trying not to be undone by the baleful sight of the noose. As the leather straps were fixed around his body, Charley and the priest continued to pray together, but the boy moaned occasionally and sighed repeatedly, as if he were hyperventilating. When Sher-iff Kelley asked Charley if he had anything final to say, he re-sponded: "Only, God have mercy on me. Please be quick."

Father McCormack then stepped away, and Sheriff Kelley led the boy forward to the edge of the fatal trap, where the actual hang-man, Deputy W. J. Wilkes, would work the hemp. The noose was placed over his head and adjusted so that the knot was located di-rectly in back of his left ear. Charley continued his mantra—"God have mercy on me. Jesus save me"—but he stopped suddenly to ask whether he should move to the right or the middle. Kelley calmly told him to remain where he was, and then placed a heavy black hood over his head and face. Now that he was in darkness, Charley's knees began to twitch, as if he was about to collapse. Through all of this, there was an ominous silence. And then a fa-miliar voice came from underneath the cap. "You are choking me a little," the boy complained, as if Kelley should have known better. The sheriff took some conciliatory steps toward him—"What's that, Charley?" he asked kindly—and he loosened the uncomfort-able noose, knowing full well, of course, that Cheyenne's new ma-chinery would do the job anyway. "All right now," Charley muttered, followed by "God have mercy on me," and then the si-lence was shattered, this time by the sound of rushing water from the tank and the clatter and bang of the trap's wooden doors falling inward, as they opened up to receive the pinioned and hooded body of young Charley Miller.

According to the press, Miller's body descended into that

opening with "frightening velocity." He weighed less than 120 pounds, so it took just short of a minute—fifty-eight and a half seconds, to be exact—to empty the water buckets that held the weights jerking away the sturdy upright underneath the trap. Miller dropped straight down—a distance of nearly six feet—and his neck was broken almost immediately. In death, Charley finally cooperated, by "stretching hemp" the way the simulations predicted.

Although the sight of the hanging body caused some to leave the gallery in a hurry and others to turn away, most of the viewers remained, observing to one another that it had gone well because it was quick, and there were no disturbing physical effects such as vomit or twitching arms and legs. Yet, as Charley's body was cut down off the rope, someone stuck his head into the courtyard to announce: "Kelley, there's a man here who wants to skin him." Kelley ordered the fellow away sharply, but the barbaric request lingered in the minds of many who heard it. When the body was removed from the rope, scientific medicine took over from law enforcement. Dr. Hunt, with stethoscope in hand, certified that at seven minutes after the drop Miller had no pulse; at ten minutes his heart slowed to only a "minimal flutter." Thirteen minutes later, at exactly eleven-forty, Charles Miller was pronounced dead. Even the *Sun*, the paper opposed to execution, said it was a job well done: "The machine worked to a nicety and Sheriff Kelley was highly complimented on his artistic job. Miller went to his death bravely. To his own natural fortitude there was added religious comfort to buoy him up in the trying ordeal."

⟫⟪

In the aftermath of the execution, some people wondered if Charley had left a will—perhaps with a story of what had really happened between the boys in the boxcar—but one was never found. Instead, he left behind in his cell a collection of small bundles, each labeled with the name of a beneficiary. Although the Wild West turned out to be his undoing, life in the Laramie

County Jail provided him with a final opportunity to make friends in a way he never had before. In a small community of jailers and inmates, where his youth, his music, and his strange talk made him the center of attention, Charley at last established a surrogate family, whom he chose to honor with his meager belongings.

There was a bundle for Sheriff Kelley, even though he had led Charley to his death. Miller's relationship to the man who controlled his daily life for eighteen months was a complex mix of antagonism and respect, not unlike many father-son relationships, something Charley had never experienced. In Miller's eyes, everybody had his job to do: his own was to escape, Kelley's was to make sure he did not, and though that struggle kept them at arm's length, they had moments of rapprochement, usually around doughnuts, checkers, and riddles. Except for the business of bringing in a girl, Kelley treated the rough New York City kid sympathetically, ensuring that he had plentiful meals and cigarettes in his last weeks, as well as time alone, away from the worst of the celebrity hounds. In the final poem he wrote for Kelley, Charley included this verse as a means of explaining why he always seemed so tough:

> You talk of my being cold-hearted,
> Or something of that kind;
> "What's the use of crying,"
> I always bear in mind.

In addition to the autograph book filled with his poetry, Charley left Kelley his favorite harmonica, the one he used to entertain himself and others in the jail that became his final home.

To Deputy Wilkes, the man who worked the rope at his execution, Miller left his other mouth organ, and the equipment he had hoarded for another big escape: his wooden key, a nail from a horseshoe, and a shank cutter, a sharp cobbler's tool used to make files. To Deputy Griffith, who walked behind him onto the scaffold, Miller willed a silver ring "acquired" along the way, a clothes

brush, and another narrative poem about his life. To O. B. Sharpless, the sympathetic "death watch" who kept him occupied with
cards and wagers on the last night of his life, Charley left his cup—
decorated with the motto "Home Sweet Home"—along with Governor Barber's letter refusing commutation. Charley's Bible,
replete with its indecent inscriptions, went to inmate Ben Bainum,
along with a small hand-mirror, something Charley liked having
around so he could see the soft down on his face turn into a coarser
beard. A deck of cards went to another inmate. And, finally, to Ed
Towse, the sympathetic ear at the *Sun*, Charley willed his most
sentimental possessions: a book, a valentine (signature unknown),
and the photographs he carried and cherished of brother Fred and
sister Carrie. (Unfortunately, none of these photographs or any of
Miller's "estate" has survived.)

Charley Miller's estate was insignificant in monetary terms, but
it had enormous emotional value to the boy who put those bundles
together on the night before he died. He sent nothing to Fred,
Willie, or Carrie—perhaps because the silence of his siblings was
by then so deafening that he could not figure out how to respond.
In the end, Charley honored the connections he had made in
Cheyenne, and his behavior toward these men was generous and
accepting, especially since he would die at their hands. Miller was
a boy for whom ownership and material things were a special luxury, making his decision to parse out his meager possessions a deliberate, self-conscious act of friendship.

The day after Charley Miller's death, newspapers in Cheyenne
sold like hotcakes because they were filled with so many pithy details about the execution as well as the boy's life, the crime, and his
trial. According to the *Sun*, "many subscribers complained" that
their newspapers were stolen on April 23, so high was the demand
for copies. For the first time, drawings of Charley Miller, "the boy
murderer," appeared not just in Cheyenne, but in a number of
cities across the nation—New York, Chicago, Denver, and San
Francisco. The *Leader* sensed that the case was historic and told its
readers why: "The criminal history of America discloses no parallel

case to that of Charley Miller, and he will go on record as one of the most remarkable specimens of humanity ever brought to public notice." Readers in New York City saw high drama in the boy's grim biography: "The life of Charles Miller, short yet fruitful in adventure furnishes a striking illustration that truth is sometimes stranger than fiction. It is a unique and thrilling story, one which in a novel would be considered distorted and exaggerated."

In Cheyenne, some felt that the "ends of justice" had been served by the execution; others did not because of the nagging issue that the person the state had killed was so young, so poor, so pathetic. Though "Kansas Charley" was undoubtedly a difficult character filled with resentment and hostility, as well as a touch of guile, the notion that he was "uncivilized" and unworthy of redemption was ultimately contradicted by his experience in Cheyenne. Charles Miller committed a terrible, callous act of violence, but he was not the brute that he was so often made out to be. In fact, in the eighteen months he spent in the Laramie County Jail, he proved himself to be no menace at all. Although he made a few desperate efforts to flee, he never acted violently, or even aggressively, toward any inmate or jailer. By his own admission, Charley Miller was a "troublesome rolling stone," but he was not innately vicious, as the law-and-order community had constantly asserted in the campaign to make the boy seem too dangerous to live, or even to be rehabilitated.

In New York City, there was a curious last-minute development in terms of Charley Miller's estate. On the morning before the execution, at the Western Union telegraph office at Fifth Avenue and 23rd Street, an agitated George Holz wrote out this message— "Give these few dollars to Charley and tell him goodbye." Then Holz handed that paper to a clerk and indicated that it needed to go immediately to Cheyenne, Wyoming, along with eighteen dollars in cash. The clerk behind the counter asked Holz why he was in such a hurry, and the old man replied: "The boy is to be hanged tomorrow and I want him to have a new suit of clothes to be buried in." Holz was the person Charley had visited in New York City, looking for help, after he left Rochester. He was also the mysterious guardian Charley had mentioned at his trial, and he actually did have a small residue of cash for the boy left by his parents. Holz told the fascinated young women who worked in the telegraph office that he owed "the boy murderer" money, but when he was asked to cough up another $1.10 to pay for sending the message along with the money, he was unwilling to do so. "Never mind the message. Just send the money. They will know who it comes from," he said. With that, Holz crumpled up his earlier dispatch and left the office.

In Cheyenne, it was never clear if Sheriff Kelley received the money for Charley before he was hanged. If it did arrive in time, it probably would have been mentioned as the boy talked with the Taggarts, but it never was. In all likelihood, the boy went to his death without knowing that there was enough money from his family to bury him in a suit of his own, not a hand-me-down. Eighteen dollars might be a spare inheritance, but it showed that Frederick Muller had had some concern for his progeny, something Charley might have liked to know. On April 24, Karl Muller—aka Kansas Charley—was buried at taxpayers' expense in Cheyenne's potter's field, an area designated for the remains of the indigent poor.

Although the *Leader* thought that Miller's hanging would do more "to discourage mob law than any event which [had] ever happened in Wyoming," not everyone was so certain about its deterrent effect. For Sheriff Kelley, the days after the execution were so difficult that he had to leave for Denver for a respite, in order to escape questioning about the awful events of April 22. When he returned, he left law enforcement entirely, went back to his grocery business, and was elected a year later to the Wyoming state legislature. Frank and Lula Taggart moved to Denver by the end of the year so that he could build a more lucrative legal practice (he became a judge), and they could expand their family (three children survived into adulthood). Lula later became involved with the National Congress of Mothers. Fred Miller, always reliable and well-liked, received a gold watch from the people of Leonardville on the occasion of his twentieth birthday, but he died five years later in the Spanish-American War, as did his younger brother, Willie. Carrie Miller, who dreaded the announcement in the Rochester newspapers of her brother's execution—Charley was explicitly identified as "the boy who worked some years ago in the *Union and Advertiser* printing office"—remained unmarried, supporting herself as a seamstress, the role for which she was prepared by the New York Orphan Asylum. She died in 1931 from pernicious anemia, a disease of the poor. Amos Barber, the one person who could have changed the end of the story, was married by Christmas 1892. His new wife was Amelia Kent, the daughter of a local banker and Cheyenne Club member whose name was never associated with any of the sentimental folderol or legal excuse-making generated by the troublesome boy tramp.

Wyoming continued to have its fair share of violent crime, but it never again executed a boy Charley Miller's age. Although Sheriff Kelley probably had a great deal to remember and say about his young charge, he granted no interviews and wrote no memoir about his personal experience with the boy murderer. Neither did Frank or Lula Taggart. This particular boy—and this particular case—had exhausted everybody, ending in a way that no one felt easy about. In the wake of a grim episode that laid bare the nation's incapacity for balancing justice with mercy, silence seemed to be the best policy. If, as the years passed, no one talked about it, then no one would remember. And that was the way it was, until now.

Afterword

I N DEATH as in life, Charley Miller only got attention as the "boy murderer." Today, that term sounds archaic, even though the phenomenon clearly persists. In the years since I began this book, homicide by adolescent boys has become familiar enough that it no longer seems unusual; instead, we are strangely inured to it. And yet, every once in a while, a particularly vicious crime captures our attention, most recently the case of Lee Boyd (John) Malvo, the seventeen-year-old accused of murder in the horrific killing spree that terrorized the Washington, D.C., area in October 2002. Malvo, much like Charley, is not a sympathetic figure. But his age and his apparently doglike devotion to John Allen Muhammed, the violent man who acted as his surrogate father, suggests that we think seriously again about the question of criminal culpability in adolescence, and whether or not "the boy sniper" should be treated in the same way as an adult one.

My point is not to compare Charley Miller to John Lee Malvo, although there may well be some similarities between them. (Malvo, for example, renamed himself, as Charley did, but not like a fictional character in a book; he called himself "John" in imitation of John Muhammed.) As a biographer, but also as a citizen, I realized that I needed to come to grips with the psychology of my subject, in this case an impecunious, taciturn boy from the nineteenth century who was noticed only because of the vicious crime he committed. Charley evokes some compassion because his life was so short, pitiful, and emotionally barren, but his brutality in the

Union Pacific boxcar also makes him difficult to embrace emotionally. Still, there was something about him—his early deprivations,
the impudent adolescent voice, the occasional flash of tender-
ness—that moved me sufficiently so that I spent a number of years
in his company trying to understand him.

One need not be a psychologist to see that Charley Miller was
poorly socialized, that a series of early losses made it difficult for
him to establish trust and human connection. Even though his
basic material needs were addressed by his asylum caretakers, he
never had much security, or the kind of unconditional love that en-
courages emotional growth and development, or the ability to em-
pathize with others. Chronic bedwetting late into adolescence was
a conspicuous sign of his mental distress. In contemporary psychological lingo, he was a "multiple-risk-factor" child, the kind
likely to make poor choices and erupt into antisocial behavior because of the accumulated stress associated with poverty, family
dysfunction, lack of consistent caregiving, harsh, erratic discipline,
and sexual abuse. Contemporary social workers, psychologists,
and psychiatrists should find no surprises here. Charley Miller
provides a template for nearly everything that can go wrong in
childhood.

But the latest advances in neuroscience provided me with another perspective on Charley's behavior that needs to be considered in taking the measure of his life or, for that matter, the
experience of any contemporary homicidal youngster. New forms
of brain and cognitive neuroimaging show that brain development
is incomplete in adolescence, that even at sixteen or seventeen a
person's brain is still growing and changing. The frontal lobe of a
teenager's brain is not the same as an adult's: it is not yet fully functioning, a difference that accounts for adolescents' characteristic
difficulties controlling impulses, reasoning logically, and resisting
the influence of others. (This is the information most relevant to
Malvo.) Given what we now know about the distinctions between
the brains of adolescents and adults, it seems fair to say that Charley
Miller didn't yet have the cognitive ability to think through the

consequences of pulling the trigger that fateful day back in 1890. At fifteen, he still had a "teenage brain," a liability that left him unable to develop any positive, realistic strategy for dealing with a situation that felt unbearable.

In addition to the general immaturity of his age group, there may also have been something about Charley's individual genetic makeup that figured in the crimes he committed. His brothers, in contrast, never displayed any violent tendencies and adjusted well to the rigors of their equally difficult early family life. According to the newest research, boys like Charley, with a history of maltreatment and abuse (recall the beatings as well as the gang rape), are more likely to become violent if they already have a genetic variation that inhibits the amount of monoamine oxidase A (MAOA), a neurotransmitter-metabolizing enzyme that affects levels of serotonin in the brain. These studies show that abused boys with reduced amounts of the enzyme were more likely to commit violent crimes then similarly abused boys with high levels of the enzyme. But the "violence gene"—if it exists—still needs to be activated by environmental stress. For example: among boys who were *never* abused, those with low levels of the enzyme were no more violent then those with lots of it. It's impossible to know now if Charley Miller had the genotype, but if he did, his propensity for violence was most likely activated by early trauma and environmental insults.

In the thick soup of ingredients that explains the behavior of a boy murderer, gender also matters. By all accounts, Charley was deeply immersed in the boy culture of his era, with its ubiquitous emphasis on swashbuckling adventurers and thieves who defied bourgeois convention and the law. These Victorian tales seem tame compared with the imaginative possibilities available to someone today: for example, "Grand Auto Theft 3," a best-selling video game that provides opportunities to imitate a drive-by shooting, a robbery, and the murder of a prostitute after having sex with her.

Even in the twenty-first century, there are aspects of Charley's behavior that feel familiar and altogether normal for a boy his age: the aspiration to become a heroic figure like a cowboy; the displays of bombast; the voracious appetite and the cigarette smoking. Unfortunately, the crime scenario also prompts a sense of déjà vu, a reminder of things we learned after the devastation at Columbine High School. Deadly violence between boys is oftentimes ignited by verbal insults and, in the Miller case, sarcasm and "put downs" may well have played a role. With time to mull over his rejection, Charley's initial admiration for the two swells turned into a silent rage that was fed by the desperate loneliness of his life. Instead of crack cocaine, today's popular drug, his vicious attack was stoked by crude whiskey and carried out with a cheap gun, another common element in many adolescent homicides. Instead of lusting for a gold Rolex, he desired a silver pocket watch.

The objects of desire change over time, but acts of acquisitive violence continue to characterize male adolescence whenever and wherever the chasm between the rich and the poor is deep and wide. Although I deplore what Charley did—it was morally indefensible to shoot two sleeping boys—his behavior was predictable, perhaps even understandable, given what we know about traumatic early-life experiences and their impact on the human psyche. Charley was a poor teenage boy whose mental landscape is not altogether unfamiliar. We have seen it before; we will see it again. What is unexpected about his story is not what it says about Charley, but what it says about us and our history.

Charley's story challenges a number of pervasive assumptions about the way the American system is supposed to work. Instead of an open, classless society, his experience provides a window on a world where opportunities were limited, social-class distinctions were meaningful, and generosity of spirit was in short supply. In history, not fiction, we have a homegrown version of Oliver Twist—in this case, a real orphan whose unseen passage from New York City into the American West symbolizes the lives of all the boys lost to history because they failed to measure up to the American dream.

Unlike Charles Dickens, I cannot manipulate the plot or make Charley's story end on a note of sentimental reconciliation and warm optimism. My rendering of his biography ends—as it began—with a harsh reality: Americans have an ugly history of executing poor children, a history that has generally been hidden from public scrutiny. In the United States we have been killing our children for more than three centuries. Victor Streib, a professor of law at Ohio Northern University, has established a historical roster of the names, ages, and offenses of those executed for crimes committed before the age of eighteen from the seventeenth century until today. From his work, I learned that since the American Civil War there have been hundreds of other cases besides Charley Miller, some involving boys as young as thirteen or fourteen. Not surprisingly, this sorry list is filled with evidence of race and social-class discrimination. In the Southern states, those assigned the death penalty in youth were almost all adolescent black males accused of killing white people; outside the South, even in places like New York and Ohio, white boys received the death penalty but were less likely to be executed.

The criminal-justice system discriminates in its use of the death penalty. This is a gritty, verifiable fact about the way crime and punishment work in this country. Historically, black men bore the brunt of the death penalty, and they continue to do so today. Charley Miller's case drew the attention it did precisely because he was *not* black, and the prospect of seeing a blond, blue-eyed boy hang by the neck unnerved many nineteenth-century Americans, stimulating some to paroxysms of Christian mercy which they rarely, if ever, extended to any young black person in similar circumstances.

Charley's story also provides historical testimony to the ways in which life-and-death decisions are persistently commingled with local politics, even in a case involving a child. Instead of a life sentence in the state penitentiary or rehabilitation back east in a special reformatory for boys, Charley was sacrificed to the larger cause of "law and order" in a volatile, immature state. This too is a familiar script in a nation where dramas of capital punishment are still played out at the state level, often in a flurry of media excitement. Judges and politicians, ranging from Amos Barber to Bill Clinton and George W. Bush, have used their power to grant or deny clemency as a way to attract votes and advance their own agendas, while making it seem that their only concern was public protection.

My retelling of Charley's story at this point in time is intended to remind us that the continued use of the juvenile death penalty is a particularly vicious kind of racial and social-class discrimination against the erring sons of the dispossessed. Charley's case mocks the canonical idea that we provide equal, disinterested treatment before the law. And his case confirms that the poor are always the most likely to be put to death because they can rarely muster the kind of savvy legal representation needed to avoid the ultimate punishment. Jurors are also less sympathetic to poor, unattractive defendants. As Mumia Abu-Jamal, a Pennsylvania death-row inmate, told the Reverend Jesse Jackson: "Them's that got the capital don't get the punishment."

—————◆—————

Charley Miller lived and died in an era when American ideas about childhood were still in flux. Less than a decade after he was hanged in Cheyenne, Americans began to develop a separate system of juvenile courts that reflected the new idea that childhood was a separate stage of life deserving of special protections. The concept behind the new juvenile justice system was simple: children did not bear the same criminal responsibility as adults because their capacity for judgment, rational thought, and moral reasoning were not fully developed. Youngsters under the age of eighteen needed to be treated in special courts where they would receive personalized guidance and sentencing at the hands of sensitive judges and trained social workers, a new, largely female profession, committed to the ideal of rehabilitation. As Barry C. Feld, a University of Minnesota criminologist, describes it, the juvenile justice system was an ambitious attempt to combine the goals of social control and social welfare in a single institution.

The judges who were at the center of the new juvenile system were expected to be authoritative, but also sympathetic and protective, willing to act as a "a wise and merciful father" to young offenders. In 1909, Judge Julian Mack, a founder of Chicago's Juvenile Protection Association, stated the new ideal: "[The juvenile court judge] must be a student of and deeply interested in the problems of philanthropy and child life, as well as a lover of children. He must be able to understand the boys' point of views [sic] and ideas of justice; he must be willing and patient enough to search out the underlying causes of the trouble and formulate the plan by which, through the cooperation, ofttimes of many agencies, the cure will be effected." Despite the paternalistic ethos of the new system and the fact that some violent boys were still handed over to the adult criminal system (especially if they were black), the juvenile courts were one of the most influential innovations of Progressive Era "Child Savers." (Kindergartens, playgrounds, and school lunch programs were others.) By 1920, forty-seven states had separate juvenile justice systems, making the United States a model for the world in terms of acting humanely, in the best interests of its children.

Although the American system was the gold standard for almost fifty years, we reversed course in the second half of the twentieth century. In the early 1960s, critics began to express concern about the ways in which judges in the juvenile court system had unlimited authority to confine young people and determine the course of their treatment. From the perspective of civil libertarians, the juvenile courts were a disaster, because young defendants were denied the same due-process protections as adults—for example, the right to a lawyer, the privilege against self-incrimination, the right to confront a witness. In 1967, the Supreme Court encapsulated these objections in *In Re Gault*, a case that had unintended consequences for our treatment of youthful offenders.

Fifteen-year-old Gerald Gault was committed to the Arizona State Industrial School until the age of twenty-one for making a dirty phone call. (Apparently, Gerald called his neighbor Mrs. Cook and asked her if she had "big bombers." Mrs. Cook, who was not amused, notified the local police.) For this distasteful but typically adolescent behavior, Gerald Gault lost his liberty for six years, even though his parents were never notified of his arrest, he was not informed of the charges against him, and he was not provided access to counsel. The presiding judge also interrogated him during the hearing, compelling him to testify against himself.

The teenager's sentence was not only severe, it was unfair. Had Gerald been an adult convicted of the same offense—a single obscene phone call—he would have been fined anywhere from five to fifty dollars, or imprisoned for a maximum of two months. In reviewing the *Gault* decision, the majority concurred that "neither the Fourteenth Amendment nor the Bill of Rights is for adults alone." Justice Abe Fortas went so far as to call the juvenile court a "kangaroo court."

In Re Gault led to some necessary and important changes in the way we handle young offenders. Today, the rights of lawbreaking juveniles are better protected, paralleling those of adults. But the well-intended reform of the juvenile justice system also fueled the notion that, if children have adult rights in court, they should also be given adult sentences, including commitment to adult prisons and the death penalty. This line of thinking picked up further steam as crime rates soared (in the early 1990s) and the nation was dazed by a cluster of hideous school shootings (in the late 1990s), the point at which I became interested in "kids who kill." In the hope of reducing violent crime through tougher punishments, many states over the past thirty years have eliminated the once widely admired American "punishment gap" between adults and juveniles. The offense—not the the offender—became the new focus, a reversal of juvenile justice priorities that has had a profound effect on how we treat and think about violent youth.

We now criminalize children in ways totally at odds with the humane improvements developed in the Progressive Era. Since the

1960s, there has been a massive shifting of juveniles back into the adult criminal justice system: an estimated two hundred thousand youngsters under the age of eighteen are tried as adults every year. This, combined with new mandatory-sentencing laws, means that the number of youths serving time in adult prisons has risen dramatically. And, in the tradition of Charley Miller, we continue to impose the death penalty for crimes committed by juveniles. Since 1973, we have executed seventeen juvenile offenders; eighty-three currently sit on death row for crimes committed before they were eighteen. Close to 50 percent of these are African American.

Although the Supreme Court in *Thompson v. Oklahoma* (1988) prohibited execution for crimes committed at age fifteen or younger, a year later, in *Stanford v. Kennedy*, the court allowed execution for crimes committed at sixteen and seventeen. This is not much of an improvement over the laws in Charley's era. What's different today is the amount of time between sentencing and execution. Charley spent only sixteen months under the shadow of death; today, the period on death row ranges from five years to two decades, a delay that turns boys into men by the time of execution. In an odd way, the contemporary opportunity for appellate consideration masks the fact that we are still putting people to death for crimes they committed in adolescence.

Though there are some regional differences—Texas, Virginia, and Florida lead the nation in their willingness to impose the juvenile death penalty, and some states, such as Kansas, New York, Montana, and Indiana, have already enacted legislation to raise the statutory minimum age to eighteen—we still have no decision from the Supreme Court that prohibits execution for crimes committed before the age of eighteen on constitutional grounds or as a measure of the moral temperature of the American public. However, major American professional groups are pushing for a change in policy: the American Bar Association is opposed to the death penalty for crimes committed under the age of eighteen; the Child Welfare League of America, the Children's Defense Fund, the American Academy of Child and Adolescent Psychiatry, the American Psychiatric Association, and the National Mental Health Association have all called for abolition of the juvenile death penalty.

In the eyes of the international community, the United States now stands out for its backwardness rather than its humanity. Although juveniles constitute only 2.4 percent of our total executions between 1973 and 2002, we executed more juveniles than all the other nations in the world combined. Notably, over half of these occurred in Texas. The only other countries that continue to execute juveniles are the Democratic Republic of the Congo, Iran, Nigeria, and Saudi Arabia. Despite our avowed commitment to extending human rights around the world, we refuse to sign a number of important international treaties and covenants that explicitly prohibit the juvenile death penalty. In truth, our government refuses to uphold the international standard of decency for the treatment of children.

The Progressive reformers of a century ago—people like Judge Mack, but also Jane Addams and Theodore Roosevelt—would be horrified by the way we have embraced the juvenile death penalty, abandoning the ideal of rehabilitation for the young. With our juvenile justice system in mothballs, we have become acclimated to the sight of young boys, occasionally as young as twelve or thirteen, standing in the dock like adults, on trial for their lives, for crimes committed before they even have fuzz on their chins. Although these cases are infrequent, they are emblematic of a larger cultural pattern: as a nation we no longer observe some of the critical distinctions between adulthood and childhood that were once a hallmark of a modern humane society. Our children not only dress like adults and know what we know about sex and human brutality, they are being punished like adults, especially when they are poor and black.

Those who insist on treating boys as adult men need to recognize that this is as ineffectual as prevention. Adolescent boys tried in the adult system recidivate at higher rates and commit more serious crimes than those tried for the very same offense in juvenile courts. Adult prisons serve the young as a kind of university where they major in violence and crime. In addition, it's unlikely that the death penalty acts as a moral stop sign, a deterrent to homicide by minors. Again, it's a matter of psychological development. In light of the characteristics associated with adolescence—poor judgment, lack of self-control, impulsiveness—young men in dangerous, volatile situations are unlikely to consider long-term outcomes before they take action with an easily accessible knife or gun.

As the behavioral sciences give us more and more insight into the complicated interactions between individual and environment, we have the capacity to be more considered, and also more compassionate, in determining what is the appropriate punishment for juvenile murderers. This will not be easy, because it involves, first and foremost, a recognition of our own responsibility for the impoverished, depressed environments that generate vicious behavior. Without continued efforts to assist poor families, improve our schools with additional psychological services, create jobs in minority communities, and reduce access to guns, we will never diminish the supply of violent teenage boys like Charley Miller. We also need to expand our understanding of "impoverishment" to include those affluent children whose garages may be filled with Audis and BMWs but whose lives are empty and disturbed because of flawed parenting and emotional isolation. It's possible for angry homicidal boys to hang out at the top as well as the bottom of the economic ladder, a lesson drawn from events at Columbine High School.

Americans need to integrate new scientific findings into our system of crime and punishment. We also need to recognize and respond to early signs of rage and psychological distress in even very young children. If there really are youngsters who are set up by their biology to become violent, then their culpability clearly is reduced, an understanding that should make us more hesitant about the imposition of the juvenile death penalty. Given what we know now about adolescent brain development and genetic variation, even the most violent youngsters deserve the opportunity to be treated with an agenda of rehabilitation (psychotherapy, drugs, and education) in special juvenile facilities. Decisions about life sentences without parole should be made when these youngsters reach maturity, on the basis of their current behavior and whether or not they pose a continued threat to the community. Even if we try offenders of all ages in one integrated criminal justice system, it should be done with appropriate modifications to accommodate young defendants and provide them with greater protections and justice.

In 1972, when the Supreme Court put a short-lived moratorium on the death penalty, Justice Thurgood Marshall wrote for the majority: "American citizens know almost nothing about capital punishment." (Marshall seemed to feel that most Americans would oppose the death penalty if they knew more about its history and use.) Thirty years later, in June 2002, in *Atkins v. Virginia*, the Supreme Court finally banned execution of the retarded on the grounds that the standard of decency had changed. In 1989, there were only two states that prohibited execution of the retarded; by 2002, the number had grown to eighteen. The *Atkins* decision is important for the future of the juvenile death penalty, because the two issues have so often moved in tandem. In *Atkins*, the majority recognized the diminished accountability of the mentally retarded as well as their tendency to act on impulse, to be followers rather than leaders, claims that may apply equally well to juveniles.

More recently, in October 2002, four justices of the Supreme Court—John Paul Stephens, David Souter, Ruth Bader Ginsburg, and Stephen Breyer—called the juvenile death penalty a "shameful practice," and "a relic of the past" that is "inconsistent with evolving standards of decency in a civilized society." Although the abolitionists on the Supreme Court are still a minority, more and more death-penalty states are raising their minimum ages to eighteen. The decision about seventeen-year-old Malvo will be important here, and the case closely watched.

For this reason, it's an apt moment to give a second life to someone like Charley Miller. From the time he lost his parents until the day he died at the hands of the state, Charley longed for security and human connection, but he failed to find either. He fell through the safety net of the nineteenth century and never landed on his feet; instead, he died in a glare of publicity, alone and abandoned, without Carrie, Fred, or Willie, but with a thick hemp rope around his neck. This tragic but true story from the nineteenth century stands as testimony to where we have been, but it also reminds us that boys like Charley exist today, some continuing to meet the same barbaric fate.

In the twenty-first century, we can and should do better than our ancestors in the 1890s. We know that, even if a youngster is not factually innocent, we should assess his guilt differently because of his age. Minors really are less culpable than adults, and that fact alone entitles juvenile offenders to more deliberative treatment and rehabilitation than the death penalty, even in the face of indefensible crimes like Charley Miller's. Today, more so than in the nineteenth century, the struggle over the juvenile death penalty tests our mettle as to whether or not we are willing to give thought and resources to understanding the complex origins of youthful violence, including our own responsibility for it. In the end, Charley's story shows us that the juvenile death penalty is more than a law, it's a larger index of how caring, fair-minded, and self-reflective American society really is.

NOTES

Prologue

My account of Miller's last hours is taken from reports in the *Cheyenne Daily Sun* and the *Cheyenne Daily Leader* on April 22–23, 1892. On the same days, the execution was reported outside Cheyenne in Denver, San Francisco, Chicago, and New York, but also in some of the smaller cities where Charley or his victims had lived, such as Rochester, New York; St. Joseph, Missouri; and Leonardville, Kansas. Despite his fame in the nineteenth century, Miller does not appear in the historical inventory of executed minors created by Victor L. Streib in *Death Penalty for Juveniles* (Bloomington, Ind., 1987), nor is the case mentioned in Robert L. Hale, *A Review of Juvenile Executions in America* (Lewiston, N.Y., 1997). However, there are some journalistic accounts of his story. Larry Brown writes about Miller strictly from the perspective of Wyoming in "Just Ice," *True West*, June 1997; "A Tale of Wyoming's Youngest Executed Felon," *Casper* (Wyoming) *Star-Tribune*, Feb. 21, 1999; and "Doughnuts to Die For," *Sentry*, April 2001. Miller is also the subject of a chapter in Stephen O'Connor, *Orphan Trains: Charles Loring Brace and the Children He Saved* (New York, 2001), a book that evaluates the life work of the founder of the Children's Aid Society.

My narrative history of Miller's life is more extensive and interpretive than these earlier accounts. My analysis is rooted in a close reading of all the published material about him in contemporaneous newspapers, especially the *Cheyenne Daily Sun* and the *Cheyenne Daily Leader*, between Sept. 1890 (the crime) and April 1892 (the execution), coupled with secondary materials that illuminate the people and the events that shaped his experience. Throughout, I have relied heavily on the words Miller spoke at trial, recorded in a typewritten transcript, available on microfilm at the Wyoming State Archives (WSA) in Cheyenne, as well as published interviews with him between Dec. 1890 and the time of his death. On the stoning of Etta Barstow, see *New York Times*, Oct. 8, 1870, and the later report, with illustration, in *Frank Leslie's Illustrated Newspaper*, Oct. 29, 1870.

CHAPTER ONE: The Cradle of Youth

Birth and death dates for the Muller family were confirmed in the New York City Municipal Archives and a newspaper report of their father's suicide in "City News," *New York Herald*, March 26, 1881. On German immigrants in late-nineteenth-century New York City, see Stanley Nadel, *Little Germany: Ethnicity, Religion and Class in New York City, 1845–89* (Urbana and Chicago, 1990); Dorothee Schneider, *Trade Unions and Community: The German Working Class in New York City, 1870–1900* (Urbana and Chicago, 1994). In *Mother Donit for the Best: Correspondence of a Nineteenth Century Orphan Asylum* (Syracuse, N.Y., 1996), editor Judith Dullberger gives voice to men like Charley's father through the letters they wrote to the asylum superintendent about their children. My portrait of childhood in this era is based on Viviana Zelizer, *Pricing the Priceless Child* (New York, 1985) who developed the formula quoted on p. 12; David Nassaw, *Children of the City: At Work and Play* (New York,1985); Stephen Mintz and Susan Kellog, *Domestic Revolutions: A Social History of American Family Life* (New York, 1989); Karin Calvert, *Children in the House: The Material Culture of Early Childhood, 1600–1900* (Boston, 1992); Priscilla Ferguson Clement, *Growing Pains: Children in the Industrial Age, 1850–90* (New York, 1997); and Julia Grant, *Raising Babies by the Book: The Education of American Mothers* (New Haven, Conn., 1998). For G. Stanley Hall's impact on American thinking, see Dorothy Ross, *G. Stanley Hall: The Psychologist as Prophet* (Chicago, 1972).

Unfortunately, no case records survive from the New York Orphan Asylum for the years when the Miller children were there. I was able to reconstruct the history of their placements and adult lives from the record book of the Children's Aid Society (CAS), still operating in New York City. Charley is number 27.205 in the CAS ledger, Fred number 26.682, and Willie number 28.90. My description of the governance, rules, and philosophy of the New York Orphan Asylum is based on annual reports contained in *Origin and History of Orphan Society in the City of New York,* compiled by Mrs. Jonathan Odell, Mrs. Woolsey Rogers, Mrs. John G. Smedberg, and Miss Janet T. Sherman (New York, 1896); *Rules and Regulations for the Internal Management of the Orphan Asylum Society in the City of New York* (New York, 1889) and also secondary material, such as Timothy A. Hasci, *Second Home: Orphan Asylums and Poor Families in America* (Cambridge, Mass., 1997). There are two obituaries in 1895 for John L. Campbell, in the *Medical Record* and the *New York Medical Journal*. Additional information was found in medical directories for New York City·available at the New York Academy of Medicine. For historical ideas about personal and domestic hygiene, see Nancy Tomes, *The Gospel of Germs: Men, Women and the Microbe in American Life* (Cambridge, Mass., 1998).

My interpretation of Carrie Miller's role as a "helper" rather than a domestic servant in the Weaver household is based on Faye Dudden, *Serving Women: Domestic Service in Nineteenth Century America* (Middletown, Conn., 1983). Information on the Weaver family was culled from the Federal Census for 1880, the *Ilion* (New York) *Citizen*, and the Syracuse University Alumni Index.

On the orphan trains that carried the Miller boys westward, see Miriam Z. Langsam, *Children West: A History of the Placing Out System of the New York Children's Aid Society, 1853–1890* (Madison, Wis., 1964); Marilyn Irvin Holt, *The Orphan Trains: Placing Out in America* (Lincoln, Nebr., 1992); and Annette R. Fry, *The Orphan Trains* (New York, 1994). On Brace, see *The Life of Charles Loring Brace Told Chiefly in His Own Letters,* compiled by Emma Brace (New York, 1894). The *Leonardville Monitor*, May 20–June 17, 1886, contained community reaction and reporting about the train that brought Fred Miller to town. On the distributions, see "The Children's Migration," *American Heritage*, 1974; and "Charles R. Fry: Grandpa and the Street Kids," in *Orphan Train Riders: Their Own Stories*, vol. 2 (Baltimore, 1992). Both are by Charles Fry's granddaughter, Annette Fry. There is a short biography of Preston Loofbourrow in *Portrait and Biographical Album of Washington, Clay and Riley County Kansas* (Chicago, 1890). His comments about the Miller boys appear in records of the CAS and in newspaper reports. I am indebted to printing historian Bill Pretzer at Old Deerfield Village for helping me understand the workings of a nineteenth-century print shop. See also William Dean Howells, "The Country Printer," in *Impressions and Experiences* (New York, 1896). On the history of Leonardville, I am indebted to Phyllis Swanson, *City of the Plains: A Story of Leonardville* (Manhattan, Kans., 1981) and Frank W. Blackman, ed., *Kansas: A Cyclopedia of State History* III (Chicago, 1912).

All of Charley's descriptions of his bedwetting are from the trial transcript. My account of medical thinking about his problems in the asylum and later in court are based on books and articles by nineteenth-century physicians: Henry Maudsley, "Illustration of a Variety of Insanity," *Journal of Mental Science*, 1868; Frederick G. Snelling, *Nocturnal Enuresis and Incontinence of Urine* (New York, 1869); M. J. Moses, "The Value of Circumcision as a Hygienic and Therapeutic Measure," *New York Medical Journal*, 1871; Henry Maudsley, *Responsibility in Mental Disease* (New York, 1874); Abraham Jacobi, "On Masturbation and Hysteria in Young Children," *American Journal of Obstetrics*, 1876; C. E. Nichols, "Incontinence of Urine of Eight Years Duration Relieved by Circumcision," *Medical Record*, 1879; N. H. Chapman, "Some of the Nervous Afflictions Which Are Likely to Follow Neglected Phimosis in Children," *Medical News*, 1882; Joseph W. Howe, *Excessive Venery: Masturbation and Continence* (New York, 1887); "Dysuris, Enuresis and Retention of Urine," in Peter Charles Remindino, *History of Circumcision from the Earliest Times to the Present, Moral and Physical Reasons for Its Performance* (Philadelphia, 1891). Theodore Dreiser's personal account is in *Dawn: A History of Myself* (New York, 1931).

Contemporary historical scholarship in the history of medicine aided my understanding of the context in which Charley was treated. On the history of circumcision, see David L. Gollaher, "From Ritual to Science: The Medical Transformation of Circumcision in America," *Journal of Social History*, 1994; Gollaher, *Circumcision: The History of the World's Most Controversial Surgery* (New York, 2000). On phimosis as a historical disease category, see Fredrick M. Hodges, "The History of Phimosis form Antiquity to the Present," in G. C. Denniston et al., *Male and Female Circumcision: Medical, Legal and Ethical Considerations in Pediatric Practice* (New York, 1999). On masturbation, see E. H. Hare, "Masturbatory Insanity: The History of an Idea," *Journal of Mental Science*, 1962; John S. and Robin Haller, *The Physician and Sexuality in Victorian America* (Urbana, Ill., 1974); and R. P. Neuman, "Masturbation, Madness and the Modern Concepts of Childhood and Adolescence," *Journal of Social History*, 1975.

Information on the family in Virginia is from the 1880 Federal Census

for Princess Anne County. My description of the Booths is patched together
from their obituaries (*Chatfield News Democrat*, Jan. 29, 1903; Oct. 3, 1907);
agricultural census for Elmira Township, Olmsted County, for 1870, 1880,
and 1885; *Plat Book of Elmira Township, Olmsted County* (Minneapolis,
1878); *Standard Atlas of Fillmore County, Minnesota* (Chicago, 1896); and a
trip to visit the original farm and Chatfield village. Hamlin Garland's accounts of farm life in this era also provided important background: *Boy Life
on the Prairie* (New York, 1899); *Prairie Folks* (New York, 1899); and *A Son
of the Middle Border* (New York, 1917). My rendering of the school situation
in Chatfield is drawn from the *Fifth Biennial Report of the Superintendent of
Public Instruction, State of Minnesota, Year Ending July 31, 1887 and 1888*
(St. Paul, 1888) and *Annual Reports to the Superintendent of Instruction,
Olmsted County, for Year Ending July 31, 1888* in the collection of the Minnesota State Historical Society. Loofbourrow told about the corroborating
letters from the unidentified teacher in the *Monitor*, Oct. 23, 1890; and
Cheyenne Daily Leader, Oct. 25, 1890. Janet Sherman's connection to
Charley Miller was established by the CAS register. On Colt, see *Portrait
and Biographical Album*.

CHAPTER TWO: Becoming "Kansas Charley"

My understanding of the subculture of tramps and tramping is based on essays in Eric H. Monkkonen, ed., *Walking to Work: Tramps in America,
1790–1935* (Lincoln, Nebr., 1984); Paul T. Ringenbach, *Tramps and Reformers, 1873–1916: The Discovery of Unemployment in New York* (West-
port, Conn., 1973); John James McCook, "The Tramp Problem: What It Is
and What to Do with It," *Proceedings of the National Conference of Charities
and Corrections* (Chicago, 1895); Josiah Flynt, *The Little Brother: A Story of
Tramp Life* (New York, 1902); Jack London, *The Road* (Santa Barbara,
Calif., 1907); and Jack Black, *You Can't Win* (New York, 1926).

The idea that youngsters carry around formulaic stories or plots in their
heads is derived from John Cawelti, *Adventure, Mystery and Romance: Formula Stories as Art and Popular Culture* (Chicago, 1976). On the significance
of dime novels among working-class boys, see Michael Denning, *Mechan-
ics Accents: Dime Novels and Working Class Culture in America* (New York,
1987). On the publishing history of this genre, see Albert Johannsen, *The
House of Beadle and Adams and Its Dime and Nickel Novels: The Story of a*

Vanished Literature (Norman, Okla., 1950). For an analysis of Jesse James as a cultural icon, see William A. Settle, Jr., *Jesse James Was His Name, or Fact and Fiction Concerning the Careers of the Notorious James Brothers of Missouri* (Columbia, Mo., 1966). For a historical account of the changing perception of the relationship between popular culture and bad behavior, see John Springhall, *Youth, Popular Culture and Moral Panics: Penny Gaffs to Gangsta Rap, 1830–1996* (New York, 1998).

An emerging historical scholarship about boys and male identity informed my perspective on Charley's adolescent life among tramping men. Most useful were E. Anthony Rotundo, *American Manhood: Transformations in Masculinity from the Revolution to the Modern Era* (New York, 1993) and Michael Kimmel, *Manhood in America: A Cultural History* (New York, 1996).

My knowledge of tramp laws in the late nineteenth century was enhanced by a senior thesis by Jennifer Scheff, an American-Studies student at Cornell, who investigated the case of Edward Alonzo Deacon, a seventeen-year-old white tramp, executed in Rochester, New York, in 1888. See also *Laws of New York*, chaps. 176 and 490; Calvin Beitel, *A Treatise on the Poor Laws of Pennsylvania* (Philadelphia, 1899).

Information on Rochester in 1889, when Charley was there, was culled from Blake McKelvey, *Rochester, The Flower City, 1855–90* (Cambridge, Mass., 1949); appropriate Rochester City Directories; and two local newspapers, the *Union & Advertiser* and *Democrat and Chronicle*. My account of George Weaver and his interest in electricity is drawn from *Ilion Citizen*, Sept. 26, 1884; *New York Evening Telegram*, March 14, 1884; and *Electrical World*, March 15, 1884. On the history of the Lawyers Cooperative Publishing Company, see Lynn Kirby, ed., *The Dream Continues: The Lawyers Cooperative Publishing Company, A 100 Year Retrospective* (Rochester, N.Y., 1982); Erwin C. Surrency, *A History of American Law Publishing* (New York, 1990); and Patti Ogden, "Mastering the Lawless Science of Our Law: A Story of Legal Citation Indexes," *Law Library Journal*, 1993.

For suggestions about the heightened desire of men for clothes and other material goods, see T. Jackson Lears and Richard Fox, *Culture of Consumption: Critical Essays in American History, 1880–1900* (New York, 1983); T. Jackson Lears, *Fables of Abundance: A Cultural History of Advertising* (New York, 1994); Stuart Blumin, *The Emergence of the Middle Class: Social Experience in the American City, 1760–1900* (Cambridge, Mass.,

1989); Thomas Schelereth, *Victorian America, 1876–1915: Transformations in Every Day Life* (New York, 1991). There is a robust academic literature on the rise of the consumer culture in late-nineteenth-century America, but most of it—such as Kathy Peiss, *Cheap Amusements: Working Class Women and Leisure in New York City, 1880–1900* (Philadelphia, 1986) and Elaine Abelson, *When Ladies Go A-Thieving: Middle-Class Shoplifters in the Victorian Department Store* (New York, 1989)—focuses on the escalating material desires of women.

· Charley's prior crimes were hard to document and never mentioned in his Cheyenne trial. However, the Lyons incident was included in a scrapbook of clippings about the Miller case kept by the acting Governor of Wyoming, Amos Barber. The report about the robbery in Lyons, New York, two years earlier appeared in the *New York Herald* after Charley's execution. Barber's scrapbook is in the Wyoming Stockgrowers Association Collection at American Heritage Center (AHC), University of Wyoming in Laramie. Using this single report as a guide, I went to the *Lyons Courant* to verify the story. Although there was no report on the robbery at the Pohls', the details provided in the story did check out in local historical sources.

The Vagrancy Docket at the Municipal Archives in Philadelphia that should include Charles Miller is missing from Jan. 1871 through Sept. 1893. My account of what happened in Philadelphia and at Holmesburg was derived from the trial transcript as well as reports on the House of Corrections in *Annual Reports of the Department of Charities and Corrections* (Philadelphia, 1890 and 1891). Jessie Bluebond-Langner, a Swarthmore College undergraduate, called my attention to reports in the *Philadelphia Press* and the *Philadelphia Inquirer* about the activities of the "Dirty Dozen" in June 1890.

My reading of the meaning of rape to a nineteenth-century boy like Charley is derived from George Chauncey, *Gay New York: Gender, Urban Culture and the Making of the Gay World* (New York, 1994). Charley might also have acquired a cheap handgun and ammunition by mail order, from catalogues such as Sears and Roebuck, but this in unlikely since he was rarely settled with an address. For the involvement of guns in homicide, see Roger Lane, *Murder in America: A History* (Columbus, Ohio, 1997) Robert Elman, *Fired in Anger* (Garden City, N.Y., 1968).

CHAPTER THREE: "Where Is My Wandering Boy Tonight?"

Despite the attribution to Horace Greeley, the slogan "Go west, young man," was actually coined by John Soule, an Indiana newspaper editor, in 1851. "The Wandering Boy"—also known as "The Absent Child"—was written by Robert Lowery, who was associated with many popular Sunday-school hymnals such as *The Fountain of Song* (1877); the song also appears in the *The Broadman Hymnal* (Baptist). See John Julian, *A Dictionary of Hymnology* (London, 1915). For information on Emerson and Fishbaugh in St. Joseph, I relied on statements made at the trial in conjunction with newspaper reports from St. Joseph (*Gazette*, *Daily News*, and *Weekly Herald*) as well as the St. Joseph city directories in the appropriate years. In *Rites of Passage: Adolescence in America, 1790 to the Present* (New York, 1973), Joseph Kett makes the important point that male adolescents in the nineteenth century experienced alternating periods of tight adult control and then almost absolute freedom, a pattern that had explosive potential.

For the train route, events leading to the murder, and the murder itself, I followed the testimony and evidence in the trial transcript as well as later interviews with Miller. In order to understand the local scene in Sidney in the hours before the murders, I turned to the local newspaper, *Sidney Telegraph*, Sep. 20–27, 1890; *History of Cheyenne County Nebraska* (Sidney, Nebr., 1986); Wayne C. Lee, *Wild Towns of Nebraska* (Caldwell, Idaho, 1988); and Albert Watkins, "Historical Sketch of Cheyenne County, Nebraska," in *Collections of the Nebraska State Historical Society* (Omaha, Nebr., 1913).

CHAPTER FOUR: Attention, at Last

Information about Charley's activities after the murder was taken from newspaper reports after his capture, the trial transcript, and interviews with him in the Cheyenne papers. Biographical material on Albert A. Stewart was found in the *Manhattan Daily Republican*, Sept. and Oct. 1890; *Kansas State College 75th Anniversary Edition*, commemorative booklet; *The Kansas Star* (Olathe, Kans., 1941); and Stewart's biographical file, Kansas State University Archives. On the entrepreneurial impulse in nineteenth-century journalism, see Michael Schudson, *Discovering the News: A Social History of American Newspapers* (New York, 1978); Gerald Baldasty, *The Commercialization of the News in the Nineteenth Century* (Madison, Wis., 1992).

On the history of murder reporting, see Karen Halttunen, *Murder Most Foul: The Killer and The American Gothic Imagination* (Cambridge, Mass., 1998); Andie Tucher, *Froth and Scum: Truth, Beauty, Goodness and the Axe Murder in America's First Mass Medium* (Chapel Hill, N.C., 1994).

A thought-provoking exploration of our social, cultural, and legal attitudes toward confessions in general is Peter Brooks, *Troubling Confessions: Speaking Guilt in Law and Literature* (Chicago, 2000). An important statement about the problems embedded in taking confessions from the young today is Steven Drizin and B. Colgan, "Let the Cameras Roll: Mandatory Videotaping of Interrogations Is the Solution to Illinois' Problem of False Confessions," *Loyola University Chicago Law Journal*, 2001.

For my understanding of Wyoming politics and the Johnson County War, I relied on Helena Huntington Smith, *The War on Powder River* (New York, 1966); Taft A. Larson, *History of Wyoming* (Lincoln, Nebr., 1965); Lewis L. Gould, "Joseph M. Carey and Wyoming Statehood," *Annals of Wyoming*, 1965; Taft A. Larson, "Wyoming Statehood," *Annals of Wyoming*, 1965; Anne Carolyn Handsen, "The Congressional Career of Senator Francis E. Warren from 1890 to 1902," *Annals of Wyoming*, 1965; and John D. W. Guice, *The Rocky Mountain Bench: The Territorial Supreme Courts of Colorado, Montana and Wyoming, 1861–1890* (New Haven, Conn., 1972).

The pretrial dueling letters from Loufbourrow and the victims' parents were published in the *Cheyenne Daily Leader*, Oct. 25 and Nov. 1, 1890.

CHAPTER FIVE: In Court

My account of the trial is drawn directly from the transcript, available at WSA; only the material exhibits and final summaries by Taggart and Stoll are missing. Information about Frank Taggart was drawn from his alumni records in Special Collections at the College of Wooster; W. R. Burton, *Past and Present of Adams County Nebraska* (Chicago, 1916); *City Directory, Hastings, Nebraska, 1882–83; Senate Journal of the Legislature of the State of Nebraska, Twenty-First Regular Session* (Lincoln, Nebr., 1889); Wyoming Bar Association file on Taggart; *History of Colorado*, vol. 3 (Chicago, 1918); and an obituary in the *Hastings Tribune*, Jan. 9, 1937. Biographies of Walter Stoll and Richard Scott appear in *Progressive Men of the State of Wyoming* (Chicago, 1903); there is also information on Stoll in *Wyoming Blue Book*, II: and his obituary, *Cheyenne Daily Leader*, June 3, 1911.

I used J. H. Trigg, *History of Cheyenne and Northern Wyoming* (Omaha, Nebr., 1876), as well as Cheyenne city directories for background on the town that was the setting of the Miller trial and execution. For example, see Johnson and McCormack, *The Cheyenne Directory, Embracing a Complete Residence and Business Guide, as well as a list of the members of the Stockgrowers Association* (Cheyenne, Wyo., 1887); *Cheyenne City and Business Directory* (Cheyenne, Wyo., 1888–92). The Club that had such an influential membership is described in great detail in Agnes Wright Spring, *The Cheyenne Club: Mecca of the Aristocrats of the Old Time Cattle Range* (Kansas City, Mo., 1961). For membership, I consulted Cheyenne Club Membership Roster, 1881–87, in Wyoming Stockgrowers Association Collection, AHC. Another source of information is *By Laws, Articles of Incorporation and House Rules, with a List of Officers and Members of the Cheyenne Club* (Cheyenne, Wyo., 1891).

CHAPTER SIX: Boys Don't Cry

All of Charley's words are taken directly from the trial transcript, and observations about his body language and demeanor from reporters' accounts. Taggart offered no explicit commentary on why he changed his strategy to push for an insanity defense. On the McNaughton Rules, see Norman Dain, *Concepts of Insanity in the United States, 1789–1865* (New Brunswick, N.J., 1964); Charles Rosenberg, *The Trial of Assassin Guiteau: Psychiatry and Law in the Gilded Age* (Chicago, 1968).

I found information on the local doctors who testified about Charley's sanity in the "Coutant Biographies" file at WSA; in *First Biennial Report of the State Board of Health* (Cheyenne, Wyo., 1911–12); and in city directories. W. W. Crook is included in *Progressive Men of the State of Wyoming* (Chicago, 1903).

CHAPTER SEVEN: The Politics of Clemency

After his trial and sentencing, covering Charley Miller's behavior in jail became a regular part of the news beat for a number of Cheyenne reporters. My account of his time in jail is based on these reports, in the *Cheyenne Daily Sun* and the *Cheyenne Daily Leader* which sometimes included interviews with Sheriff Kelley, or just snippets of conversation intended to reveal what the boy was really like.

Herman Groesbeck is included in the *Wyoming Blue Book*, II, and obituary in *Laramie Republican-Boomerang*, June 26, 1929. Groesbeck's papers are available at AHC but they include no reference to the Miller case. The only public indication that he opposed the hanging is the one I quote on page 213, from the *Daily Sun*, April 21, 1892.

The biography of Amos Barber has been extracted from his alumni records at the University of Pennsylvania; *History of the Medical Class of 1883, University of Pennsylvania*, compiled by F. C. Johnson, 1905; and *Progressive Men of the State of Wyoming*. On Barber and his early association with the cattle growers, see Phil Roberts, "The Fetterman Hospital Association: Cooperative Health Care on the Range in the 1880s," *Montana Magazine of Western History*, 1994; and "Cowboys for a Health Cooperative: The Fetterman Hospital Association and Health Care Coverage on the Range," in Roberts, ed. *Readings in Wyoming History* (Laramie, Wyo., 1993).

The petition from the trustees of the New York Orphan Society is part of a larger file of clemency petitions sent to Amos Barber about the Miller case; this plea, along with others from E. Louisa Smith, Adelia Conduitte, Ethelburt Talbot, Sidney Dillon, George Weaver, Esther Weaver, and Alice Downs Clark, is available in the Miller file at WSA. To establish the social class of the signatories on the New York petition, I used standard genealogical sources to check their lineage. These signatories included Pauline de Lentilhoff, Katherine Hone Blatchford, Elizabeth Ellen Auchincloss, Euphemia Sloane Coffin, and Cora Dillon Wycoff.

On the WCTU, see Ruth Bordin, *Frances Willard: A Biography* (Chapel Hill, N.C., 1986); Frances Willard, *Glimpses of Fifty Year: The Autobiography of An American Woman* (Chicago, 1889).

Elizabeth Cady Stanton's reaction to achieving suffrage in Wyoming appeared in *Westminister Review*, July–Dec. 1870. For accounts by historians of this landmark accomplishment, see Taft A. Larson, "The Equality State," in *Wyoming: A Bi-Centennial History* (Nashville, Tenn., 1977); Larson, "Woman Suffrage in Western America," *Utah Historical Quarterly*, 1970; Katherine A. Morton, "A Historical Review of Woman Suffrage," *Annals of Wyoming*, 1940.

Since there are no surviving organizational records of WCTU activity in Wyoming, I relied on newspapers and reports from state locals in the *Union Signal*, the national newspaper of the organization. Therese A. Jenkins reported to the *Union Signal* for the state in the period of the Miller trial. Her work is described in the entry under her name in Frances E. Willard and Mary Livermore, *A Woman of the Century: fourteen hundred seventy biographical sketches accompanied by portraits of leading American women of all walks of life* (Buffalo, N.Y., 1893) and in an obituary in the *Wyoming State Tribune*, Feb. 28, 1927; a biographical file at WSA; and in "Brides of the Open Range" in *The Wyoming Society of the Colonial Dames of America Pioneer Biographies*, II (Sheridan, Wyo., 1959). Amalia Post is also included in *A Woman of the Century* and there is an obituary in the *Cheyenne Daily Leader*, Jan. 29, 1897. Information on E. Louisa Smith was culled from the 1880 Federal Census and the 1875 and 1895 Kansas Agricultural Census for Jackson Township, Anderson County. Her letter is in the Miller clemency file, WSA. John Wesley Hoyt was an 1849 graduate of Ohio Wesleyan who studied medicine in Cincinnatti, taught chemistry at Antioch College, and became the founder and first president of the Wyoming Academy of Arts and Sciences. Elizabeth Sampson Hoyt had no college degree but she wrote articles for national magazines and spoke publicly on weighty subjects, such as "The Limits of Intellectual Cognition" and "A New Theory of the Immaculate Conception." While her husband was president of the state university, she lectured there on logic and psychology, and in 1890 she received a Ph.D. from the University of Denver. John Wesley Hoyt spoke adamantly in favor of woman suffrage at Association Hall in Philadelphia in 1882. Elizabeth Hoyt served the WCTU in Wyoming as superintendent of purity work, and she is also included in the *History of Woman Suffrage* (New York, 1881) by Elizabeth Cady Stanton, Susan B. Anthony, and Matilda Gage. For biographical information on the Hoyts, see James Raymond Shumacher, "The Life, Educational Work and Contributions of John Wesley Hoyt," unpublished Ph.D. dissertation, University of Wyoming, 1970.

In explaining the sentiment of Kansas women, I relied on many different sources. For ideas about the death penalty in that state, see Louise Barry, "Legal Hangings in Kansas," *Kansas Historical Quarterly*, 1950; Harvey Hougan, "The Strange Career of the Kansas Hangman: A History of Capital Punishment in the Sunflower State to 1944," unpublished Ph.D. dissertation, Kansas State University, 1979. On the history of the WCTU in Kansas, I consulted Agnes D. Hays, *The White Ribbon in the Sunflower State: A Biography of Courageous Conviction, 1878–1953* (Topeka, Kans., 1953); and Eva M. Murphy, "The Women's Christian Temperance Union," *Kansas Historical Collections*, 1907–8. Unfortunately, records for WCTU locals in Kansas are also unavailable. As a result, I searched *Our Messenger*, the official newspaper of the Kansas WCTU, for interest in the Miller case. *Our Messenger* reported pro-Miller activity on the part of the State Executive Committee in May 1891. For identifying prominent WCTU women in Kansas, I turned to Howard D. Berrett, *Who's Who in Topeka* (Topeka, Kans., 1905). Information about Olive Bray was drawn from *Our Messenger* and *The Waif*, 1891–92, and her obituary, *Topeka Capital*, March 3, 1920. Adelia Conduitte's letter is in the Miller clemency file, WSA, along with those of the male petitioners I describe.

Ethelburt Talbot's biography can be found in John A. Garraty and Marc C. Carnes, eds., *American National Biography* (New York, 1999), and his papers at the AHC. His memoir, *My People of the Plains* (New York, 1906), provides an interesting perspective on early Wyoming settlement.

Sidney Dillon's biography is culled from Garraty and Carnes, eds., *American National Biography*; obituary, *New York Times*, June 10, 1892; and Maury Klien, *The Birth of a Railroad, 1862–93* (New York, 1987).

Robert Desty, the legal strategist behind the clemency effort, is mentioned in Erwin C. Surrency, *A History of American Law Publishing* (New York, 1990); and Patti Ogden, "Mastering the Lawless Science of Our Law: A Story of Legal Citation Indexes," *Law Library Journal*, 1993. There is also a biographical entry in J. H. Lamb, *Lamb's Biographical Dictionary of the United States*, II (Boston, 1900–1903), and an obituary in *Rochester Democrat and Chronicle*, Sept. 28, 1895. The Weaver petition, with its citations to Desty, appears to have been widely circulated, probably even in the nation's capital. I was able to track down almost all of the signatories by using biographical sources such as *The Red Book* (Albany, N.Y., 1892).

On the issue of landmark ages for boys in nineteenth-century America, I turned to Joseph Kett, *Rites of Passage* (New York, 1973). In addition to Victor L. Streib, *Juvenile Death Penalty in America* (Bloomington, Ind., 1987), others who substantiate the execution of juveniles in nineteenth-century America are Daniel Allen Hearn, *Legal Execution in New York State, 1639–1963* (Jefferson, N.C., 1997); entries under "Juveniles" in Louis J. Palmer, *Encyclopedia of Capital Punishment in the United States* (Jefferson, N.C. 2001); and Edward H. Lawson, *Encyclopedia of Human Rights* (Washington, D.C., 1996).

For general background on American thinking about the death penalty, the most important sources are Hugo Adam Bedau, ed., *The Death Penalty in America: An Anthology* (New York, 1964); Phillip English Mackey, *Voices Against Death: American Opposition to Capital Punishment, 1787–1975* (New York, 1976); Louis P. Masur, *Rites of Execution: Capital Punishment and the Transformation of American Culture, 1776–1865* (New York, 1989); and Stuart Banner, *The Death Penalty: An American History* (Cambridge, Mass., 2002).

CHAPTER EIGHT: Acting Out

The account of the two escapes is drawn from *Cheyenne Daily Sun* and *Cheyenne Daily Leader*, Sept. 27–29, 1891; Jan. 1–6, 1892. For the Supreme Court case, *Miller v. State*, see 3 *Wyoming Reports*, 1892. There is also a summary in *Daily Leader* Feb. 19, 1892, and a copy of the "Decision Against Retrial" in the Miller file, WSA. All of the briefs presented in the case, by defense and prosecution, are in the WSA file.

From the language used at the Cheyenne Debating Club, and also some of the women's pleas for clemency, it would seem that many of Charley Miller's supporters were familiar with religious arguments found in Marvin Bovee's *Christ and the Gallows; or Reasons for the Abolition of Capital Punishment* (New York, 1870), a popular abolitionist text. Strangely, there was not a great deal of talk about the merits of a reformatory for Charley, perhaps because Wyoming had none. If he had been granted clemency, Miller would probably have spent his life in the state penitentiary in Laramie. A reconstruction of the inmate population at Laramie in 1891–92 reveals that there were two inmates as young as seventeen: one jailed for killing livestock and then discharged; the other, a burglar, who escaped, was recaptured and then held for nearly thirty years. See Elnora Frye, *Atlas of Wyoming Outlaws at the Territorial Penitentiary* (Laramie, Wyo., 1990); Board of Charities and Reform, *Description and History of Convicts* (Wyoming Territory, 1873–98), WSA. On Jesse Pomeroy, see Harold Schecter, *Fiend: The Shocking True Story of America's Youngest Serial Killer* (New York, 2000).

Letters from Esther Weaver and Frank Bond to Barber are both in the Miller clemency file, WSA. Bond's surveying and engineering activities were well known in Wyoming and established through his biographical file at WSA; *Wyoming Blue Book*, II (Cheyenne, Wyo., 1974); John C. Thompson, "In Old Wyoming," *Wyoming State Tribune* (Cheyenne), July 27, 1940; "Former Wyoming Man at Head of Geographic Board," *Casper Tribune-Herald*, July 8, 1929. Information on William A. Richards can also be found in a biographical file at WSA; *Wyoming Blue Book*, II; and obituary, *Cheyenne Daily Leader*, July 27, 1912.

Throughout the period of his incarceration, the threat of lynching Miller seemed quite real; I borrowed the term "rough justice" from Michael James Pfeifer, "Lynching and Criminal Justice in Regional Context: Iowa, Wyoming and Louisiana, 1878–1946," unpublished Ph.D. dissertation, University of Iowa, 1998. For J. P. Julian's obituary, see *Wyoming State Tribune*, Jan. 7, 1932. On changing attitudes toward methods and places of execution, see Banner, *The Death Penalty: An American History*.

CHAPTER NINE: A Stormy April

Discussion about a tramp menace appears in the *Cheyenne Daily Leader* beginning April 7, 1892. The standard source on the Johnson County War is Smith, *The War on Powder River* and Larson, *History of Wyoming*. On Amos Barber and his association with the cattle growers, see Patrick S. McGreevy, "Amos Barber, Charles Penrose, and the War on Powder River," *Surgery*, 1973. Conversations with Phil Roberts, Department of History, University of Wyoming, were critical in sustaining my judgment that Amos Barber was well aware of, and involved in, the 1892 invasion. However, Barber's posthumous biographies universally praise him for being the person who saved Wyoming from anarchy because of his firm stand in favor of law and order; they also claim for him army service, which is not supported by evidence, according to Roberts.

The Taggart-Emerson exchange was in *Cheyenne Daily Leader*, April 15, 1892; the unsigned proposal that Miller be granted clemency but never receive parole, in *Cheyenne Daily Leader*, April 17, 1892; Barber's final letter of denial, in *Cheyenne Daily Sun*, April 23, 1892, the day after the execution. Based on newspaper reports in the last few weeks and days of Miller's life, I was able to develop a partial list of those who supported clemency, but I was never able to ascertain how many of the pro-clemency women actually had WCTU connections, because of the absence of state and local membership records.

CHAPTER TEN: "I Can Die Game"

My account of Charley's behavior in the last month of his life relies on coverage in the *Cheyenne Daily Leader* and the *Cheyenne Daily Sun* from the end of March (Barber's first denial of commutation) until the execution. The account of Sheriff Kelley was drawn from Courant biographies, WSA; newspaper reports and interviews; and his obituary, *Cheyenne Daily Leader*, Dec. 9, 1925. At WSA, a biographical file on Ed Towse reveals that he left Cheyenne the year after the execution. The Taggarts' departure for Denver was reported in the *Cheyenne Daily Sun*, Dec. 1, 1892; the Barber-Kent nuptials, Dec. 13, 1892. Information on Fred and Willie Miller's deaths is from the register of the CAS; to the best of my knowledge, Carrie Miller was buried in the Mount Hope Cemetery in Rochester in 1931.

Afterword

My thinking about the issue of brain development in violent youth has been influenced by my Cornell colleagues in the department of human development, and by presentations and conversations at the fall-2000 meeting in Chicago of the John D. & Catherine T. MacArthur Foundation Research Network on Adolescent Development and Juvenile Justice. There is an excellent summary of current research on the "teenage brain" in Laurence Steinberg, *Adolescence*, 6th ed. (Boston, 2002) and an important synthesis of the many ways in which developmental psychology and juvenile justice should intersect in Thomas Grisso and Robert Schwartz, *Youth on Trial: A Developmental Perspective on Juvenile Justice* (Chicago, 2002).

The case for reforming the juvenile justice system so that it acknowledges and accomodates the realities of adolescence is made convincingly in journal articles co-authored by attorneys and psychologists, such as Elizabeth S. Scott and T. Grisso, "Adolescent Development and Juvenile Justice Reform," *Journal of Criminal Law & Criminology*, 1977 and Elizabeth S. Scott and Laurence Steinberg, "Blaming Youth," *Texas Law Review*, 2003. In an important study in *Law and Human Behavior* (on press), Thomas Grisso, Laurence Steinberg, and other members of the MacArthur Foundation Research Network on Adolescent Development suggests that immaturity does make adolescents, especially under the age of sixteen, incompetent to stand trials the same way as adults.

In addition to his historic inventory, Victor Streib is a tireless advocate for abolition of the contemporary juvenile death penalty. See his "Moratorium on the Death Penalty for Juveniles," *Law and Contemporary Problems*, 1998; "Emerging Issues in Juvenile Death Penalty Law," *Ohio Northern*

Law Review, 2000. For up-to-the-minute information, readers may also want to consult Streib's "The Juvenile Death Penalty Today: Death Sentences and Executions for Juvenile Crimes, 1973–2001," at http://www.law.onu.edu/faculty/streib/juvdeath.pdf and also the American Bar Association's http://www.abanet.org/crimjust/juvjus/juvdp.html. The quote from Abu-Jamal is in Jesse Jackson, *Legal Lynching: Racism, Injustice, and the Death Penalty* (New York, 1996).

On the history of the juvenile justice system, see Sanford J. Fox, "Juvenile Justice Reform: An Historical Perspective," *Stanford Law Review*, 1969–70; Stephen Schlossman, *Love and the American Delinquent: The Theory and Practice of "Progressive" Juvenile Justice, 1825–1920* (Chicago, 1977); Merril Sobie, *The Creation of Juvenile Justice: A History of New York's Children's Law* (Albany, N.Y., 1987); Office of Juvenile Justice and Delinquency Prevention, *Juvenile Justice: A Century of Change* (Washington, D.C., 1999); Steven Drizin and D. Tannehaus, "Owing to the Extreme Youth of the Accused: The Changing Legal Response to Juvenile Homicide," *Journal of Criminal Law & Criminology*, forthcoming 2003.

On *In Re Gault* and the criminalization of children, see Norman Dorsen and Daniel A. Rezneck, "*In Re Gault* and the Future of Juvenile Law," *Family Law Quarterly*, 1967; Gary B. Melton, "Taking Gault Seriously: Toward a New Juvenile Court," *Nebraska Law Review*, 1989; Thomas J. Bernard, *The Cycle of Juvenile Justice* (New York, 1992); Margaret Talbot, "The Maximum Security Adolescent," *New York Times*, Sept. 10, 2000.

For those interested in reading more about the contemporary problem with violent youth, see Barry C. Feld, *Bad Kids: Race and the Transformation of the Juvenile Court* (Oxford, 1999); James Garbarino, *Lost Boys: Why Our Sons Turn Violent and How We Can Save Them* (New York, 1999). On the complex issue of age, rights, and responsibilities in the law, see Group for the Advancement of Psychiatry, *How Old Is Old Enough? The Ages of Rights and Responsibilities* (New York, 1989); Laura Purdy, *In Their Best Interest? The Case Against Equal Rights for Children* (New York, 1992); and Elizabeth S. Scott, "The Legal Construction of Adolescence," *Hofstra Law Review*, 2000.

On the issue of the juvenile death penalty as a deterrent, my thinking has been shaped by Franklin E. Zimring and Gordon Hawkins, *Deterrence: The Legal Threat in Crime Control* (Chicago, 1973); and Michael L. Radelet and Ronald Akers, "Deterrence and the Death Penalty: The Views of

Experts," *Journal of Criminal Law and Criminology*, 1996. On the critical issue of recidivism in the juvenile justice system versus the criminal courts, see Donna M. Bishop and Charles E. Frazier, "The Transfer of Juveniles to Criminal Court: Does It Make a Difference?," *Crime & Delinquency*, 1996; and Jeffrey Fagan, "The Comparative Advantage of Juvenile Versus Criminal Court Sanctions on Recidivism Among Adolescent Felony Offenders," *Law & Policy*, 1996.

INDEX

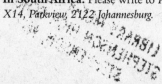